GLENCOE

Pre-Algebra
An Integrated Transition to Algebra & Geometry

Study Guide Masters

GLENCOE
McGraw-Hill

New York, New York   Columbus, Ohio   Woodland Hills, California   Peoria, Illnois

Glencoe/McGraw-Hill

A Division of The **McGraw·Hill** Companies

Send all inquiries to:
Glencoe/McGraw-Hill
936 Eastwind Drive
Westerville, OH 43081-3329

ISBN: 0-07-821691-5

Pre-Algebra
Study Guide Masters

1 2 3 4 5 6 7 8 9 10 066 03 02 01 00 99

Contents

1-1 Study Guide
Problem-Solving Strategy: Make a Plan

The Four-Step Plan

1. **Explore** the problem. Read and ask questions about what you know and what you need to know.
2. **Plan** your method of solution. Estimate the answer and decide how you will solve the problem.
3. **Solve** the problem using your plan.
4. **Examine** your solution. Ask yourself whether it answers the question or makes sense for the problem.

Solve each problem using the four-step plan.

1. **Engineering** Geothermal energy is heat from inside the earth. Underground temperatures usually rise 9°C for each 300 feet of depth. For the ground temperature to rise 90°C, how deep would you have to dig?

2. **Transportation** A DC-11 jumbo jet carries 342 passengers with 36 in first class seating and the rest in coach. On a certain day, a first class ticket from Los Angeles to Chicago costs $750, and a coach ticket costs $450. What will be the ticket sales for the airline if the flight is full?

3. **Retail** At the Woodward Park School bookstore, a ball point pen costs 28¢ and a notepad costs 23¢. What could you buy and spend exactly 74¢?

4. **Geography** On Kenny's map, each inch represents 30 miles. Raleigh, NC, is about 12 inches from Atlanta, GA. About how many miles is this?

5. **Fundraising** Emily sold 332 boxes of candy in two weeks for her band trip. If she sold the same number of boxes each day, how many boxes of candy did Emily sell each day?

6. **Catering** Swan Catering Services offers banquet facilities and food service. They charge $6 per person for a cold buffet. If the Everetts invite 75 people to a retirement party, how much should they budget for the cold buffet?

1

1-1 Study Guide

Problem-Solving Strategy: Make a Plan

The Four-Step Plan

1. **Explore** the problem. Read and ask questions about what you know and what you need to know.
2. **Plan** your method of solution. Estimate the answer and decide how you will solve the problem.
3. **Solve** the problem using your plan.
4. **Examine** your solution. Ask yourself whether it answers the question or makes sense for the problem.

Solve each problem using the four-step plan.

1. **Engineering** Geothermal energy is heat from inside the earth. Underground temperatures usually rise 9°C for each 300 feet of depth. For the ground temperature to rise 90°C, how deep would you have to dig? **3,000 feet**

2. **Transportation** A DC-11 jumbo jet carries 342 passengers with 36 in first class seating and the rest in coach. On a certain day, a first class ticket from Los Angeles to Chicago costs $750, and a coach ticket costs $450. What will be the ticket sales for the airline if the flight is full? **$164,700**

3. **Retail** At the Woodward Park School bookstore, a ball point pen costs 28¢ and a notepad costs 23¢. What could you buy and spend exactly 74¢? **2 tablets and 1 pen**

4. **Geography** On Kenny's map, each inch represents 30 miles. Raleigh, NC, is about 12 inches from Atlanta, GA. About how many miles is this? **about 360 miles**

5. **Fundraising** Emily sold 332 boxes of candy in two weeks for her band trip. If she sold the same number of boxes each day, how many boxes of candy did Emily sell each day? **23 boxes**

6. **Catering** Swan Catering Services offers banquet facilities and food service. They charge $6 per person for a cold buffet. If the Everetts invite 75 people to a retirement party, how much should they budget for the cold buffet? **$450**

1-2 Study Guide
Order of Operations

Student Edition
Pages 11–15

There are rules for the order of operations.

> 1. Do all operations within grouping symbols first; start with the innermost grouping symbols.
> 2. Next, do all multiplications and divisions from left to right.
> 3. Then, do all additions and subtractions from left to right.

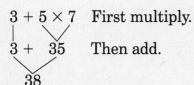

$3 + 5 \times 7$ First multiply.

$3 + 35$ Then add.

38

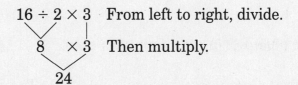

$16 \div 2 \times 3$ From left to right, divide.

8×3 Then multiply.

24

Name the operation that should be done first. Then find the value.

1. $24 \div 3 + 6$

2. $6 \times 9 - 7$

3. $14 \div 2 \times 7$

4. $13 + 28 \div 4 + 5$

5. $(22 + 6) \times 8$

6. $16 \div (8 - 4)$

Find the value of each expression.

7. $25 \div 5 - 2$

$5 \quad - 2$

_____

8. $7 + 3 - 5$

$10 \quad - 5$

_____

9. $7 \times 9 + 6$

$63 \quad + 6$

_____

10. $(12 - 8) \div 4 + 6$

11. $6 \times 8 \div 12 + 3$

12. $5 + 8 \times 2 - 7$

13. $24 + 6 \times 2$

14. $12 \times 5 \div 4$

15. $13 + 5 \times 4$

16. $50 - 28 \div 4 \times 7$

17. $36 - 3 \times 2 \times 4$

18. $60 \div 12 \times (4 - 1)$

19. $(100 - 25) \times 2 + 25$

20. $3 \times 7 - 5 + 4$

21. $9 \times 4 \div 2 - 10$

1-2 Study Guide

Order of Operations

There are rules for the order of operations.

> 1. Do all operations within grouping symbols first; start with the innermost grouping symbols.
> 2. Next, do all multiplications and divisions from left to right.
> 3. Then, do all additions and subtractions from left to right.

$3 + 5 \times 7$ First multiply.

$3 + 35$ Then add.

38

$16 \div 2 \times 3$ From left to right, divide.

8×3 Then multiply.

24

Name the operation that should be done first. Then find the value.

1. $24 \div 3 + 6$
   divide; 14

2. $6 \times 9 - 7$
   multiply; 47

3. $14 \div 2 \times 7$
   divide; 49

4. $13 + 28 \div 4 + 5$
   divide; 25

5. $(22 + 6) \times 8$
   add; 224

6. $16 \div (8 - 4)$
   subtract; 4

Find the value of each expression.

7. $25 \div 5 - 2$
   $5 - 2$
   3

8. $7 + 3 - 5$
   $10 - 5$
   5

9. $7 \times 9 + 6$
   $63 + 6$
   69

10. $(12 - 8) \div 4 + 6$ **7**

11. $6 \times 8 \div 12 + 3$ **7**

12. $5 + 8 \times 2 - 7$ **14**

13. $24 + 6 \times 2$ **36**

14. $12 \times 5 \div 4$ **15**

15. $13 + 5 \times 4$ **33**

16. $50 - 28 \div 4 \times 7$ **1**

17. $36 - 3 \times 2 \times 4$ **12**

18. $60 \div 12 \times (4 - 1)$ **15**

19. $(100 - 25) \times 2 + 25$
    175

20. $3 \times 7 - 5 + 4$ **20**

21. $9 \times 4 \div 2 - 10$ **8**

1-3 Study Guide
Variables and Expressions

A variable is used to represent some number. The value of an expression may be changed by replacing a variable with different numbers. An expression may contain more than one variable. Remember to use the order of operations when evaluating expressions.

Example: Evaluate $5a - 2b$ if
$a = 3$ and $b = 2$.
$$5a - 2b = 5(3) - 2(2)$$
$$= 15 - 4$$
$$= 11$$

Example: Evaluate $5a - 2b$ if
$a = 10$ and $b = 0$.
$$5a - 2b = 5(10) - 2(0)$$
$$= 50 - 0$$
$$= 50$$

Evaluate each expression if $a = 1$, $b = 2$, $x = 5$, and $y = 10$.

1. $y - a$

2. $y - b$

3. $x + y$

4. $a + b$

5. ab

6. ax

7. bx

8. xy

9. $ab + y$

10. $ax - b$

11. $bx - y$

12. $xy + ab$

13. $\dfrac{y}{b}$

14. $\dfrac{y}{x}$

15. $\dfrac{x}{a} + x$

16. $\dfrac{y}{a} - bx$

17. $5a$

18. $5b$

19. $10y + y$

20. $10b - a$

Evaluate each expression if $a = 3$, $b = 5$, $x = 2$, and $y = 4$.

21. $a \times 7$

22. $b \times 8$

23. $2 \times x + y$

24. $a + 6 \times b$

25. $5x - y$

26. $2b - 2a$

27. $6x \div y$

28. $x + y \times 7 \div 2$

29. $a \times x + b \times y$

30. $2ab$

31. $b + x \times a$

32. $4x \div y$

1-3 Study Guide

Variables and Expressions

A variable is used to represent some number. The value of an expression may be changed by replacing a variable with different numbers. An expression may contain more than one variable. Remember to use the order of operations when evaluating expressions.

Example: Evaluate $5a - 2b$ if
$a = 3$ and $b = 2$.
$5a - 2b = 5(3) - 2(2)$
$= 15 - 4$
$= 11$

Example: Evaluate $5a - 2b$ if
$a = 10$ and $b = 0$.
$5a - 2b = 5(10) - 2(0)$
$= 50 - 0$
$= 50$

Evaluate each expression if $a = 1$, $b = 2$, $x = 5$, and $y = 10$.

1. $y - a$ **9**

2. $y - b$ **8**

3. $x + y$ **15**

4. $a + b$ **3**

5. ab **2**

6. ax **5**

7. bx **10**

8. xy **50**

9. $ab + y$ **12**

10. $ax - b$ **3**

11. $bx - y$ **0**

12. $xy + ab$ **52**

13. $\frac{y}{b}$ **5**

14. $\frac{y}{x}$ **2**

15. $\frac{x}{a} + x$ **10**

16. $\frac{y}{a} - bx$ **0**

17. $5a$ **5**

18. $5b$ **10**

19. $10y + y$ **110**

20. $10b - a$ **19**

Evaluate each expression if $a = 3$, $b = 5$, $x = 2$, and $y = 4$.

21. $a \times 7$ **21**

22. $b \times 8$ **40**

23. $2 \times x + y$ **8**

24. $a + 6 \times b$ **33**

25. $5x - y$ **6**

26. $2b - 2a$ **4**

27. $6x \div y$ **3**

28. $x + y \times 7 \div 2$ **16**

29. $a \times x + b \times y$ **26**

30. $2ab$ **30**

31. $b + x \times a$ **11**

32. $4x \div y$ **2**

1-4 Study Guide
Properties

Three Properties of Addition

Commutative   The order of adding does not change the sum. $15 + 23 = 23 + 15$

Associative   Grouping numbers differently does not change the sum. $(18 + 2) + 8 = 18 + (2 + 8)$

Identity   Adding zero to a number does not change its value. $68 + 0 = 68$

Four Properties of Multiplication

Commutative   The order of multiplying does not change the product. $3 \times 5 = 5 \times 3$

Associative   Grouping numbers differently does not change the product. $(3 \times 2) \times 4 = 3 \times (2 \times 4)$

Identity   Multiplying a number by 1 does not change its value. $5 \times 1 = 5$

Zero   Zero times any number equals zero. $16 \times 0 = 0$

Name the addition property shown by each statement.

1. $300 + 0 = 300$

2. $96 + 4 = 4 + 96$

3. $0 + 36 = 36$

4. $(6 + 2) + 4 = 6 + (2 + 4)$

5. $20 + (12 + 2) = (20 + 12) + 2$

6. $27 + 45 = 45 + 27$

7. $75 + 25 = 25 + 75$

8. $2115 = 2115 + 0$

9. $(3 + 7) + 6 = 3 + (7 + 6)$

10. $x + y = y + x$

11. $y + 0 = y$

12. $x + (y + z) = (x + y) + z$

Name the multiplication property shown by each statement.

13. $3 \times 2 = 2 \times 3$

14. $(6 \times 3) \times 4 = 6 \times (3 \times 4)$

15. $7 \times 1 = 7$

16. $0 \times 8 = 0$

17. $76 \times 13 = 13 \times 76$

18. $42 \times 0 = 0$

19. $xy = yx$

20. $x(yz) = (xy)z$

21. $1 \times y = y$

1-4 Study Guide
Properties

Three Properties of Addition

Commutative The order of adding does not change the sum.
$15 + 23 = 23 + 15$

Associative Grouping numbers differently does not change the sum.
$(18 + 2) + 8 = 18 + (2 + 8)$

Identity Adding zero to a number does not change its value.
$68 + 0 = 68$

Four Properties of Multiplication

Commutative The order of multiplying does not change the product. $3 \times 5 = 5 \times 3$

Associative Grouping numbers differently does not change the product.
$(3 \times 2) \times 4 = 3 \times (2 \times 4)$

Identity Multiplying a number by 1 does not change its value. $5 \times 1 - 5$

Zero Zero times any number equals zero. $16 \times 0 = 0$

Name the addition property shown by each statement.

1. $300 + 0 = 300$
Identity

2. $96 + 4 = 4 + 96$
Commutative

3. $0 + 36 = 36$
Identity

4. $(6 + 2) + 4 = 6 + (2 + 4)$
Associative

5. $20 + (12 + 2) = (20 + 12) + 2$
Associative

6. $27 + 45 = 45 + 27$
Commutative

7. $75 + 25 = 25 + 75$
Commutative

8. $2115 = 2115 + 0$
Identity

9. $(3 + 7) + 6 = 3 + (7 + 6)$
Associative

10. $x + y = y + x$
Commutative

11. $y + 0 = y$
Identity

12. $x + (y + z) = (x + y) + z$
Associative

Name the multiplication property shown by each statement.

13. $3 \times 2 = 2 \times 3$
Commutative

14. $(6 \times 3) \times 4 = 6 \times (3 \times 4)$
Associative

15. $7 \times 1 = 7$
Identity

16. $0 \times 8 = 0$
Zero

17. $76 \times 13 = 13 \times 76$
Commutative

18. $42 \times 0 = 0$
Zero

19. $xy = yx$
Commutative

20. $x(yz) = (xy)z$
Associative

21. $1 \times y = y$
Identity

1-5 Study Guide
The Distributive Property

The distributive property involves multiplication and addition. It states that the sum of two products with a common factor is equal to the sum of the other factors times the common factor.

$$(12 \times 5) + (4 \times 5) = (12 + 4) \times 5$$

Notice that the two products on the left have a common factor, 5.

The distributive property is used to combine like terms in algebraic expressions. Two or more terms with the same variables are combined by adding the coefficients.

$$12a + 4a = (12 + 4)a = 16a$$
$$b + 6b = (1 + 6)b = 6b$$

Use the distributive property to find the value of each of the following.

1. $(3 \times 8) + (3 \times 2)$

2. $(2 \times 9) + (2 \times 11)$

3. $(13 \times 6) + (7 \times 6)$

4. $(59 \times 5) + (41 \times 5)$

5. $(25 \times 731) + (25 \times 129)$

6. $(486 \times 40) + (144 \times 40)$

7. $(6 \times 31) + (6 \times 147)$

8. $(7 \times 4) + (7 \times 9) + (7 \times 8)$

Simplify each expression.

9. $8y + 2y$

10. $9m + 2m$

11. $13a + 7a$

12. $5x + x$

13. $d + 10d$

14. $z + z$

15. $8y + 2y + 3y$

16. $9m + 2m + 3m$

17. $13a + 7a + 2a$

18. $8y + 2y + y$

19. $m + 2m + m$

20. $a + a + 2a$

1-5 Study Guide
The Distributive Property

The distributive property involves multiplication and addition. It states that the sum of two products with a common factor is equal to the sum of the other factors times the common factor.

$$(12 \times 5) + (4 \times 5) = (12 + 4) \times 5$$

Notice that the two products on the left have a common factor, 5.

The distributive property is used to combine like terms in algebraic expressions. Two or more terms with the same variables are combined by adding the coefficients.

$$12a + 4a = (12 + 4)a = 16a$$
$$b + 6b = (1 + 6)b = 6b$$

Use the distributive property to find the value of each of the following.

1. $(3 \times 8) + (3 \times 2)$ **30**

2. $(2 \times 9) + (2 \times 11)$ **40**

3. $(13 \times 6) + (7 \times 6)$ **120**

4. $(59 \times 5) + (41 \times 5)$ **500**

5. $(25 \times 731) + (25 \times 129)$ **21,500**

6. $(486 \times 40) + (144 \times 40)$ **25,200**

7. $(6 \times 31) + (6 \times 147)$ **1068**

8. $(7 \times 4) + (7 \times 9) + (7 \times 8)$ **147**

Simplify each expression.

9. $8y + 2y$ **10y**

10. $9m + 2m$ **11m**

11. $13a + 7a$ **20a**

12. $5x + x$ **6x**

13. $d + 10d$ **11d**

14. $z + z$ **2z**

15. $8y + 2y + 3y$ **13y**

16. $9m + 2m + 3m$ **14m**

17. $13a + 7a + 2a$ **22a**

18. $8y + 2y + y$ **11y**

19. $m + 2m + m$ **4m**

20. $a + a + 2a$ **4a**

1-6 Study Guide
Variables and Equations

The solution of an equation is the number or numbers that make it true. When you have found the solution of an equation, you have solved it.

One way to solve an equation is to guess a number and then check to see if your guess is correct.

Example: Solve $m + 13 = 20$

First guess: 33 $33 + 13 = 46$
So 33 is not the solution.

Next guess: 10 $10 + 13 = 23$
So 10 is not the solution.
But, 10 is closer than 33.

Next guess: 7 $7 + 13 = 20$
So 7 is the solution to the equation.

Name the number that is a solution of the given equation.

1. $19 \times p = 95$; 0, 1, 2, 3, 4, 5, 6

2. $11 - q = 8$; 1, 3, 5, 7

3. $51 \div r = 17$; 0, 3, 6, 9, 12

4. $21 + j = 31$; 0, 5, 10, 15, 20

5. $28 = 4 \times s$; 1, 3, 5, 7, 9

6. $13 - t = 9$; 0, 2, 4, 6, 8, 10

7. $100 = h + 25$; 0, 25, 50, 75

8. $g \times 9 = 0$; 0, 3, 6, 9, 12

Solve each equation mentally.

9. $m + 21 = 35$

10. $17 - c = 2$

11. $150 = 15 \times s$

12. $9 = a \div 2$

13. $h + 23 = 32$

14. $c - 12 = 50$

15. $81 = 9 \times t$

16. $3 = 12 \div t$

17. $82 + a = 102$

18. $11 = h - 7$

19. $6 \times a = 48$

20. $u \div 4 = 20$

6

1-6 Study Guide

Variables and Equations

The solution of an equation is the number or numbers that make it true. When you have found the solution of an equation, you have solved it.

One way to solve an equation is to guess a number and then check to see if your guess is correct.

Example: Solve $m + 13 = 20$

First guess: 33 $33 + 13 = 46$
    So 33 is not the solution.

Next guess: 10 $10 + 13 = 23$
    So 10 is not the solution.
    But, 10 is closer than 33.

Next guess: 7 $7 + 13 = 20$
    So 7 is the solution to the equation.

Name the number that is a solution of the given equation.

1. $19 \times p = 95$; 0, 1, 2, 3, 4, 5, 6   **5**

2. $11 - q = 8$; 1, 3, 5, 7   **3**

3. $51 \div r = 17$; 0, 3, 6, 9, 12   **3**

4. $21 + j = 31$; 0, 5, 10, 15, 20   **10**

5. $28 = 4 \times s$; 1, 3, 5, 7, 9   **7**

6. $13 - t = 9$; 0, 2, 4, 6, 8, 10   **4**

7. $100 = h + 25$; 0, 25, 50, 75   **75**

8. $g \times 9 = 0$; 0, 3, 6, 9, 12   **0**

Solve each equation mentally.

9. $m + 21 = 35$
   $m = 14$

10. $17 - c = 2$
    $c = 15$

11. $150 = 15 \times s$
    $s = 10$

12. $9 = a \div 2$
    $a = 18$

13. $h + 23 = 32$
    $h = 9$

14. $c - 12 = 50$
    $c = 62$

15. $81 = 9 \times t$
    $t = 9$

16. $3 = 12 \div t$
    $t = 4$

17. $82 + a = 102$
    $a = 20$

18. $11 = h - 7$
    $h = 18$

19. $6 \times a = 48$
    $a = 8$

20. $u \div 4 = 20$
    $u = 80$

1-7 Study Guide
Integration: Geometry
Ordered Pairs

An ordered pair of numbers, such as the point (5, 2), can be graphed as follows.

Move right 5 units.

⌐────────► (5, 2)
            ▲
            └─── **Then move up 2 units.**

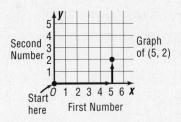

Describe the location of each point with respect to the point (0, 0).

1. (4, 4)   **2.** (1, 4)   **3.** (6, 5)

4. (5, 3)   **5.** (0, 2)   **6.** (2, 1)

7. (3, 0)   **8.** (2, 6)   **9.** (3, 3)

Use the grid at the right to name the point for each ordered pair.

10. (4, 4)   **11.** (5, 3)

12. (3, 0)   **13.** (1, 6)

14. (2, 2)   **15.** (3, 4)

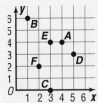

Use the grid at the right to find the ordered pair for each labeled point.

16. A   **17.** G

18. B   **19.** H

20. C   **21.** I

22. D   **23.** J

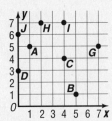

1-7 Study Guide

Integration: Geometry
Ordered Pairs

An ordered pair of numbers, such as the
point (5, 2), can be graphed as follows.

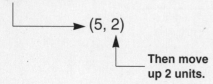

Move right 5 units.

→ (5, 2)

**Then move
up 2 units.**

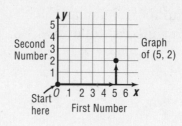

Second Number

Graph of (5, 2)

Start here   First Number

*Describe the location of each point with respect to the point
(0, 0).*

1. (4, 4) **4 units right,
4 units up**

2. (1, 4) **1 unit right,
4 units up**

3. (6, 5) **6 units right,
5 units up**

4. (5, 3) **5 units right,
3 units up**

5. (0, 2) **2 units up**

6. (2, 1) **2 units right,
1 unit up**

7. (3, 0) **3 units right**

8. (2, 6) **2 units right,
6 units up**

9. (3, 3) **3 units right,
3 units up**

*Use the grid at the right to name the point for each ordered
pair.*

10. (4, 4) **A**

11. (5, 3) **D**

12. (3, 0) **C**

13. (1, 6) **B**

14. (2, 2) **F**

15. (3, 4) **E**

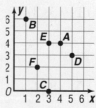

*Use the grid at the right to find the ordered pair for each
labeled point.*

16. A **(1, 5)**

17. G **(7, 5)**

18. B **(5, 1)**

19. H **(2, 7)**

20. C **(4, 4)**

21. I **(4, 7)**

22. D **(0, 3)**

23. J **(0, 6)**

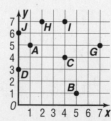

1-8 Study Guide

Solving Equations Using Inverse Operations

Addition and subtraction are **inverse** operations. Because of this, these four equations give the same information.

$$10 + 5 = 15 \qquad 5 + 10 = 15 \qquad 15 - 5 = 10 \qquad 15 - 10 = 5$$

Multiplication and division are also inverse operations.

$$4 \times 5 = 20 \qquad 5 \times 4 = 20 \qquad 20 \div 5 = 4 \qquad 20 \div 4 = 5$$

To solve a single-operation equation, write and solve the related equation that has the variable all by itself on one side of the equal sign.

$$x + 5 = 15 \rightarrow 15 - 5 = x \qquad 4 \times n = 20 \rightarrow 20 \div 4 = n$$

Write the three related equations for each given equation.

1. $7 \times 6 = 42$

2. $50 - 30 = 20$

3. $56 \div 8 = 7$

4. $13 + 3 = 16$

5. $6 + m = 10$

6. $12 = 3y$

7. $d = 32 \div 8$

8. $12 = t - 3$

Solve each equation by using the inverse operation. Use a calculator where necessary.

9. $6x = 42$

10. $42 = 7y$

11. $42 \div z = 6$

12. $13 + a = 23$

13. $b - 13 = 23$

14. $23 - c = 13$

15. $56 - p = 0$

16. $56 + q = 56$

17. $r - 0 = 56$

18. $30 = 10k$

19. $30 \div h = 10$

20. $j \times 3 = 30$

1-8 Study Guide

Solving Equations Using Inverse Operations

Addition and subtraction are **inverse** operations. Because of this, these four equations give the same information.

$10 + 5 = 15$ $5 + 10 = 15$ $15 - 5 = 10$ $15 - 10 = 5$

Multiplication and division are also inverse operations.

$4 \times 5 = 20$ $5 \times 4 = 20$ $20 \div 5 = 4$ $20 \div 4 = 5$

To solve a single-operation equation, write and solve the related equation that has the variable all by itself on one side of the equal sign.

$x + 5 = 15 \rightarrow 15 - 5 = x$ $4 \times n = 20 \rightarrow 20 \div 4 = n$

Write the three related equations for each given equation.

1. $7 \times 6 = 42$
   $6 \times 7 = 42$, $42 \div 7 = 6$, $42 \div 6 = 7$

2. $50 - 30 = 20$
   $50 - 20 = 30$, $20 + 30 = 50$, $30 + 20 = 50$

3. $56 \div 8 = 7$
   $56 \div 7 = 8$, $7 \times 8 = 56$, $8 \times 7 = 56$

4. $13 + 3 = 16$
   $3 + 13 = 16$, $16 - 3 = 13$, $16 - 13 = 3$

5. $6 + m = 10$
   $m + 6 = 10$, $10 - m = 6$, $10 - 6 = m$

6. $12 = 3y$
   $12 = y \times 3$, $y = 12 \div 3$, $3 = 12 \div y$

7. $d = 32 \div 8$
   $8 = 32 \div d$, $8 \times d = 32$, $d \times 8 = 32$

8. $12 = t - 3$
   $t - 12 = 3$, $3 + 12 = t$, $12 + 3 = t$

Solve each equation by using the inverse operation. Use a calculator where necessary.

9. $6x = 42$
   $x = 7$

10. $42 = 7y$
   $y = 6$

11. $42 \div z = 6$
   $z = 7$

12. $13 + a = 23$
   $a = 10$

13. $b - 13 = 23$
   $b = 36$

14. $23 - c = 13$
   $c = 10$

15. $56 - p = 0$
   $p = 56$

16. $56 + q = 56$
   $q = 0$

17. $r - 0 = 56$
   $r = 56$

18. $30 = 10k$
   $k = 3$

19. $30 \div h = 10$
   $h = 3$

20. $j \times 3 = 30$
   $j = 10$

1-9 Study Guide
Inequalities

An **inequality** is a number sentence which states that two expressions are *not* equal. Four symbols for inequality are $>$, $<$, $\geq$, and $\leq$. Notice that the point of the V-shaped symbol points toward the lesser expression.

$2 + 2 > 3$ Two plus two is greater than 3.
$2 + 2 \geq 3$ Two plus two is greater than or equal to 3.
$2 + 2 \geq 4$ Two plus two is greater than or equal to 4.
$2 + 2 < 5$ Two plus two is less than 5.
$2 + 2 \leq 5$ Two plus two is less than or equal to 5.
$2 + 2 \leq 4$ Two plus two is less than or equal to 4.

Translate each statement into an algebraic inequality.

1. x is less than 10.

2. 20 is greater than or equal to y.

3. 14 is greater than a.

4. b is less than or equal to 8.

5. 6 is less than the product of f and 20.

6. The sum of t and 9 is greater than or equal to 36.

7. 7 more than w is less than or equal to 10.

8. 19 decreased by p is greater than or equal to 2.

Name the numbers that are a solutions of the given inequality.

9. $r > 10$; 5, 10, 15, 20

10. $t \geq 10$; 5, 10, 15, 20

11. $2 + n < 5$; 0, 1, 2, 3, 4

12. $2 + m \leq 5$; 0, 1, 2, 3, 4

13. $6 + m \geq 10$; 3, 4, 5, 6, 7

14. $6 + m \leq 10$; 3, 4, 5, 6, 7

15. $30 \leq 5d$; 4, 5, 6, 7, 8

16. $30 \geq 5d$; 4, 5, 6, 7, 8

1-9 Study Guide
Inequalities

Student Edition
Pages 46–49

An **inequality** is a number sentence which states that two expressions are *not* equal. Four symbols for inequality are $>$, $<$, $\geq$, and $\leq$. Notice that the point of the V-shaped symbol points toward the lesser expression.

$2 + 2 > 3$ Two plus two is greater than 3.
$2 + 2 \geq 3$ Two plus two is greater than or equal to 3.
$2 + 2 \geq 4$ Two plus two is greater than or equal to 4.
$2 + 2 < 5$ Two plus two is less than 5.
$2 + 2 \leq 5$ Two plus two is less than or equal to 5.
$2 + 2 \leq 4$ Two plus two is less than or equal to 4.

Translate each statement into an algebraic inequality.

1. x is less than 10.
$x < 10$

2. 20 is greater than or equal to y.
$20 \geq y$

3. 14 is greater than a.
$14 > a$

4. b is less than or equal to 8.
$b \leq 8$

5. 6 is less than the product of f and 20.
$6 < 20f$

6. The sum of t and 9 is greater than or equal to 36.
$t + 9 \geq 36$

7. 7 more than w is less than or equal to 10.
$w + 7 \leq 10$

8. 19 decreased by p is greater than or equal to 2.
$19 - p \geq 2$

Name the numbers that are a solutions of the given inequality.

9. $r > 10$; 5, 10, 15, 20
15, 20

10. $t \geq 10$; 5, 10, 15, 20
10, 15, 20

11. $2 + n < 5$; 0, 1, 2, 3, 4
0, 1, 2

12. $2 + m \leq 5$; 0, 1, 2, 3, 4
0, 1, 2, 3

13. $6 + m \geq 10$; 3, 4, 5, 6, 7
4, 5, 6, 7

14. $6 + m \leq 10$; 3, 4, 5, 6, 7
3, 4

15. $30 \leq 5d$; 4, 5, 6, 7, 8
6, 7, 8

16. $30 \geq 5d$; 4, 5, 6, 7, 8
4, 5, 6

1-10 Study Guide

Integration: Statistics
Gathering and Recording Data

To make a frequency table:

  a. collect the data.
  b. tally the results.
  c. count the tallies.

Birthdays

Month	Tally	Frequency
Jan	⁙	5
Feb	⁙ III	8
March	IIII	4
April	⁙ ⁙ I	11
May	⁙ III	
June	⁙ ⁙ II	
July	⁙ ⁙ I	
Aug	⁙ ⁙ III	
Sept	⁙ IIII	
Oct	⁙ II	
Nov	⁙ ⁙	
Dec	⁙ III	

1. Complete the frequency table for the number of birthdays per month.

2. Which four months had the greatest number of birthdays?

3. Compare the number of birthdays in the first six months to the number in the second six months.

4. Complete the frequency table for the number of books read.

Favorite books	Tally	Frequency
Science Fiction	⁙ ⁙ ⁙ I	16
Mystery	⁙ ⁙ II	
Biography	⁙ ⁙ III	
Romance	⁙ ⁙ ⁙	
Sports	⁙ IIII	
Historical Novel	⁙ ⁙ ⁙ IIII	

5. How many people responded to this survey?

6. What percent chose mysteries? (Round to the nearest whole percent.)

7. What is the ratio of those who chose romances to those who chose sports?

8. Complete the frequency table for these scores.

Math Quiz Scores

82	78	91	67	72
75	81	68	90	75
83	72	77	71	65
55	93	73	76	81
90	88	78	75	60

Range	Tally	Frequency
95–100		
90–94	IIII	
85–89	I	
80–84	IIII	
75–79	⁙ II	
70–74	IIII	
65–69	III	
below 65	II	

1-10 Study Guide

Integration: Statistics
Gathering and Recording Data

To make a frequency table:

  a. collect the data.
  b. tally the results.
  c. count the tallies.

Birthdays

Month	Tally	Frequency
Jan	ⅢⅢ	5
Feb	ⅢⅢ Ⅲ	8
March	ⅢⅠ	4
April	ⅢⅢ ⅢⅢ Ⅰ	11
May	ⅢⅢ Ⅲ	**8**
June	ⅢⅢ ⅢⅢ Ⅱ	**12**
July	ⅢⅢ ⅢⅢ Ⅰ	**11**
Aug	ⅢⅢ ⅢⅢ Ⅲ	**13**
Sept	ⅢⅢ ⅢⅠ	**9**
Oct	ⅢⅢ Ⅱ	**7**
Nov	ⅢⅢ ⅢⅢ	**10**
Dec	ⅢⅢ Ⅲ	**8**

1. Complete the frequency table for the number of birthdays per month.

2. Which four months had the greatest number of birthdays?
   April, June, July, August

3. Compare the number of birthdays in the first six months to the number in the second six months.
   48 < 58

4. Complete the frequency table for the number of books read.

5. How many people responded to this survey? **84**

6. What percent chose mysteries? (Round to the nearest whole percent.) **14%**

Favorite books	Tally	Frequency
Science Fiction	ⅢⅢ ⅢⅢ ⅢⅢ Ⅰ	16
Mystery	ⅢⅢ ⅢⅢ Ⅱ	**12**
Biography	ⅢⅢ ⅢⅢ Ⅲ	**13**
Romance	ⅢⅢ ⅢⅢ ⅢⅢ	**15**
Sports	ⅢⅢ ⅢⅢ	**9**
Historical Novel	ⅢⅢ ⅢⅢ ⅢⅢ ⅢⅠ	**19**

7. What is the ratio of those who chose romances to those who chose sports? **15:9 or 5:3**

8. Complete the frequency table for these scores.

Math Quiz Scores

82	78	91	67	72
75	81	68	90	75
83	72	77	71	65
55	93	73	76	81
90	88	78	75	60

Range	Tally	Frequency
95–100		**0**
90–94	ⅢⅠ	**4**
85–89	Ⅰ	**1**
80–84	ⅢⅠ	**4**
75–79	ⅢⅢ Ⅱ	**7**
70–74	ⅢⅠ	**4**
65–69	Ⅲ	**3**
below 65	Ⅱ	**2**

2-1 Study Guide

Integers and Absolute Value

Situations that involve growth or increase are usually represented by positive integers.

Situations Represented by Positive Integers
Profit of $50 → +50
Deposit of $400 → +400
Increase of 20 → +20

Situations that involve decline or decrease are usually represented by negative integers.

Situations Represented by Negative Integers
Loss of $30 → −30
Withdrawal of $250 → −250
Decrease of 40 → −40

Write the integer that describes the situation.

1. loss of 8 yards

2. 4° rise in temperature

3. 50-foot drop in altitude

4. debt of $500

5. deposit of $70

6. gain of 10 pounds

Graph each set of numbers on the number line provided.

7. $\{-4, -1, 3\}$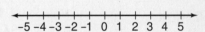

8. $\{-2, 0, 5\}$

Write the absolute value of each integer.

9. -3

10. 14

11. 20

12. -5

Write the two integers that have the given absolute value.

13. 6

14. 1

15. 15

16. 8

17. 3

18. 12

19. 30

20. 21

Simplify.

21. $|4| - |-2|$

22. $|-8| + |-3|$

23. $|-15| - |6|$

24. $|-7| \cdot |-11|$

25. $|12| \cdot |-4|$

26. $|-36| \div |-9|$

2-1 Study Guide

Integers and Absolute Value

Situations that involve growth or increase are usually represented by positive integers.

Situations Represented by Positive Integers
Profit of $50 → +50
Deposit of $400 → +400
Increase of 20 → +20

Situations that involve decline or decrease are usually represented by negative integers.

Situations Represented by Negative Integers
Loss of $30 → −30
Withdrawal of $250 → −250
Decrease of 40 → −40

Write the integer that describes the situation.

1. loss of 8 yards **−8**

2. 4° rise in temperature **+4**

3. 50-foot drop in altitude **−50**

4. debt of $500 **−500**

5. deposit of $70 **+70**

6. gain of 10 pounds **+10**

Graph each set of numbers on the number line provided.

7. $\{-4, -1, 3\}$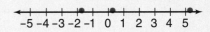

8. $\{-2, 0, 5\}$

Write the absolute value of each integer.

9. −3 **3**

10. 14 **14**

11. 20 **20**

12. −5 **5**

Write the two integers that have the given absolute value.

13. 6 **−6, 6**

14. 1 **−1, 1**

15. 15 **−15, 15**

16. 8 **−8, 8**

17. 3 **−3, 3**

18. 12 **−12, 12**

19. 30 **−30, 30**

20. 21 **−21, 21**

Simplify.

21. $|4| - |{-2}|$ **2**

22. $|{-8}| + |{-3}|$ **11**

23. $|{-15}| - |6|$ **9**

24. $|{-7}| \cdot |{-11}|$ **77**

25. $|12| \cdot |{-4}|$ **48**

26. $|{-36}| \div |{-9}|$ **4**

2-2 Study Guide

Integration: Geometry
The Coordinate System

A horizontal number line and a vertical number line that meet at zero are shown in the figure at the right.

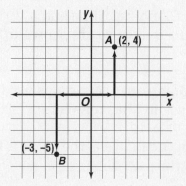

Such a **coordinate system** is used for maps and graphs, and has many uses in mathematics.

Point A in the figure is the point for the **ordered pair** (2, 4).

To find point A, start at 0 and move to the point for 2 on the horizontal number line. Then move *up* 4 units. To find point B, start at 0 and move to the point for -3 on the horizontal number line. Then move *down* 5 units.

Use the coordinate system at the right to name the ordered pair for each point.

1. A 2. B 3. C

4. D 5. E 6. F

7. G 8. H 9. J

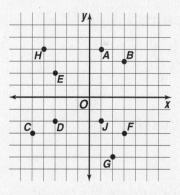

Use the coordinate system at the right. Graph and label each point. Name the quadrant in which each point is located.

10. $K(5, 2)$ 11. $L(-1, 3)$ 12. $M(4, -4)$

13. $N(-2, -6)$ 14. $P(3, 0)$ 15. $Q(0, -2)$

16. $R(6, -2)$ 17. $S(-5, 2)$ 18. $T(1, 5)$

2-2 Study Guide

Student Edition
Pages 72–76

Integration: Geometry
The Coordinate System

A horizontal number line and a vertical number line that meet at zero are shown in the figure at the right.

Such a **coordinate system** is used for maps and graphs, and has many uses in mathematics.

Point A in the figure is the point for the **ordered pair** (2, 4).

To find point A, start at 0 and move to the point for 2 on the horizontal number line. Then move *up* 4 units. To find point B, start at 0 and move to the point for -3 on the horizontal number line. Then move *down* 5 units.

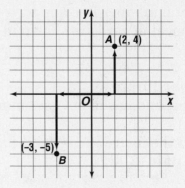

Use the coordinate system at the right to name the ordered pair for each point.

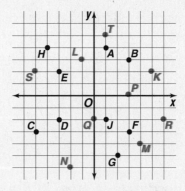

1. A **(1, 4)**

2. B **(3, 3)**

3. C **(-5, -3)**

4. D **(-3, -2)**

5. E **(-3, 2)**

6. F **(3, -3)**

7. G **(2, -5)**

8. H **(-4, 4)**

9. J **(1, -2)**

Use the coordinate system at the right. Graph and label each point. Name the quadrant in which each point is located.

10. $K(5, 2)$
I

11. $L(-1, 3)$
II

12. $M(4, -4)$
IV

13. $N(-2, -6)$
III

14. $P(3, 0)$
none

15. $Q(0, -2)$
none

16. $R(6, -2)$
IV

17. $S(-5, 2)$
II

18. $T(1, 5)$
I

Pre-Algebra

2-3 Study Guide

Comparing and Ordering Integers

The graphs of -4, -1, 3, and 5 are shown on the number line.

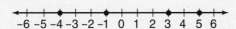

The following statements can be made about the numbers and their graphs.

-4 is graphed to the left of -1, so -4 < -1.
-1 is graphed to the left of 5, so -1 < 5.
3 is graphed to the right of -1, so 3 > -1.
5 is graphed to the right of -4, so 5 > -4.

Write >, <, or = in each ☐.

1. 4 ☐ -4   **2.** 8 ☐ 12   **3.** -7 ☐ -5

4. 2 ☐ -1   **5.** -8 ☐ -8   **6.** -4 ☐ 3

7. -3 ☐ -8   **8.** -11 ☐ -10   **9.** 6 ☐ -9

10. -12 ☐ 7   **11.** 9 ☐ -9   **12.** 5 ☐ -5

Order the numbers in each set from least to greatest.

13. {4, -4, 2, -1}   **14.** {-5, 0, -3, 1}

15. {-9, -6, -12, -7}   **16.** {-1, 3, -5, -7}

17. {-5, 5, -4, 4}   **18.** {2, -3, 0, 4}

Cross out one number in each group so that the rest of the numbers are in order. More than one answer is possible.

19. -3, -2, 0, -1, 3, 4   **20.** 5, 4, 3, 1, 0, -3, -2, -4

21. -6, -4, -2, 0, 4, 2, 6   **22.** 15, 10, 0, 5, -5, -10, -15

23. -1, -2, 0, 1, 2, 3, 4   **24.** 9, 7, 5, -5, -9, -7, -11

                                       Pre-Algebra

2-3 Study Guide
Comparing and Ordering Integers

The graphs of −4, −1, 3, and 5 are shown on the number line.

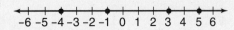

The following statements can be made about the numbers and their graphs.

-4 is graphed to the left of −1, so −4 < −1.
-1 is graphed to the left of 5, so −1 < 5.
3 is graphed to the right of −1, so 3 > −1.
5 is graphed to the right of −4, so 5 > −4.

Write >, <, or = in each ☐.

1. 4 $\boxed{>}$ −4

2. 8 $\boxed{<}$ 12

3. −7 $\boxed{<}$ −5

4. 2 $\boxed{>}$ −1

5. −8 $\boxed{=}$ −8

6. −4 $\boxed{<}$ 3

7. −3 $\boxed{>}$ −8

8. −11 $\boxed{<}$ −10

9. 6 $\boxed{>}$ −9

10. −12 $\boxed{<}$ 7

11. 9 $\boxed{>}$ −9

12. 5 $\boxed{>}$ −5

Order the numbers in each set from least to greatest.

13. {4, −4, 2, −1} **{−4, −1, 2, 4}**

14. {−5, 0, −3, 1} **{−5, −3, 0, 1}**

15. {−9, −6, −12, −7}
    {−12, −9, −7, −6}

16. {−1, 3, −5, −7}
    {−7, −5, −1, 3}

17. {−5, 5, −4, 4} **{−5, −4, 4, 5}**

18. {2, −3, 0, 4} **{−3, 0, 2, 4}**

Cross out one number in each group so that the rest of the numbers are in order. More than one answer is possible.

19. −3, −2, 0, −1, 3, 4 **0 or −1**

20. 5, 4, 3, 1, 0, −3, −2, −4 **−3 or −2**

21. −6, −4, −2, 0, 4, 2, 6 **4 or 2**

22. 15, 10, 0, 5, −5, −10, −15 **0 or 5**

23. −1, −2, 0, 1, 2, 3, 4 **−1 or −2**

24. 9, 7, 5, −5, −9, −7, −11
    −7 or −9

2-4 Study Guide
Adding Integers

To add integers with different signs, find the difference of their absolute values. The sum has the same sign as the addend with the greater absolute value.

$$7 + (-2) = 5 \qquad -7 + 2 = -5$$

To add integers with the same sign, add their absolute values. The sum has the same sign as the addends.

$$8 + 3 = 11 \qquad -8 + (-3) = -11$$

To add more than two integers, follow these three steps:
1. Add all the positive integers.
2. Add all the negative integers.
3. Add these two sums together.

$$-3 + 2 + (-6) = 2 + (-3) + (-6) \qquad -8x + 9x + (-3)x = [-8 + (-3)]x + 9x$$
$$= 2 + (-9) \qquad\qquad\qquad = -11x + 9x$$
$$= -7 \qquad\qquad\qquad\qquad = -2x$$

Add.

1. $6 + 4$

2. $1 + 4$

3. $-3 + (-2)$

4. $-6 + 4$

5. $-1 + (-5)$

6. $2 + (-4)$

7. $-2 + 2$

8. $5 + (-3)$

Solve each equation.

9. $-2 + (-1) + 6 = x$

10. $-5 + 3 + 3 = y$

11. $4 + 3 + (-2) = d$

12. $r = 9 + (-4) + 3$

13. $m = -3 + (-8) + 11$

14. $c = 2 + (-7) + (-1)$

Simplify each expression.

15. $-4x + 7x + (-6)x$

16. $8f + (-2f) + (-5)f$

17. $-7e + (-10)e + 7e$

18. $3y + 6y + (-10)y$

19. $-10t + 9t + 3t$

20. $5d + (-1)d + (-8)d$

2-4 Study Guide
Adding Integers

> To add integers with different signs, find the difference of their absolute values. The sum has the same sign as the addend with the greater absolute value.

$$7 + (-2) = 5 \qquad -7 + 2 = -5$$

> To add integers with the same sign, add their absolute values. The sum has the same sign as the addends.

$$8 + 3 = 11 \qquad -8 + (-3) = -11$$

> To add more than two integers, follow these three steps:
> 1. Add all the positive integers.
> 2. Add all the negative integers.
> 3. Add these two sums together.

$$-3 + 2 + (-6) = 2 + (-3) + (-6) \qquad -8x + 9x + (-3)x = [-8 + (-3)]x + 9x$$

$$= 2 + (-9) \qquad\qquad\qquad = -11x + 9x$$

$$= -7 \qquad\qquad\qquad\qquad = -2x$$

Add.

1. $6 + 4$ **10**

2. $1 + 4$ **5**

3. $-3 + (-2)$ **-5**

4. $-6 + 4$ **-2**

5. $-1 + (-5)$ **-6**

6. $2 + (-4)$ **-2**

7. $-2 + 2$ **0**

8. $5 + (-3)$ **2**

Solve each equation.

9. $-2 + (-1) + 6 = x$
   $x = 3$

10. $-5 + 3 + 3 = y$
    $y = 1$

11. $4 + 3 + (-2) = d$
    $d = 5$

12. $r = 9 + (-4) + 3$
    $r = 8$

13. $m = -3 + (-8) + 11$
    $m = 0$

14. $c = 2 + (-7) + (-1)$
    $c = -6$

Simplify each expression.

15. $-4x + 7x + (-6)x$
    $-3x$

16. $8f + (-2f) + (-5)f$
    $1f$ or f

17. $-7e + (-10)e + 7e$
    $-10e$

18. $3y + 6y + (-10)y$
    $-1y$ or $-y$

19. $-10t + 9t + 3t$
    $2t$

20. $5d + (-1)d + (-8)d$
    $-4d$

2-5 Study Guide
Subtracting Integers

Student Edition
Pages 89–93

To subtract an integer, add its opposite.

$15 - 20 = 15 + (-20)$ **To subtract 20,** $5 - (-9) = 5 + 9$ **To subtract -9,**
$\qquad = -5$ **add -20.** $= 14$ **add 9.**

Write an addition expression for each of the following.

1. $9 - 16$ **2.** $12 - (-8)$ **3.** $-7 - (-7)$

4. $-3 - 18$ **5.** $\frac{4}{9} - \frac{4}{9}$ **6.** $-3.5 - (-4.7)$

Simplify each expression.

7. $-5x - 5x$ **8.** $7y - (-12y)$ **9.** $4z - 15z$

10. $-6ab - (-11ab)$ **11.** $-21rs - (-14rs)$ **12.** $17np - (-9np)$

13. $42d - (-18d)$ **14.** $-17w - (-36w)$ **15.** $36c - (-81c)$

16. $-83k - (-38k)$ **17.** $-56t - (-41t)$ **18.** $15xy - (-6xy)$

19. $45p - 63p$ **20.** $-35f - (-35f)$ **21.** $-53uv - 32uv$

Solve each equation.

22. $5 - 11 = n$ **23.** $x = 9 - (-2)$ **24.** $d = 11 - 3$

25. $20 - 15 = a$ **26.** $b = 15 - 20$ **27.** $-15 - 20 = c$

28. $p = 3 - 3$ **29.** $q = -3 - 3$ **30.** $-3 - (-3) = r$

31. $50 - (-25) = d$ **32.** $-75 - 50 = e$ **33.** $-25 - (-50) = f$

                  Pre-Algebra

2-5 Study Guide

Subtracting Integers

To subtract an integer, add its opposite.

$15 - 20 = 15 + (-20)$
$\qquad = -5$

To subtract 20, add -20.

$5 - (-9) = 5 + 9$
$\qquad = 14$

To subtract -9, add 9.

Write an addition expression for each of the following.

1. $9 - 16$ **9 + (-16)**

2. $12 - (-8)$ **12 + 8**

3. $-7 - (-7)$ **-7 + 7**

4. $-3 - 18$
-3 + (-18)

5. $\frac{4}{9} - \frac{4}{9}$ $\frac{4}{9} + \left(-\frac{4}{9}\right)$

6. $-3.5 - (-4.7)$
-3.5 + 4.7

Simplify each expression.

7. $-5x - 5x$ **-10x**

8. $7y - (-12y)$ **19y**

9. $4z - 15z$ **-11z**

10. $-6ab - (-11ab)$ **5ab**

11. $-21rs - (-14rs)$
-7rs

12. $17np - (-9np)$
26np

13. $42d - (-18d)$ **60d**

14. $-17w - (-36w)$ **19w**

15. $36c - (-81c)$ **117c**

16. $-83k - (-38k)$ **-45k**

17. $-56t - (-41t)$ **-15t**

18. $15xy - (-6xy)$ **21xy**

19. $45p - 63p$ **-18p**

20. $-35f - (-35f)$ **0**

21. $-53uv - 32uv$
-85uv

Solve each equation.

22. $5 - 11 = n$
n = -6

23. $x = 9 - (-2)$
x = 11

24. $d = 11 - 3$
d = 8

25. $20 - 15 = a$
a = 5

26. $b = 15 - 20$
b = -5

27. $-15 - 20 = c$
c = -35

28. $p = 3 - 3$
p = 0

29. $q = -3 - 3$
q = -6

30. $-3 - (-3) = r$
r = 0

31. $50 - (-25) = d$
d = 75

32. $-75 - 50 = e$
e = -125

33. $-25 - (-50) = f$
f = 25

Pre-Algebra

2-6 Study Guide

Problem Solving Strategy: Look for a Pattern

Example: At Fairview High School the bell rings at 7:35, 8:22, 8:25, 9:12, and 9:15 each weekday morning. When do the next three bells ring?

Bell	1	2	3	4	5
Time	7:35	8:22	8:25	9:12	9:15

Explore The chart shows the times that the bell rings.

Plan Since bell schedules often follow patterns, look for a pattern. Once you find a pattern, you can determine the next three bells.

Solve Notice that each class period is forty-seven minutes long and there is three minutes between each class. According to this pattern, the next three bells will be at 10:02, 10:05, and 10:52.

Examine The first class begins at 7:35. The class periods are forty-seven minutes in length, so dismissal bell will ring at 8:22. Having three minutes between classes, you must be in the next class by 8:25. Continuing this pattern, you will see that the sixth, seventh, and eighth bells ring at 10:02, 10:05, and 10:52.

Solve. Look for a pattern.

1. Find the next two integers in the set.
   {3, 5, 9, 17, 33, _____, _____}

2. Jon ran 1 lap on the first day. He ran 2 laps on the second day, 4 laps on the third day, and 8 laps on the fourth day. How many laps should he run on the seventh day?

3. The following chart shows the scores at the baseball game.

Cubs	0	1	2	4	0	1	3
Reds	4	3	2	0	4	3	?

   If the pattern continues, how many runs will the Reds score in the bottom of the 7th inning?

4. Ellie is using the following chart to help her calculate the discount on T-shirts.

T-shirts	1	2	3
Discount	$1.75	$3.25	$4.75

   Mr. Smith would like to order 8 T-shirts. How much of a discount should Ellie give him?

2-6 Study Guide
Problem Solving Strategy: Look for a Pattern

Student Edition
Pages 94–97

Example: At Fairview High School the bell rings at 7:35, 8:22, 8:25, 9:12, and 9:15 each weekday morning. When do the next three bells ring?

Bell	1	2	3	4	5
Time	7:35	8:22	8:25	9:12	9:15

Explore The chart shows the times that the bell rings.

Plan Since bell schedules often follow patterns, look for a pattern. Once you find a pattern, you can determine the next three bells.

Solve Notice that each class period is forty-seven minutes long and there is three minutes between each class. According to this pattern, the next three bells will be at 10:02, 10:05, and 10:52.

Examine The first class begins at 7:35. The class periods are forty-seven minutes in length, so dismissal bell will ring at 8:22. Having three minutes between classes, you must be in the next class by 8:25. Continuing this pattern, you will see that the sixth, seventh, and eighth bells ring at 10:02, 10:05, and 10:52.

Solve. Look for a pattern.

1. Find the next two integers in the set. {3, 5, 9, 17, 33, **65**, **129**}

2. Jon ran 1 lap on the first day. He ran 2 laps on the second day, 4 laps on the third day, and 8 laps on the fourth day. How many laps should he run on the seventh day? **64**

3. The following chart shows the scores at the baseball game.

Cubs	0	1	2	4	0	1	3
Reds	4	3	2	0	4	3	?

If the pattern continues, how many runs will the Reds score in the bottom of the 7th inning? **1**

4. Ellie is using the following chart to help her calculate the discount on T-shirts.

T-shirts	1	2	3
Discount	$1.75	$3.25	$4.75

Mr. Smith would like to order 8 T-shirts. How much of a discount should Ellie give him? **$12.25**

2-7 Study Guide
Multiplying Integers

The product of two integers with different signs is negative.

$$8 \times {}^-2 = {}^-16 \qquad \bigg| \qquad {}^-8 \times 2 = {}^-16$$

The product of two integers with same signs is positive.

$$5 \times 6 = 30 \qquad \bigg| \qquad {}^-5 \times ({}^-6) = 30$$

State whether each statement is true or false.

1. The product of two positive integers is positive.

2. The product of two negative integers is negative.

3. The product of a negative and a positive integer is positive.

4. The product of one negative and two positive integers is negative.

State whether each product is positive or negative.

5. 6×7

6. $^-3 \times 4$

7. $^-5 \times ({}^-2)$

8. $8 \times ({}^-8)$

9. $^-7 \times ({}^-9)$

10. 11×4

11. $^-3 \times ({}^-12)$

12. 2×7

13. $3 \times ({}^-8)$

Solve each equation

14. $x = {}^-4 \times ({}^-15)$

15. $y = {}^-8 \times 7$

16. $x = 3 \times ({}^-6)$

17. $^-4 \times 5 \times 2 = c$

18. $3 \times ({}^-9) \times ({}^-2) = d$

19. $2 \times ({}^-5) \times ({}^-5) = n$

20. $^-22 \times ({}^-12) = t$

21. $s = {}^-18 \times 32$

22. $w = 15 \times ({}^-25)$

2-7 Study Guide

Multiplying Integers

The product of two integers with different signs is negative.

$$8 \times {}^-2 = {}^-16 \qquad {}^-8 \times 2 = {}^-16$$

The product of two integers with same signs is positive.

$$5 \times 6 = 30 \qquad {}^-5 \times ({}^-6) = 30$$

State whether each statement is true or false.

1. The product of two positive integers is positive. **true**

2. The product of two negative integers is negative. **false**

3. The product of a negative and a positive integer is positive. **false**

4. The product of one negative and two positive integers is negative. **true**

State whether each product is positive or negative.

5. 6×7 **positive**

6. ${}^-3 \times 4$ **negative**

7. ${}^-5 \times ({}^-2)$ **positive**

8. $8 \times ({}^-8)$ **negative**

9. ${}^-7 \times ({}^-9)$ **positive**

10. 11×4 **positive**

11. ${}^-3 \times ({}^-12)$ **positive**

12. 2×7 **positive**

13. $3 \times ({}^-8)$ **negative**

Solve each equation

14. $x = {}^-4 \times ({}^-15)$
    $x = 60$

15. $y = {}^-8 \times 7$
    $y = {}^-56$

16. $x = 3 \times ({}^-6)$
    $x = {}^-18$

17. ${}^-4 \times 5 \times 2 = c$
    $c = {}^-40$

18. $3 \times ({}^-9) \times ({}^-2) = d$
    $d = 54$

19. $2 \times ({}^-5) \times ({}^-5) = n$
    $n = 50$

20. ${}^-22 \times ({}^-12) = t$
    $t = 264$

21. $s = {}^-18 \times 32$
    $s = {}^-576$

22. $w = 15 \times ({}^-25)$
    $w = {}^-375$

2-8 Study Guide

Dividing Integers

When dividing two integers with different signs, the result is negative.

Examples: $35 \div (-7) = -5$

$$-\frac{30}{5} = -6$$

When dividing two integers with the same sign, the result is positive.

Examples: $-35 \div (-7) = 5$

$$\frac{30}{5} = 6$$

State whether each quotient is positive or negative. Then find the quotient

1. $132 \div 11$

2. $-108 \div 12$

3. $-80 \div (-16)$

4. $98 \div (-14)$

5. $30 \div (-3)$

6. $-88 \div 8$

7. $-120 \div (-15)$

8. $196 \div 14$

9. $81 \div (-3)$

State whether each statement is true or false.

10. The quotient of two negative numbers is positive.

11. The quotient of one positive and one negative number is negative.

Divide.

12. $12 \div (-6)$

13. $-15 \div 3$

14. $14 \div 2$

15. $(-21) \div (-7)$

16. $30 \div (-5)$

17. $0 \div 6$

18. $64 \div 8$

19. $-81 \div 9$

20. $-49 \div (-7)$

2-8 Study Guide
Dividing Integers

When dividing two integers with different signs, the result is negative.

Examples: $35 \div (-7) = -5$

$$-\frac{30}{5} = -6$$

When dividing two integers with the same sign, the result is positive.

Examples: $-35 \div (-7) = 5$

$$\frac{30}{5} = 6$$

State whether each quotient is positive or negative. Then find the quotient

1. $132 \div 11$ **positive; 12**

2. $-108 \div 12$ **negative; -9**

3. $-80 \div (-16)$ **positive; 5**

4. $98 \div (-14)$ **negative; -7**

5. $30 \div (-3)$ **negative; -10**

6. $-88 \div 8$ **negative; -11**

7. $-120 \div (-15)$ **positive; 8**

8. $196 \div 14$ **positive; 14**

9. $81 \div (-3)$ **negative; -27**

State whether each statement is true or false.

10. The quotient of two negative numbers is positive. **true**

11. The quotient of one positive and one negative number is negative. **true**

Divide.

12. $12 \div (-6)$ **-2**

13. $-15 \div 3$ **-5**

14. $14 \div 2$ **7**

15. $(-21) \div (-7)$ **3**

16. $30 \div (-5)$ **-6**

17. $0 \div 6$ **0**

18. $64 \div 8$ **8**

19. $-81 \div 9$ **-9**

20. $-49 \div (-7)$ **7**

3-1 Study Guide
Problem-Solving Strategy: Eliminate Possibilities

Dan, Ellie, and Ian each went on a vacation. One went to Mexico, one went to Florida, and one went to Canada. Ian did not go to Florida or Canada. Ellie did not go to Florida. Find where each went for vacation.

Explore We need to find out where each person went on vacation.

Plan Make a chart to organize the information. Mark an X to eliminate a possibility.

Solve Since Ian did not go to Florida or Canada, he must have gone to Mexico. By using the second clue and eliminating possibilities, we find that Ellie went to Canada and that Dan went to Florida.

	Mexico	Canada	Florida
Dan	X	X	O
Ellie	X	O	X
Ian	O	X	X

Examine Check the results with the clues. There is no conflict with any of the given clues.

Pick an answer by eliminating as many possibilities as possible.

1. 462   765   612   87   223   492
   534   591   688   638   333   692
   a. It is an even number divisible by 6.
   b. It is larger than 400 and smaller than 600.
   c. The sum of the digits is 15.

2. 12   248   76   3   240
   504   7   26   48   25
   86   592   50   9   72
   a. It is not divisible by 6.
   b. It is even.
   c. It is divisible by 4.
   d. The sum of its digits is 14.

3. Theo, Sue, and Lenita each had breakfast. One had toast, one had pancakes, and one had eggs. Use the clues to find out who had what for breakfast.
   a. Lenita did not have pancakes.
   b. Theo did not have eggs or pancakes.

4. Ross is twice as tall as Enrico. Enrico is 6 inches taller than Tony. Which answer could be the heights of the three boys?
   a. Ross, 64 in.; Enrico, 29 in.; Tony, 32 in.
   b. Ross, 32 in.; Enrico, 64 in.; Tony, 67 in.
   c. Ross, 64 in.; Enrico, 32 in.; Tony, 26 in.

3-1 Study Guide

Problem-Solving Strategy: Eliminate Possibilities

Dan, Ellie, and Ian each went on a vacation. One went to Mexico, one went to Florida, and one went to Canada. Ian did not go to Florida or Canada. Ellie did not go to Florida. Find where each went for vacation.

Explore We need to find out where each person went on vacation.

Plan Make a chart to organize the information. Mark an X to eliminate a possibility.

Solve Since Ian did not go to Florida or Canada, he must have gone to Mexico. By using the second clue and eliminating possibilities, we find that Ellie went to Canada and that Dan went to Florida.

	Mexico	Canada	Florida
Dan	X	X	O
Ellie	X	O	X
Ian	O	X	X

Examine Check the results with the clues. There is no conflict with any of the given clues.

Pick an answer by eliminating as many possibilities as possible.

1. 462 765 612 87 223 492
   534 591 688 638 333 692
   a. It is an even number divisible by 6.
   b. It is larger than 400 and smaller than 600.
   c. The sum of the digits is 15. **492**

2. 12 248 76 3 240
   504 7 26 48 25
   86 592 50 9 72
   a. It is not divisible by 6.
   b. It is even.
   c. It is divisible by 4.
   d. The sum of its digits is 14. **248**

3. Theo, Sue, and Lenita each had breakfast. One had toast, one had pancakes, and one had eggs. Use the clues to find out who had what for breakfast.
   a. Lenita did not have pancakes.
   b. Theo did not have eggs or pancakes.
   Theo-toast; Lanita-eggs; Sue-pancakes

4. Ross is twice as tall as Enrico. Enrico is 6 inches taller than Tony. Which answer could be the heights of the three boys?
   a. Ross, 64 in.; Enrico, 29 in.; Tony, 32 in.
   b. Ross, 32 in.; Enrico, 64 in.; Tony, 67 in.
   c. Ross, 64 in.; Enrico, 32 in.; Tony, 26 in. **C**

3-2 Study Guide

Solving Equations by Adding or Subtracting

Method: 1. Identify the variable.
2. To get the variable by itself, add the same number to or subtract the same number from each side of the equation.
3. Check the solution.

Example: Solve $x + (-2) = 6$.

$$x + (-2) = 6$$
$$x + (-2) - (-2) = 6 - (-2)$$ **Subtract -2 from each side. The solution is 8.**
$$x = 8$$

Check: $x + (-2) = 6$ **In the original equation, replace x with 8.**
$$8 + (-2) \stackrel{?}{=} 6$$
$$6 = 6 ✔$$

```
←+—+—+—+—+—+—+—+—+—●—+—+→
 -1 0  1  2  3  4  5  6  7  8  9
```

Example: Solve $x - 9 = -13$.

$$x - 9 = -13$$
$$x - 9 + 9 = -13 + 9$$ **Add 9 to each side. The solution is -4.**
$$x = -4$$

Check: $x - 9 = -13$ **In the original equation, replace x with -4.**
$$-4 - 9 \stackrel{?}{=} -13$$
$$-13 = -13 ✔$$

```
←+—+—●—+—+—+—+—+—+—+—+→
 -5 -4 -3 -2 -1  0  1  2  3  4  5
```

Solve each equation and check your solution. Then graph the solution on the number line.

1. $x + 5 = 2$

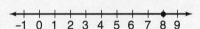

2. $11 + w = 10$

```
←+—+—+—+—+—+—+—+—+—+—+→
 -5 -4 -3 -2 -1  0  1  2  3  4  5
```

3. $a - 7 = -5$

```
←+—+—+—+—+—+—+—+—+—+—+→
 -5 -4 -3 -2 -1  0  1  2  3  4  5
```

4. $b + (-13) = -13$

```
←+—+—+—+—+—+—+—+—+—+—+→
 -5 -4 -3 -2 -1  0  1  2  3  4  5
```

5. $-3 + h = -7$

```
←+—+—+—+—+—+—+—+—+—+—+→
 -5 -4 -3 -2 -1  0  1  2  3  4  5
```

6. $y - (-9) = 12$

```
←+—+—+—+—+—+—+—+—+—+—+→
 -5 -4 -3 -2 -1  0  1  2  3  4  5
```

Pre-Algebra

3-2 Study Guide

Student Edition
Pages 124–128

Solving Equations by Adding or Subtracting

Method: 1. Identify the variable.
2. To get the variable by itself, add the same number to or subtract the same number from each side of the equation.
3. Check the solution.

Example: Solve $x + (-2) = 6$.

$$x + (-2) = 6$$
$$x + (-2) - (-2) = 6 - (-2)$$ Subtract -2 from each side. The solution is 8.
$$x = 8$$

Check: $x + (-2) = 6$
$$8 + (-2) \stackrel{?}{=} 6$$ In the original equation, replace x with 8.
$$6 = 6 ✔$$

Example: Solve $x - 9 = -13$.

$$x - 9 = -13$$
$$x - 9 + 9 = -13 + 9$$ Add 9 to each side. The solution is -4.
$$x = -4$$

Check: $x - 9 = -13$
$$-4 - 9 \stackrel{?}{=} -13$$ In the original equation, replace x with -4.
$$-13 = -13 ✔$$

Solve each equation and check your solution. Then graph the solution on the number line.

1. $x + 5 = 2$ **$x = {}^-3$**

2. $11 + w = 10$ **$w = {}^-1$**

3. $a - 7 = {}^-5$ **$a = 2$**

4. $b + (-13) = {}^-13$ **$b = 0$**

5. $^-3 + h = {}^-7$ **$h = {}^-4$**

6. $y - (-9) = 12$ **$y = 3$**

Pre-Algebra

3-3 Study Guide

Solving Equations by Multiplying or Dividing

Method: 1. Identify the variable.
2. Multiply or divide each side of the equation by the same nonzero number to get the variable by itself.
3. Check the solution.

Example: Solve $-7x = 42$.

$$-7x = 42$$

$$\frac{-7x}{-7} = \frac{42}{-7} \quad \text{Divide each side by -7.}$$

$$x = -6 \quad \text{The solution is -6.}$$

Example: Solve $\frac{y}{2} = -2$.

$$\frac{y}{2} = -2$$

$$\frac{y}{2} \cdot (2) = -2 \cdot (2) \quad \text{Multiply each side by 2.}$$

$$y = -4 \quad \text{The solution is -4.}$$

Check: $-7x = 42$

$$-7(-6) \overset{?}{=} 42$$

$$42 = 42 ✔$$

Check: $\frac{y}{2} = -2$

$$\frac{-4}{2} \overset{?}{=} -2$$

$$-2 = -2 ✔$$

Solve each equation and check your solution. Then graph the solution on the number line.

1. $-3a = 15$

2. $-t = 5$

3. $-1 = \frac{n}{4}$

4. $7r = 28$

5. $0 = \frac{h}{7}$

6. $24 = -8m$

7. $-11b = 44$

8. $\frac{a}{-2} = -1$

3-3 Study Guide

Solving Equations by Multiplying or Dividing

Method:
1. Identify the variable.
2. Multiply or divide each side of the equation by the same nonzero number to get the variable by itself.
3. Check the solution.

Example: Solve $-7x = 42$.

$-7x = 42$

$\dfrac{-7x}{-7} = \dfrac{42}{-7}$ **Divide each side by -7.**

$x = -6$ **The solution is -6.**

Example: Solve $\dfrac{y}{2} = -2$.

$\dfrac{y}{2} = -2$

$\dfrac{y}{2} \cdot (2) = -2 \cdot (2)$ **Multiply each side by 2.**

$y = -4$ **The solution is -4.**

Check: $-7x = 42$

$-7(-6) \overset{?}{=} 42$

$42 = 42$ ✔

Check: $\dfrac{y}{2} = -2$

$\dfrac{-4}{2} \overset{?}{=} -2$

$-2 = -2$ ✔

Solve each equation and check your solution. Then graph the solution on the number line.

1. $-3a = 15$ $a = -5$

2. $-t = 5$ $t = -5$

3. $-1 = \dfrac{n}{4}$ $n = -4$

4. $7r = 28$ $r = 4$

5. $0 = \dfrac{h}{7}$ $h = 0$

6. $24 = -8m$ $m = -3$

7. $-11b = 44$ $b = -4$

8. $\dfrac{a}{-2} = -1$ $a = 2$

T 21

3-4 Study Guide
Using Formulas

A **formula** shows the relationship between certain quantities. The formula for the distance traveled by a moving object is $d = rt$. In the formula, d represents distance in kilometers (km), r represents the rate in kilometers per hour (km/h), and t represents the time in hours (h).

Example: Suppose r is 40 kilometers per hour and t is 3 hours. Find the distance traveled (d).

$d = rt$

$d = 40 \times 3$ Replace *r* with 40 and *t* with 3.

$d = 120$ The distance traveled is 120 kilometers.

Use the formula d = rt to find the indicated variables.

1. $r = 60$ km/h; $t = 4$ h; d

2. $d = 100$ km; $t = 2$ h; r

3. $r = 55$ km/h; $d = 110$ km; t

4. $r = 35$ km/h; $t = 3$ h; d

5. $d = 210$ km; $t = 7$ h; r

6. $r = 80$ km/h; $d = 320$ km; t

The formula $I = \dfrac{V}{R}$ shows the relationship between the current in amperes (I), the voltage in volts (V), and the resistance in ohms (R) in an electrical circuit.

Use the formula I = $\dfrac{V}{R}$ to find the current for each of the following. (Current is measured in amperes.)

7. V: 60 volts; R: 3 ohms

8. V: 90 volts; R: 3 ohms

9. V: 100 volts; R: 2 ohms

10. V: 120 volts; R: 3 ohms

3-4 Study Guide
Using Formulas

A **formula** shows the relationship between certain quantities. The formula for the distance traveled by a moving object is $d = rt$. In the formula, d represents distance in kilometers (km), r represents the rate in kilometers per hour (km/h), and t represents the time in hours (h).

Example: Suppose r is 40 kilometers per hour and t is 3 hours. Find the distance traveled (d).

$d = rt$

$d = 40 \times 3$ **Replace r with 40 and t with 3.**

$d = 120$ The distance traveled is 120 kilometers.

Use the formula $d = rt$ to find the indicated variables.

1. $r = 60$ km/h; $t = 4$ h; d **$d = 240$ km**   2. $d = 100$ km; $t = 2$ h; r **$r = 50$ km/h**

3. $r = 55$ km/h; $d = 110$ km; t **$t = 2$ h**   4. $r = 35$ km/h; $t = 3$ h; d **$d = 105$ km**

5. $d = 210$ km; $t = 7$ h; r **$r = 30$ km/h**   6. $r = 80$ km/h; $d = 320$ km; t **$t = 4$ h**

The formula $I = \dfrac{V}{R}$ shows the relationship between the current in amperes (I), the voltage in volts (V), and the resistance in ohms (R) in an electrical circuit.

Use the formula $I = \dfrac{V}{R}$ to find the current for each of the following. (Current is measured in amperes.)

7. V: 60 volts; R: 3 ohms **20 amperes**   8. V: 90 volts; R: 3 ohms **30 amperes**

9. V: 100 volts; R: 2 ohms **50 amperes**   10. V: 120 volts; R: 3 ohms **40 amperes**

3-5 Study Guide

Integration: Geometry
Area and Perimeter

Student Edition
Pages 139–144

The perimeter of a rectangle equals twice the sum of the measure of the two sides.

$$P = a + a + b + b$$
$$= 2a + 2b, \text{ or } 2(a + b)$$

Example: Find the perimeter of the rectangle.

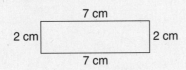

$$P = 2(7 \text{ cm} + 2 \text{ cm})$$
$$= 18 \text{ cm}$$

The area of a rectangle equals the product of the measure of the two sides.

$$A = a \times b$$

Example: Find the area of the rectangle.

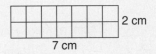

$$A = 2 \text{ cm} \times 7 \text{ cm}$$
$$= 14 \text{ cm}^2$$

Find the perimeter and area of each rectangle.

1.
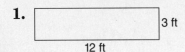
3 ft
12 ft

2.
3 cm
5 cm

3.
10 yd
15 yd

4.
6 m
9 m

5.
3 in.
7 in.

6.
18 cm
20 cm

Tell whether each expression would give you the perimeter or the area of the rectangle.

7. xy

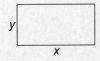
y
x

8. $(x + 1)(x + 2)$

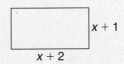
x + 1
x + 2

9. $y + 2x + y$

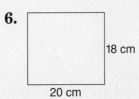
x
y

10. $4x$

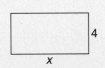
4
x

11. $2(a + b)$

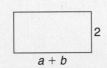
2
a + b

12. $2(w + 2w)$

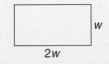
w
2w

3-5 Study Guide

Integration: Geometry
Area and Perimeter

The perimeter of a rectangle equals twice the sum of the measure of the two sides.

$$P = a + a + b + b$$
$$= 2a + 2b, \text{ or } 2(a + b)$$

Example: Find the perimeter of the rectangle.

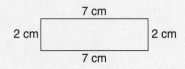

$$P = 2(7 \text{ cm} + 2 \text{ cm})$$
$$= 18 \text{ cm}$$

The area of a rectangle equals the product of the measure of the two sides.

$$A = a \times b$$

Example: Find the area of the rectangle.

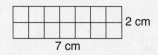

$$A = 2 \text{ cm} \times 7 \text{ cm}$$
$$= 14 \text{ cm}^2$$

Find the perimeter and area of each rectangle.

1.
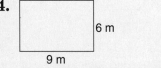

A = 36 ft² P = 30 ft

2.
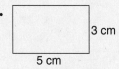

A = 15 cm²
P = 16 cm

3.
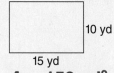

A = 150 yd²
P = 50 yd

4.
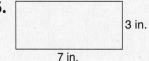

A = 54 m² P = 30 m

5.
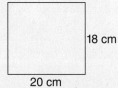

A = 21 in² P = 20 in.

6.

A = 360 cm²
P = 76 cm

Tell whether each expression would give you the perimeter or the area of the rectangle.

7. xy **area**

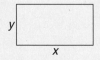

8. $(x + 1)(x + 2)$ **area**

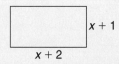

9. $y + 2x + y$ **perimeter**

10. $4x$ **area**

11. $2(a + b)$ **area**

12. $2(w + 2w)$ **perimeter**

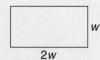

3-6 Study Guide

Solving Inequalities by Adding or Subtracting

An **inequality** is a mathematical sentence that contains one of these symbols: $<$, $>$, $\leq$, $\geq$, or $\neq$. The meaning of each is given at the right.

Symbol	Meaning
$<$	less than
$>$	greater than
$\leq$	less than or equal to
$\geq$	greater than or equal to
$\neq$	not equal to

The same steps used to solve equations are used to solve inequalities.

Example: Solve $x + 6 > 11$.

$$x + 6 > 11$$
$$x + 6 - 6 > 11 - 6 \quad \text{Subtract 6 from each side.}$$
$$x > 5$$

Check: Pick a number greater than 5. Use 8.

$$x + 6 \overset{?}{>} 11$$
$$8 + 6 \overset{?}{>} 11 \quad \text{Replace } x \text{ with the number 8.}$$
$$14 > 11 \quad \text{The statement is true, so it checks.}$$

The solution to an inequality with one variable can be shown on a number line. A closed dot is used when the point is included in the solution. An open circle is used when the point is *not* included in the solution.

Examples: $x - 3 \leq {}^-6$
$$x \leq {}^-3$$

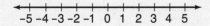
–5 –4 –3 –2 –1 0

$x - 3 > {}^-6$
$$x > {}^-3$$

–4 –3 –2 –1 0 1

Solve each inequality and check your solution. Then graph the solution on the number line.

1. ${}^-1 > x + 3$

–5 –4 –3 –2 –1 0 1 2 3 4 5

2. $t + 9 \geq 6$

–5 –4 –3 –2 –1 0 1 2 3 4 5

3. ${}^-5 \leq r - 3$

–5 –4 –3 –2 –1 0 1 2 3 4 5

4. ${}^-7 + m \geq {}^-9$

–5 –4 –3 –2 –1 0 1 2 3 4 5

5. $b - 14 < {}^-10$

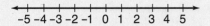
–5 –4 –3 –2 –1 0 1 2 3 4 5

6. $8 + y \geq 6$

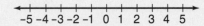
–5 –4 –3 –2 –1 0 1 2 3 4 5

3-6 Study Guide

Solving Inequalities by Adding or Subtracting

An **inequality** is a mathematical sentence that contains one of these symbols: $<, >, \leq, \geq,$ or $\neq$. The meaning of each is given at the right.

Symbol	Meaning
$<$	less than
$>$	greater than
$\leq$	less than or equal to
$\geq$	greater than or equal to
$\neq$	not equal to

The same steps used to solve equations are used to solve inequalities.

Example: Solve $x + 6 > 11$.

$$x + 6 > 11$$
$$x + 6 - 6 > 11 - 6 \quad \text{Subtract 6 from}$$
$$x > 5 \qquad\qquad \text{each side.}$$

Check: Pick a number greater than 5. Use 8.

$$x + 6 \overset{?}{>} 11$$
$$8 + 6 \overset{?}{>} 11 \quad \text{Replace } x \text{ with the number 8.}$$
$$14 > 11 \qquad \text{The statement is true, so it checks.}$$

The solution to an inequality with one variable can be shown on a number line. A closed dot is used when the point is included in the solution. An open circle is used when the point is *not* included in the solution.

Examples: $x - 3 \leq {}^-6$ $x - 3 > {}^-6$
            $x \leq {}^-3$ $x > {}^-3$

```
←─┼─┼─●─┼─┼─┼→        ←─┼─○─┼─┼─┼─┼→
 -5 -4 -3 -2 -1  0      -4 -3 -2 -1  0  1
```

Solve each inequality and check your solution. Then graph the solution on the number line.

1. $^-1 > x + 3$ $x < {}^-4$

```
←──○─┼─┼─┼─┼─┼─┼─┼─┼─┼→
 -5 -4 -3 -2 -1  0  1  2  3  4  5
```

2. $t + 9 \geq 6$ $t \geq {}^-3$

```
←─┼─┼─●─┼─┼─┼─┼─┼─┼─┼─┼→
 -5 -4 -3 -2 -1  0  1  2  3  4  5
```

3. $^-5 \leq r - 3$ $r \geq {}^-2$

```
←─┼─┼─┼─●─┼─┼─┼─┼─┼─┼─┼→
 -5 -4 -3 -2 -1  0  1  2  3  4  5
```

4. $^-7 + m \geq {}^-9$ $m \geq {}^-2$

```
←─┼─┼─┼─●─┼─┼─┼─┼─┼─┼─┼→
 -5 -4 -3 -2 -1  0  1  2  3  4  5
```

5. $b - 14 < {}^-10$ $b < 4$

```
←─┼─┼─┼─┼─┼─┼─┼─┼─○─┼→
 -5 -4 -3 -2 -1  0  1  2  3  4  5
```

6. $8 + y \geq 6$ $y \geq {}^-2$

```
←─┼─┼─┼─●─┼─┼─┼─┼─┼─┼─┼→
 -5 -4 -3 -2 -1  0  1  2  3  4  5
```

                   Pre-Algebra

3-7 Study Guide

Solving Inequalities by Multiplying or Dividing

● When you multiply or divide each side of an inequality by a *positive* number, you get a new inequality with the same solutions.

$$3h < {}^-12$$
$$3h \div 3 < {}^-12 \div 3$$
$$h < {}^-4$$

$$\frac{h}{5} > 10$$
$$\frac{h}{5} \cdot 5 > 10 \cdot 5$$
$$h > 50$$

When you multiply or divide each side by a *negative* number, you must reverse the inequality symbol. Otherwise, the new inequality will not have the same solutions.

$$-3h < {}^-12$$
$$-3h \div ({}^-3) > {}^-12 \div ({}^-3)$$
$$h > 4$$

$$\frac{h}{-5} > 10$$
$$\frac{h}{-5} \cdot ({}^-5) < 10 \cdot ({}^-5)$$
$$h < {}^-50$$

● **Do the two inequalities have the same solutions? Write yes or no.**

1. $2x < 14$
$x > 7$

2. $-x < 0$
$x > 0$

3. $3x < 9$
$x < 3$

4. $-5x > 0$
$x > 0$

5. $-4x < 4$
$x > {}^-1$

6. $-3x > {}^-3$
$x > 1$

Solve each inequality and check your solution.

7. $7x < 84$

8. $9x > 81$

9. $\frac{h}{3} < {}^-10$

10. $6p < 12$

11. $\frac{h}{4} > {}^-7$

12. $0 > {}^-5c$

13. $-2d > 4$

14. $-2d > {}^-4$

15. $-2d < {}^-4$

● **16.** $\frac{a}{-3} < 9$

17. $\frac{a}{-3} > {}^-9$

18. $\frac{a}{3} < {}^-9$

3-7 Study Guide

Solving Inequalities by Multiplying or Dividing

When you multiply or divide each side of an inequality by a *positive* number, you get a new inequality with the same solutions.

$$3h < -12$$
$$3h \div 3 < -12 \div 3$$
$$h < -4$$

$$\frac{h}{5} > 10$$
$$\frac{h}{5} \cdot 5 > 10 \cdot 5$$
$$h > 50$$

When you multiply or divide each side by a *negative* number, you must reverse the inequality symbol. Otherwise, the new inequality will not have the same solutions.

$$-3h < -12$$
$$-3h \div (-3) > -12 \div (-3)$$
$$h > 4$$

$$\frac{h}{-5} > 10$$
$$\frac{h}{-5} \cdot (-5) < 10 \cdot (-5)$$
$$h < -50$$

Do the two inequalities have the same solutions? Write <u>yes</u> or <u>no</u>.

1. $2x < 14$
$x > 7$ **no**

2. $-x < 0$
$x > 0$ **yes**

3. $3x < 9$
$x < 3$ **yes**

4. $-5x > 0$
$x > 0$ **no**

5. $-4x < 4$
$x > -1$ **yes**

6. $-3x > -3$
$x > 1$ **no**

Solve each inequality and check your solution.

7. $7x < 84$ **$x < 12$**

8. $9x > 81$ **$x > 9$**

9. $\frac{h}{3} < -10$ **$h < -30$**

10. $6p < 12$ **$p < 2$**

11. $\frac{h}{4} > -7$ **$h > -28$**

12. $0 > -5c$ **$c > 0$**

13. $-2d > 4$ **$d < -2$**

14. $-2d > -4$ **$d < 2$**

15. $-2d < -4$ **$d > 2$**

16. $\frac{a}{-3} < 9$ **$a > -27$**

17. $\frac{a}{-3} > -9$ **$a < 27$**

18. $\frac{a}{3} < -9$ **$a < -27$**

3-8 Study Guide

Applying Equations and Inequalities

Compare these two examples. On the left, an equation is used to find the solution. On the right, an inequality is used.

Example: The record low temperature for Bakersville is −35°F. This is 5 times the record low for Springtown. What is the record low for Springtown?	**Example:** The record high temperature for Bakersville is 120°F. This is more than 2 times the record high for Springtown. What is the record high for Springtown?
Explore Bakersville's low is 5 times Springtown's.	**Explore** Bakersville's high is *more than* 2 times Springtown's.
Plan $B = 5 \times S$	**Plan** $B > 2 \times S$
Solve $-35 = 5 \times S$ $$\frac{-35}{5} = S$$ $$-7 = S$$ Springtown's low is −7°F.	**Solve** $120 > 2 \times S$ $$\frac{120}{2} > S$$ $$60 > S$$ Springtown's high is *less than* 60°F.
Examine Check the answer in the original problem.	**Examine** Check whether the answer should include *less than* or *more than*.

Choose the equation or inequality that could be used to solve each problem.

1. On the way to school it was 10°F. It dropped 13 degrees by the end of the day. What is the temperature at the end of the day?

   A. $10 + t = -13$ **B.** $10 - 13 = t$
   C. $10 + t < -13$ **D.** $10 - 13 > t$

2. Football practice begins in 6 weeks. Ted wants to gain at least 12 pounds. How much must he gain per week?

   A. $g \leq 6 \times 12$ **B.** $g \leq 12 \div 6$
   C. $g \geq 6 \times 12$ **D.** $g \geq 12 \div 6$

3. The radio Andrea wants costs $16 less than a cassette player. How much does the radio cost?

   A. $r = c + 16$ **B.** $r = c - 16$
   C. $r > c + 16$ **D.** $r < c + 16$

4. Randy invested $2000 in 150 shares of stock last year. This is twice what the stock is worth today. What is the present value of the stock?

   A. $p < 2000 \times 2$ **B.** $p > 2000 \div 2$
   C. $p = 2000 \times 2$ **D.** $p = 2000 \div 2$

3-8 Study Guide

Applying Equations and Inequalities

Compare these two examples. On the left, an equation is used to find the solution. On the right, an inequality is used.

Example: The record low temperature for Bakersville is ⁻35°F. This is 5 times the record low for Springtown. What is the record low for Springtown?

Explore Bakersville's low is 5 times Springtown's.

Plan $B = 5 \times S$

Solve $^-35 = 5 \times S$

$\dfrac{^-35}{5} = S$

$^-7 = S$

Springtown's low is ⁻7°F.

Examine Check the answer in the original problem.

Example: The record high temperature for Bakersville is 120°F. This is more than 2 times the record high for Springtown. What is the record high for Springtown?

Explore Bakersville's high is *more than* 2 times Springtown's.

Plan $B > 2 \times S$

Solve $120 > 2 \times S$

$\dfrac{120}{2} > S$

$60 > S$

Springtown's high is *less than* 60°F.

Examine Check whether the answer should include *less than* or *more than*.

Choose the equation or inequality that could be used to solve each problem.

1. On the way to school it was 10°F. It dropped 13 degrees by the end of the day. What is the temperature at the end of the day?

   A. $10 + t = ^-13$ **B.** $10 - 13 = t$
   C. $10 + t < ^-13$ **D.** $10 - 13 > t$

2. Football practice begins in 6 weeks. Ted wants to gain at least 12 pounds. How much must he gain per week?

   A. $g \le 6 \times 12$ **B.** $g \le 12 \div 6$
   C. $g \ge 6 \times 12$ **D.** $g \ge 12 \div 6$

3. The radio Andrea wants costs $16 less than a cassette player. How much does the radio cost?

   A. $r = c + 16$ **B.** $r = c - 16$
   C. $r > c + 16$ **D.** $r < c + 16$

4. Randy invested $2000 in 150 shares of stock last year. This is twice what the stock is worth today. What is the present value of the stock?

   A. $p < 2000 \times 2$ **B.** $p > 2000 \div 2$
   C. $p = 2000 \times 2$ **D.** $p = 2000 \div 2$

4-1 Study Guide
Factors and Monomials

The **factors** of a whole number divide that number with no remainder.

> 3 is a factor of 12 because $12 \div 3 = 4$ with no remainder.
> 3 is not a factor of 16 because $16 \div 3 = 5$ with a remainder of 1.

Because $12 \div 3 = 4$, with no remainder, we say that 12 is divisible by 3.

> A number is divisible by:
> ● 2 if the ones digit is divisible by 2.
> ● 3 if the sum of the digits is divisible by 3.
> ● 5 if the ones digit is 0 or 5.
> ● 6 if the number is divisible by 2 *and* 3.
> ● 10 if the ones digit is 0.

A **monomial** is an integer, a variable, or a product of integers or variables.

> Expressions like -537 and $8ac$ are monomials.
> Expressions like $4t + 5$ and $-2(3x - 3)$ are not monomials.

Using divisibility rules, state whether each number is divisible by 2, 3, 5, 6, or 10.

1. 1060

2. 996

3. 285

4. 705

5. 32

6. 64,230

7. 1645

8. 3241

9. 42,246

Determine whether each expression is a monomial. Explain why or why not.

10. $-3mn$

11. $-4x + y$

12. 672

13. $65cde$

14. k

15. $-9(3x - 2)$

4-1 Study Guide

Factors and Monomials

The **factors** of a whole number divide that number with no remainder.

> 3 is a factor of 12 because $12 \div 3 = 4$ with no remainder.
> 3 is not a factor of 16 because $16 \div 3 = 5$ with a remainder of 1.

Because $12 \div 3 = 4$, with no remainder, we say that 12 is divisible by 3.

> A number is divisible by:
> - 2 if the ones digit is divisible by 2.
> - 3 if the sum of the digits is divisible by 3.
> - 5 if the ones digit is 0 or 5.
> - 6 if the number is divisible by 2 *and* 3.
> - 10 if the ones digit is 0.

A **monomial** is an integer, a variable, or a product of integers or variables.

> Expressions like -537 and $8ac$ are monomials.
> Expressions like $4t + 5$ and $-2(3x - 3)$ are not monomials.

Using divisibility rules, state whether each number is divisible by 2, 3, 5, 6, or 10.

1. 1060 **2, 5, 10**

2. 996 **2, 3, 6**

3. 285 **3, 5**

4. 705 **3, 5**

5. 32 **2**

6. 64,230 **2, 3, 5, 6, 10**

7. 1645 **5**

8. 3241 **none**

9. 42,246 **2, 3, 6**

Determine whether each expression is a monomial. Explain why or why not.

10. $-3mn$ **Yes; it is the product of an integer and a variable.**

11. $-4x + y$ **No; it involves addition.**

12. 672 **Yes; it is an integer.**

13. $65cde$ **Yes; it is the product of an integer and variables.**

14. k **Yes; it is a variable.**

15. $-9(3x - 2)$ **No; it involves subtraction.**

4-2 Study Guide
Powers and Exponents

Student Edition
Pages 175–179

Expressions such as 4^2, a^3, 2^n, and $(x + 3)^5$ are written using exponents. In 4^2, the base is 4, and the exponent is 2.

The exponent tells you how many times to use the base as a factor.

$3^4 = 3 \cdot 3 \cdot 3 \cdot 3$, or 81   The number named by 3^4 is 81.

Write each product using exponents.

1. $5 \cdot 5 \cdot 5$

2. $6 \cdot 6 \cdot 6 \cdot 6 \cdot 6$

3. $7 \cdot 7 \cdot 7 \cdot 7 \cdot 7 \cdot 7 \cdot 7 \cdot 7$

4. $2 \cdot 2 \cdot 2 \cdot 3 \cdot 3$

5. $2 \cdot 2 \cdot 2 \cdot 2 \cdot 2 \cdot 2 \cdot 2$

6. $2 \cdot 2 \cdot 2 \cdot 2 \cdot 2 \cdot 5 \cdot 5 \cdot 5$

7. $m \cdot m \cdot m \cdot m \cdot m \cdot m$

8. $n \cdot n \cdot n \cdot n \cdot n \cdot y \cdot y \cdot y \cdot y$

9. $q \cdot q \cdot q \cdot p \cdot p \cdot p \cdot p$

10. $2 \cdot t \cdot t \cdot t \cdot t \cdot t \cdot t$

11. $9 \cdot 9 \cdot 9 \cdot 9 \cdot 9 \cdot 9$

12. $4 \cdot 4 \cdot 6 \cdot 6 \cdot x \cdot x \cdot x \cdot v \cdot v$

Write each power as the product of the same factor.

13. 5^3

14. a^5

15. 1^4

16. $(-j)^2$

17. $(y - 2)^2$

18. 7^2

19. $(-4)^3$

20. 5^{22}

4-2 Study Guide

Powers and Exponents

Expressions such as 4^2, a^3, 2^n, and $(x + 3)^5$ are written using exponents. In 4^2, the base is 4, and the exponent is 2.

The exponent tells you how many times to use the base as a factor.

$3^4 = 3 \cdot 3 \cdot 3 \cdot 3$, or 81   The number named by 3^4 is 81.

Write each product using exponents.

1. $5 \cdot 5 \cdot 5$ $\mathbf{5^3}$

2. $6 \cdot 6 \cdot 6 \cdot 6 \cdot 6$ $\mathbf{6^5}$

3. $7 \cdot 7 \cdot 7 \cdot 7 \cdot 7 \cdot 7 \cdot 7 \cdot 7$ $\mathbf{7^8}$

4. $2 \cdot 2 \cdot 2 \cdot 3 \cdot 3$ $\mathbf{2^3 \cdot 3^2}$

5. $2 \cdot 2 \cdot 2 \cdot 2 \cdot 2 \cdot 2 \cdot 2$ $\mathbf{2^7}$

6. $2 \cdot 2 \cdot 2 \cdot 2 \cdot 2 \cdot 5 \cdot 5 \cdot 5$ $\mathbf{2^5 \cdot 5^3}$

7. $m \cdot m \cdot m \cdot m \cdot m \cdot m$ $\mathbf{m^6}$

8. $n \cdot n \cdot n \cdot n \cdot n \cdot y \cdot y \cdot y \cdot y$ $\mathbf{n^5 \cdot y^4}$

9. $q \cdot q \cdot q \cdot p \cdot p \cdot p \cdot p$ $\mathbf{q^3 \cdot p^4}$

10. $2 \cdot t \cdot t \cdot t \cdot t \cdot t \cdot t$ $\mathbf{2 \cdot t^6}$

11. $9 \cdot 9 \cdot 9 \cdot 9 \cdot 9 \cdot 9$ $\mathbf{9^6}$

12. $4 \cdot 4 \cdot 6 \cdot 6 \cdot x \cdot x \cdot x \cdot v \cdot v$ $\mathbf{4^2 6^2 x^3 v^2}$

Write each power as the product of the same factor.

13. 5^3 $\mathbf{5 \cdot 5 \cdot 5}$

14. a^5
$\mathbf{a \cdot a \cdot a \cdot a \cdot a}$

15. 1^4 $\mathbf{1 \cdot 1 \cdot 1 \cdot 1}$

16. $(-j)^2$ $\mathbf{(-j)(-j)}$

17. $(y - 2)^2$
$\mathbf{(y - 2)(y - 2)}$

18. 7^2 $\mathbf{7 \cdot 7}$

19. $(-4)^3$
$\mathbf{(-4)(-4)(-4)}$

20. 5^{22}
$\mathbf{\underbrace{5 \cdot 5 \cdot \ldots \cdot 5}_{\textbf{22 factors}}}$

4-3 Study Guide
Problem-Solving Strategy: Draw a Diagram

There are four baseball teams in a single elimination tournament. How many baseball games will be played during the tournament?

Explore   There are 4 teams in the single elimination tournament. The problem asks how many games will be played.

Plan   Draw a diagram to show how the winning teams will advance through the tournament. A diagram will help to count the number of games.

Solve

Team A

Team B

Team C

Team D

Notice that 2 games are played in the first round and 1 final game is played for the championship
$$2 + 1 = 3$$
There will be 3 games played in the tournament.

Examine   Each team loses exactly once except the champion. Therefore, $4 - 1$ or 3 games are played. The answer is correct.

Solve. Use any strategy.

1. If a coin is tossed three times, how many different combinations of heads and tails are possible?

2. An airport services seven different airlines and nine different types of airplanes. In how many different ways can a person fly out of the airport?

3. Twelve bowlers will be participating in the annual single elimination bowling tournament. How many games will be played during the tournament?

4. A certain buffet restaurant serves six different entrees, eight kinds of beverages, and four types of desserts. How many different combinations for dinner are possible if each includes an entree, a beverage, and a dessert?

4-3 Study Guide
Problem-Solving Strategy: Draw a Diagram

Student Edition
Pages 181–183

There are four baseball teams in a single elimination tournament. How many baseball games will be played during the tournament?

Explore   There are 4 teams in the single elimination tournament. The problem asks how many games will be played.

Plan   Draw a diagram to show how the winning teams will advance through the tournament. A diagram will help to count the number of games.

Solve   Team A

Team B

Team C

Team D

Notice that 2 games are played in the first round and 1 final game is played for the championship
$$2 + 1 = 3$$
There will be 3 games played in the tournament.

Examine   Each team loses exactly once except the champion. Therefore, 4 − 1 or 3 games are played. The answer is correct.

Solve. Use any strategy.

1. If a coin is tossed three times, how many different combinations of heads and tails are possible? **HHH, HHT, HTH, HTT, THH, THT, TTH, TTT**

2. An airport services seven different airlines and nine different types of airplanes. In how many different ways can a person fly out of the airport? **63 ways**

3. Twelve bowlers will be participating in the annual single elimination bowling tournament. How many games will be played during the tournament? **11 games**

4. A certain buffet restaurant serves six different entrees, eight kinds of beverages, and four types of desserts. How many different combinations for dinner are possible if each includes an entree, a beverage, and a dessert? **192 combinations**

4-4 Study Guide
Prime Factorization

Student Edition
Pages 184–188

A **factor tree** can be used to find the **prime factorization** of a composite number. Test prime numbers as factors in order from least to greatest. Test 2, 3, 5, 7, and so on.

$$
\begin{array}{c}
75 \\
3 \times 25 \\
3 \times 5 \times 5
\end{array}
\quad \textbf{Are all the factors prime?}
$$

$$
\begin{aligned}
30y^2x &= 2 \cdot 15 \cdot y^2 \cdot x \\
&= 2 \cdot 3 \cdot 5 \cdot y \cdot y \cdot x
\end{aligned}
$$

Complete each factor tree.

1.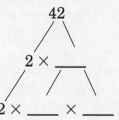

2.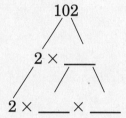

3.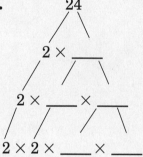

4.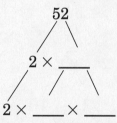

5.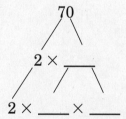

6.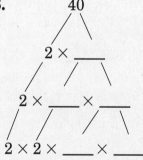

Factor completely.

7. 36

8. -28

9. 50

10. $54xyz$

11. $81m^2n$

12. $100a^2b^2$

13. $-164st^3$

14. $102f^3g^2$

15. $-72rt$

16. $200xy^3$

17. $-225w^2vu$

18. $140cd^2$

Pre-Algebra

A **factor tree** can be used to find the **prime factorization** of a composite number. Test prime numbers as factors in order from least to greatest. Test 2, 3, 5, 7, and so on.

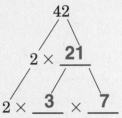

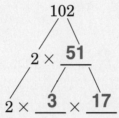

$$30y^2x = 2 \cdot 15 \cdot y^2 \cdot x$$
$$= 2 \cdot 3 \cdot 5 \cdot y \cdot y \cdot x$$

Are all the factors prime?

Complete each factor tree.

1.
```
        42
       /  \
      2 × 21
     /    / \
    2 × 3 × 7
```

2.
```
       102
      /   \
     2 × 51
    /    / \
   2 × 3 × 17
```

3.
```
        24
       /  \
      2 × 12
     /    / \
    2 ×  2 × 6
   /    /   / \
  2 × 2 × 2 × 3
```

4.
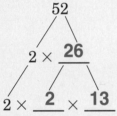
```
        52
       /  \
      2 × 26
     /    / \
    2 × 2 × 13
```

5.
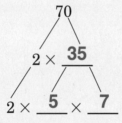
```
        70
       /  \
      2 × 35
     /    / \
    2 × 5 × 7
```

6.
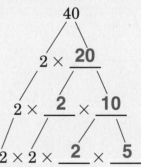
```
         40
        /  \
       2 × 20
      /    / \
     2 × 2 × 10
    /    /   / \
   2 × 2 × 2 × 5
```

Factor completely.

7. 36 **2 · 2 · 3 · 3**

8. –28 **–1 · 2 · 2 · 7**

9. 50 **2 · 5 · 5**

10. $54xyz$ **2 · 3 · 3 · 3 · x · y · z**

11. $81m^2n$ **3 · 3 · 3 · 3 · m · m · n**

12. $100a^2b^2$ **2 · 2 · 5 · 5 · a · a · b · b**

13. $-164st^3$ **–1 · 2 · 2 · 41 · s · t · t · t**

14. $102f^3g^2$ **2 · 3 · 17 · f · f · f · g · g**

15. $-72rt$ **–2 · 2 · 2 · 3 · 3 · r · t**

16. $200xy^3$ **2 · 2 · 2 · 5 · 5 · x · y · y · y**

17. $-225w^2vu$ **–3 · 3 · 5 · 5 · w · w · v · u**

18. $140cd^2$ **2 · 2 · 5 · 7 · c · d · d**

4-5 Study Guide

Greatest Common Factor (GCF)

Step 1
Factor each number completely.

Step 2
Circle all pairs of factors that the numbers have in common.

Step 3
Find the product of the common factors circled in Step 2.

Find the GCF of 24 and 56.

$$24 = 2 \cdot 12 \qquad 56 = 2 \cdot 28$$
$$= 2 \cdot 2 \cdot 6 \qquad = 2 \cdot 2 \cdot 14$$
$$= 2 \cdot 2 \cdot 2 \cdot 3 \qquad = 2 \cdot 2 \cdot 2 \cdot 7$$

$$24 = \boxed{2} \cdot \boxed{2} \cdot \boxed{2} \cdot 3$$
$$56 = \boxed{2} \cdot \boxed{2} \cdot \boxed{2} \cdot 7$$

$$2 \cdot 2 \cdot 2 = 8$$

8 is the GCF.

Find the GCF of $15xy^2$ and $18x^2y$.

$$15xy^2 = 3 \cdot 5 \cdot x \cdot y \cdot y$$

$$18x^2y = 2 \cdot 9 \cdot x \cdot x \cdot y$$
$$= 2 \cdot 3 \cdot 3 \cdot x \cdot x \cdot y$$

$$15xy^2 = 3 \cdot 5 \cdot x \cdot y \cdot y$$

$$18x^2y = 2 \cdot 3 \cdot 3 \cdot x \cdot x \cdot y$$

$$3 \cdot x \cdot y = 3xy$$

$3xy$ is the GCF.

Find the GCF of each set of numbers or monomials.

1. 8, 10

2. 15, 24

3. 42, 54

4. 22, 55

5. 21, 49

6. 75, 100

7. $8n$, $18n$

8. $15vw^2$, $27v^3w$

9. $125ab$, $200a^2b^2$

10. $26r^2$, $91s^2$, $13rs$

11. $48xy$, $72x^3y^3$

12. $15m^3n^2$, $30mn$, $135m^2n^2$

4-5 Study Guide
Greatest Common Factor (GCF)

Student Edition
Pages 190–194

Step 1
Factor each number
completely.

Step 2
Circle all pairs of
factors that the numbers
have in common.

Step 3
Find the product
of the common factors
circled in Step 2.

Find the GCF of 24 and 56.

$24 = 2 \cdot 12$ $56 = 2 \cdot 28$ $24 = \boxed{2} \cdot \boxed{2} \cdot \boxed{2} \cdot 3$ $2 \cdot 2 \cdot 2 = 8$
$\quad = 2 \cdot 2 \cdot 6$ $\quad = 2 \cdot 2 \cdot 14$
$\quad = 2 \cdot 2 \cdot 2 \cdot 3$ $\quad = 2 \cdot 2 \cdot 2 \cdot 7$ $56 = \boxed{2} \cdot \boxed{2} \cdot \boxed{2} \cdot 7$ **8 is the GCF.**

Find the GCF of $15xy^2$ and $18x^2y$.

$15xy^2 = 3 \cdot 5 \cdot x \cdot y \cdot y$ $15xy^2 = 3 \cdot 5 \cdot x \cdot y \cdot y$ $3 \cdot x \cdot y = 3xy$

$18x^2y = 2 \cdot 9 \cdot x \cdot x \cdot y$ $18x^2y = 2 \cdot 3 \cdot 3 \cdot x \cdot x \cdot y$ **$3xy$ is the GCF.**
$\quad = 2 \cdot 3 \cdot 3 \cdot x \cdot x \cdot y$

Find the GCF of each set of numbers or monomials.

1. 8, 10 **2**

2. 15, 24 **3**

3. 42, 54 **6**

4. 22, 55 **11**

5. 21, 49 **7**

6. 75, 100 **25**

7. $8n, 18n$ **$2n$**

8. $15vw^2, 27v^3w$ **$3vw$**

9. $125ab, 200a^2b^2$ **$25ab$**

10. $26r^2, 91s^2, 13rs$ **13**

11. $48xy, 72x^3y^3$ **$24xy$**

12. $15m^3n^2, 30mn,$
$135m^2n^2$ **$15mn$**

Pre-Algebra

4-6 Study Guide
Simplifying Fractions

> To write a fraction in simplest form, divide both the numerator and denominator by their GCF. A fraction is in simplest form when the GCF of the numerator and the denominator is 1.

Write $\dfrac{36}{40}$ in simplest form.

$\dfrac{36}{40} = \dfrac{\cancel{2} \cdot \cancel{2} \cdot 3 \cdot 3}{\cancel{2} \cdot \cancel{2} \cdot 2 \cdot 5}$ **The slashes indicate that the numerator and denominator are divided by 2 · 2, the GCF.**

$= \dfrac{9}{10}$ **The fraction is simplified since the GCF is 1.**

Write $\dfrac{15a^2c^3}{3ac^4}$ simplest form.

$\dfrac{15a^2c^3}{3ac^4} = \dfrac{\cancel{3} \cdot 5 \cdot \cancel{a} \cdot a \cdot \cancel{c} \cdot \cancel{c} \cdot \cancel{c}}{\cancel{3} \cdot \cancel{a} \cdot \cancel{c} \cdot \cancel{c} \cdot \cancel{c} \cdot c}$ **Divide $15a^2c^3$ and $3ac^4$ by $3 \cdot a \cdot c \cdot c \cdot c$, the GCF.**

$= \dfrac{5a}{c}$ **Because the GCF is 1, the fraction is simplified.**

Write each fraction in simplest form. If the fraction is already in simplest form, write simplified.

1. $\dfrac{14}{20}$

2. $\dfrac{16}{35}$

3. $\dfrac{16}{20}$

4. $\dfrac{10}{40}$

5. $\dfrac{16}{36}$

6. $\dfrac{45}{48}$

7. $\dfrac{23}{55}$

8. $\dfrac{49}{56}$

9. $\dfrac{13}{26}$

10. $\dfrac{3x^3}{12x^4}$

11. $\dfrac{9x^2}{16y^3}$

12. $\dfrac{4p^2q^3}{12pq}$

13. $\dfrac{3ab}{15a^2b^3}$

14. $\dfrac{-3r^2s^5}{-12r^3s^6}$

15. $\dfrac{7m^3n^{12}}{15mn^8}$

16. $\dfrac{-13p^4q^3}{26p^5q^7}$

17. $\dfrac{12a^4m^3}{16a^3m^8}$

18. $\dfrac{6q^3v^3}{18q^2v^4}$

4-6 Study Guide
Simplifying Fractions

Student Edition
Pages 196–199

> To write a fraction in simplest form, divide both the numerator and denominator by their GCF. A fraction is in simplest form when the GCF of the numerator and the denominator is 1.

Write $\frac{36}{40}$ in simplest form.

$\frac{36}{40} = \frac{\cancel{2} \cdot \cancel{2} \cdot 3 \cdot 3}{\cancel{2} \cdot \cancel{2} \cdot 2 \cdot 5}$ **The slashes indicate that the numerator and denominator are divided by 2 · 2, the GCF.**

$= \frac{9}{10}$ **The fraction is simplified since the GCF is 1.**

Write $\frac{15a^2c^3}{3ac^4}$ simplest form.

$\frac{15a^2c^3}{3ac^4} = \frac{\cancel{3} \cdot 5 \cdot \cancel{a} \cdot a \cdot \cancel{c} \cdot \cancel{c} \cdot \cancel{c}}{\cancel{3} \cdot \cancel{a} \cdot \cancel{c} \cdot \cancel{c} \cdot \cancel{c} \cdot c}$ **Divide $15a^2c^3$ and $3ac^4$ by $3 \cdot a \cdot c \cdot c \cdot c$, the GCF.**

$= \frac{5a}{c}$ **Because the GCF is 1, the fraction is simplified.**

Write each fraction in simplest form. If the fraction is already in simplest form, write simplified.

1. $\frac{14}{20}$ **$\frac{7}{10}$**

2. $\frac{16}{35}$ **simplified**

3. $\frac{16}{20}$ **$\frac{4}{5}$**

4. $\frac{10}{40}$ **$\frac{1}{4}$**

5. $\frac{16}{36}$ **$\frac{4}{9}$**

6. $\frac{45}{48}$ **$\frac{15}{16}$**

7. $\frac{23}{55}$ **simplified**

8. $\frac{49}{56}$ **$\frac{7}{8}$**

9. $\frac{13}{26}$ **$\frac{1}{2}$**

10. $\frac{3x^3}{12x^4}$ **$\frac{1}{4x}$**

11. $\frac{9x^2}{16y^3}$ **simplified**

12. $\frac{4p^2q^3}{12pq}$ **$\frac{pq^2}{3}$**

13. $\frac{3ab}{15a^2b^3}$ **$\frac{1}{5ab^2}$**

14. $\frac{-3r^2s^5}{-12r^3s^6}$ **$\frac{1}{4rs}$**

15. $\frac{7m^3n^{12}}{15mn^8}$ **$\frac{7m^2n^4}{15}$**

16. $\frac{-13p^4q^3}{26p^5q^7}$ **$-\frac{1}{2pq^4}$**

17. $\frac{12a^4m^3}{16a^3m^8}$ **$\frac{3a}{4m^5}$**

18. $\frac{6q^3v^3}{18q^2v^4}$ **$\frac{q}{3v}$**

4-7 Study Guide
Using the Least Common Multiple (LCM)

Follow these steps to find the **least common multiple (LCM)** of two or more numbers or algebraic expressions.

Step 1
Factor each number or monomial completely.

Step 2
Write the prime factorization as powers.

Step 3
Multiply the greatest power of each number or variable to find the LCM.

Find the LCM of $30a$ and $45b^2$.

$30a = 2 \cdot 3 \cdot 5 \cdot a$
$45b^2 = 3 \cdot 3 \cdot 5 \cdot b \cdot b$

$30a = 2^1 \cdot 3^1 \cdot 5^1 \cdot a^1$
$45b^2 = 3^2 \cdot 5^1 \cdot b^2$

$\mathbf{LCM} = 2^1 \cdot 3^2 \cdot 5^1 \cdot a^1 \cdot b^2$
$= 2 \cdot 9 \cdot 5 \cdot a \cdot b^2$
$= 90ab^2$

You can use the LCM to compare two fractions. To compare two fractions, write them as equal fractions with the same denominator by multiplying or dividing the numerator and denominator by the same *nonzero* number.

Which is greater, $\frac{3}{5}$ or $\frac{2}{3}$?

$$\overset{\times 3}{\frac{3}{5}} = \underset{\times 3}{\frac{9}{15}}$$

$$\overset{\times 5}{\frac{2}{3}} = \underset{\times 5}{\frac{10}{15}}$$

Since $\frac{9}{15} < \frac{10}{15}$, $\frac{3}{5} < \frac{2}{3}$.

Find the LCM of each set of numbers or algebraic expressions.

1. 4, 6

2. 6, 9

3. 21, 9

4. 6, 10

5. 20, 25

6. 15, 20

7. 12, 36

8. 20, 30

9. $4x, 3x$

10. $3c^2, 7c$

11. $16w^2, 72$

12. $4f, 10f^2, 12f^2$

Write < or > in each box to make a true statement.

13. $\frac{2}{3} \square \frac{6}{24}$

14. $\frac{2}{5} \square \frac{3}{4}$

15. $\frac{5}{8} \square \frac{5}{6}$

16. $\frac{7}{10} \square \frac{3}{4}$

17. $\frac{4}{6} \square \frac{3}{12}$

18. $\frac{6}{9} \square \frac{2}{7}$

4-7 Study Guide

Using the Least Common Multiple (LCM)

Follow these steps to find the **least common multiple (LCM)**
of two or more numbers or algebraic expressions.

Step 1
Factor each number
or monomial completely.

Step 2
Write the prime
factorization as powers.

Step 3
Multiply the greatest
power of each number or
variable to find the LCM.

Find the LCM of $30a$ and $45b^2$.

$30a = 2 \cdot 3 \cdot 5 \cdot a$
$45b^2 = 3 \cdot 3 \cdot 5 \cdot b \cdot b$

$30a = 2^1 \cdot 3^1 \cdot 5^1 \cdot a^1$
$45b^2 = 3^2 \cdot 5^1 \cdot b^2$

$\mathbf{LCM} = 2^1 \cdot 3^2 \cdot 5^1 \cdot a^1 \cdot b^2$
$= 2 \cdot 9 \cdot 5 \cdot a \cdot b^2$
$= 90ab^2$

You can use the LCM to compare two fractions. To compare two
fractions, write them as equal fractions with the same
denominator by multiplying or dividing the numerator and
denominator by the same *nonzero* number.

Which is greater, $\frac{3}{5}$ or $\frac{2}{3}$?

$\overset{\times\,3}{\frac{3}{5} = \frac{9}{15}}\underset{\times\,3}{}$

$\overset{\times\,5}{\frac{2}{3} = \frac{10}{15}}\underset{\times\,5}{}$

Since $\frac{9}{15} < \frac{10}{15}$, $\frac{3}{5} < \frac{2}{3}$.

Find the LCM of each set of numbers or algebraic expressions.

1. $4, 6$ **12**

2. $6, 9$ **18**

3. $21, 9$ **63**

4. $6, 10$ **30**

5. $20, 25$ **100**

6. $15, 20$ **60**

7. $12, 36$ **36**

8. $20, 30$ **60**

9. $4x, 3x$ **$12x$**

10. $3c^2, 7c$ **$21c^2$**

11. $16w^2, 72$ **$144w^2$**

12. $4f, 10f^2, 12f^2$ **$60f^2$**

Write < or > in each box to make a true statement.

13. $\frac{2}{3}$ $\boxed{>}$ $\frac{6}{24}$

14. $\frac{2}{5}$ $\boxed{<}$ $\frac{3}{4}$

15. $\frac{5}{8}$ $\boxed{<}$ $\frac{5}{6}$

16. $\frac{7}{10}$ $\boxed{<}$ $\frac{3}{4}$

17. $\frac{4}{6}$ $\boxed{>}$ $\frac{3}{12}$

18. $\frac{6}{9}$ $\boxed{>}$ $\frac{2}{7}$

4-8 Study Guide

Multiplying and Dividing Monomials

Student Edition
Pages 205–209

To multiply powers with the same base, add the exponents.

Examples:
$$x^4 \cdot x^8 = x^{4+8}$$
$$= x^{12}$$

$$(4x^2)(2x^5) = (4 \cdot 2)(x^2 \cdot x^5)$$
$$= 8(x^{2+5})$$
$$= 8x^7$$

To divide powers with the same base, subtract the exponents.

Examples:
$$\frac{4^8}{4^5} = 4^{8-5}$$
$$= 4^3$$

$$\frac{x^5}{x^3} = x^{5-3}$$
$$= x^2$$

Find each product or quotient. Express your answer in exponential form.

1. $8^2 \cdot 8^3$

2. $x^5 \cdot x^1$

3. $10^2 \cdot 10^7$

4. $(3x^2)(2x^4)$

5. $y^3(y^2x)$

6. $a^3 \cdot a^3$

7. $n^1 \cdot n^3$

8. $20^3 \cdot 20^5$

9. $(4x^3)(-2x^5)$

10. $\dfrac{a^5}{a^2}$

11. $\dfrac{10^4}{10^2}$

12. $\dfrac{h^8}{h^4}$

13. $\dfrac{t^9}{t^3}$

14. $\dfrac{(-d)^3}{(-d)^2}$

15. $\dfrac{c^3}{c^1}$

16. $\dfrac{x^4x^3}{x^5}$

17. $\dfrac{5^6}{5^3}$

18. $\dfrac{6^7}{6^2}$

34

4-8 Study Guide

Multiplying and Dividing Monomials

To multiply powers with the same base, add the exponents.

Examples: $x^4 \cdot x^8 = x^{4+8}$

$\qquad = x^{12}$

$(4x^2)(2x^5) = (4 \cdot 2)(x^2 \cdot x^5)$

$\qquad = 8(x^{2+5})$

$\qquad = 8x^7$

To divide powers with the same base, subtract the exponents.

Examples: $\dfrac{4^8}{4^5} = 4^{8-5}$

$\qquad = 4^3$

$\dfrac{x^5}{x^3} = x^{5-3}$

$\qquad = x^2$

***Find each product or quotient. Express your answer in
exponential form.***

1. $8^2 \cdot 8^3$ $\mathbf{8^5}$

2. $x^5 \cdot x^1$ $\boldsymbol{x^6}$

3. $10^2 \cdot 10^7$ $\mathbf{10^9}$

4. $(3x^2)(2x^4)$ $\boldsymbol{6x^6}$

5. $y^3(y^2x)$ $\boldsymbol{y^5x}$

6. $a^3 \cdot a^3$ $\boldsymbol{a^6}$

7. $n^1 \cdot n^3$ $\boldsymbol{n^4}$

8. $20^3 \cdot 20^5$ $\mathbf{20^8}$

9. $(4x^3)(-2x^5)$ $\boldsymbol{-8x^8}$

10. $\dfrac{a^5}{a^2}$ $\boldsymbol{a^3}$

11. $\dfrac{10^4}{10^2}$ $\mathbf{10^2}$

12. $\dfrac{h^8}{h^4}$ $\boldsymbol{h^4}$

13. $\dfrac{t^9}{t^3}$ $\boldsymbol{t^6}$

14. $\dfrac{(-d)^3}{(-d)^2}$ $\boldsymbol{-d}$

15. $\dfrac{c^3}{c^1}$ $\boldsymbol{c^2}$

16. $\dfrac{x^4x^3}{x^5}$ $\boldsymbol{x^2}$

17. $\dfrac{5^6}{5^3}$ $\mathbf{5^3}$

18. $\dfrac{6^7}{6^2}$ $\mathbf{6^5}$

4-9 Study Guide
Negative Exponents

Definition of Negative Exponents
For any nonzero number a and any integer n,
$a^{-n} = \dfrac{1}{a^n}$

Using the definition, $10^{-6} = \dfrac{1}{10^6}$ and $x^{-2} = \dfrac{1}{x^2}$

The definition also shows that $\dfrac{1}{10^6} = 10^{-6}$ and $\dfrac{1}{x^2} = x^{-2}$.

Represent each expression using positive exponents.

1. 3^{-1} **2.** $e^{-4}f$ **3.** w^{-2}

4. $\dfrac{1}{5^{-2}}$ **5.** $(-4)^{-3}$ **6.** $7(xy)^{-1}$

Write each fraction as an exponent with negative exponents.

7. $\dfrac{b}{a^7}$ **8.** $\dfrac{6}{2^3}$ **9.** $\dfrac{1}{6^3}$

10. $\dfrac{1}{100}$ **11.** $\dfrac{1}{u}$ **12.** $\dfrac{s}{r^3 t^2}$

Evaluate each expression.

13. 2^x if $x = -4$ **14.** $(3b)^{-3}$ if $b = -2$ **15.** $5w^{-2}$ if $w = 3$

4-9 Study Guide

Negative Exponents

Definition of Negative Exponents
For any nonzero number a and any integer n,
$a^{-n} = \dfrac{1}{a^n}$

Using the definition, $10^{-6} = \dfrac{1}{10^6}$ and $x^{-2} = \dfrac{1}{x^2}$

The definition also shows that $\dfrac{1}{10^6} = 10^{-6}$ and $\dfrac{1}{x^2} = x^{-2}$.

Represent each expression using positive exponents.

1. 3^{-1} $\dfrac{1}{3}$

2. $e^{-4}f$ $\dfrac{f}{e^4}$

3. w^{-2} $\dfrac{1}{w^2}$

4. $\dfrac{1}{5^{-2}}$ 5^2

5. $(-4)^{-3}$ $\dfrac{1}{(-4)^3}$

6. $7(xy)^{-1}$ $\dfrac{7}{(xy)}$

Write each fraction as an exponent with negative exponents.

7. $\dfrac{b}{a^7}$ ba^{-7}

8. $\dfrac{6}{2^3}$ $6 \cdot 2^{-3}$

9. $\dfrac{1}{6^3}$ 6^{-3}

10. $\dfrac{1}{100}$ 10^{-2}

11. $\dfrac{1}{u}$ u^{-1}

12. $\dfrac{s}{r^3t^2}$ $sr^{-3}t^{-2}$

Evaluate each expression.

13. 2^x if $x = -4$ $\dfrac{1}{16}$

14. $(3b)^{-3}$ if $b = -2$ $\dfrac{-1}{216}$

15. $5w^{-2}$ if $w = 3$ $\dfrac{5}{9}$

5-1 Study Guide
Rational Numbers

The set of **whole numbers** includes 0, 1, 2, 3, ...

The set of **integers** includes . . . , $^-2$, $^-1$, 0, 1, 2, ...

Any number that can be written as a fraction is called a **rational number**.

To express a decimal as a fraction or mixed number, write the digits of the decimal as the numerator and use the appropriate power of ten (10, 100, 1000, · · ·) as the denominator. Simplify if necessary.

Examples: Express each decimal as a fraction in simplest form.

a. $0.125 = \dfrac{125}{1000} = \dfrac{1}{8}$

So, $0.125 = \dfrac{1}{8}$.

b. $0.\overline{7}$

Let $N = 0.777 \ldots$ Multiply N by 10 since one digit repeats.

Then $10N = 7.777 \ldots$

$10N = 7.777 \ldots$ Subtract N from $10N$ to eliminate the repeating part.

$\underline{-\ \ 1N = 0.777 \ldots}$

$9N = 7$

$N = \dfrac{7}{9}$

Express each decimal as a fraction or mixed number in simplest form.

1. 0.8

2. $^-0.4$

3. 0.09

4. $0.\overline{48}$

5. 0.15

6. 0.25

7. $^-0.\overline{81}$

8. 0.88

9. $0.\overline{6}$

10. 0.845

11. $5.\overline{36}$

12. $7.\overline{16}$

Name the set(s) of numbers to which each number belongs. (Use the symbols W = whole numbers, I = integers, and R = rationals.)

13. 2

14. $^-4$

15. 4.169

16. $-\dfrac{1}{4}$

17. $-2\dfrac{3}{5}$

18. 0.32

19. $\dfrac{18}{3}$

20. $^-8.0$

5-1 Study Guide
Rational Numbers

Student Edition
Pages 224–228

The set of **whole numbers** includes 0, 1, 2, 3, ...

The set of **integers** includes . . . , $-2, -1, 0, 1, 2, ...$

Any number that can be written as a fraction is called a **rational number**.

To express a decimal as a fraction or mixed number, write the digits of the decimal as the numerator and use the appropriate power of ten (10, 100, 1000, · · ·) as the denominator. Simplify if necessary.

Examples: Express each decimal as a fraction in simplest form.

a. $0.125 = \dfrac{125}{1000} = \dfrac{1}{8}$

So, $0.125 = \dfrac{1}{8}$.

b. $0.\overline{7}$

Let $N = 0.777 . . . .$

Then $10N = 7.777 . . . .$

$$\begin{array}{r} 10N = 7.777 . . . \\ - \quad 1N = 0.777 . . . \\ \hline 9N = 7 \\ N = \dfrac{7}{9} \end{array}$$

Multiply *N* by 10 since one digit repeats.

Subtract *N* from 10*N* to eliminate the repeating part.

Express each decimal as a fraction or mixed number in simplest form.

1. 0.8 $\dfrac{4}{5}$

2. -0.4 $-\dfrac{2}{5}$

3. 0.09 $\dfrac{9}{100}$

4. $0.\overline{48}$ $\dfrac{16}{33}$

5. 0.15 $\dfrac{3}{20}$

6. 0.25 $\dfrac{1}{4}$

7. $-0.\overline{81}$ $-\dfrac{81}{99}$

8. 0.88 $\dfrac{22}{25}$

9. $0.\overline{6}$ $\dfrac{2}{3}$

10. 0.845 $\dfrac{169}{200}$

11. $5.\overline{36}$ $5\dfrac{12}{33}$

12. $7.\overline{16}$ $7\dfrac{16}{99}$

Name the set(s) of numbers to which each number belongs. (Use the symbols W = whole numbers, I = integers, and R = rationals.)

13. 2 **W, I, R**

14. -4 **I, R**

15. 4.169 **R**

16. $-\dfrac{1}{4}$ **R**

17. $-2\dfrac{3}{5}$ **R**

18. 0.32 **R**

19. $\dfrac{18}{3}$ **W, I, R**

20. -8.0 **I, R**

Pre-Algebra

5-2 Study Guide
Estimating Sums and Differences

You can use rounding to estimate sums and differences. Round each number to a convenient place-value position.

$4.25 + 3.56$
$4.25 + 3.56 \rightarrow 4 + 4 = 8$
$4.25 + 3.56$ is about 8.

$\$187.45 - \$53.81$
$\$187.45 - \$53.81 \rightarrow 190 - 50 = 140$
$\$187.45 - \$53.81$ is about $\$140$.

To estimate sums and differences of mixed numbers, round each mixed number to the nearest whole number. To estimate sums and differences of proper fractions, round each fraction to 0, $\frac{1}{2}$, or 1.

$15\frac{17}{19} - 7\frac{3}{43} \rightarrow 16 - 7 = 9$

$\frac{12}{25} + \frac{7}{65} + \frac{34}{35} \rightarrow \frac{1}{2} + 0 + 1 = 1\frac{1}{2}$

Round to the nearest whole number.

1. 9.23

2. 3.045

3. 17.792

4. 634.572

5. $37\frac{5}{29}$

6. $6\frac{5}{6}$

7. $13\frac{1}{7}$

8. $4\frac{8}{9}$

Round each fraction to 0, $\frac{1}{2}$, or 1.

9. $\frac{17}{35}$

10. $\frac{5}{9}$

11. $\frac{2}{11}$

12. $\frac{15}{16}$

Estimate each sum or difference.

13. $24.02 + 17.46$

14. $74.63 - 65.89$

15. $10\frac{17}{20} - 8\frac{2}{9}$

16. $28\frac{1}{6} - 4\frac{9}{17}$

17. $2\frac{4}{11} + \frac{6}{31}$

18. $21\frac{6}{7} + 5\frac{8}{27}$

5-2 Study Guide
Estimating Sums and Differences

You can use rounding to estimate sums and differences. Round
each number to a convenient place-value position.

$4.25 + 3.56$

$4.25 + 3.56 \rightarrow 4 + 4 = 8$

$4.25 + 3.56$ is about 8.

$\$187.45 - \$53.81$

$\$187.45 - \$53.81 \rightarrow 190 - 50 = 140$

$\$187.45 - \$53.81$ is about $\$140$.

To estimate sums and differences of mixed numbers, round
each mixed number to the nearest whole number. To estimate
sums and differences of proper fractions, round each fraction
to 0, $\frac{1}{2}$, or 1.

$15\frac{17}{19} - 7\frac{3}{43} \rightarrow 16 - 7 = 9$

$\frac{12}{25} + \frac{7}{65} + \frac{34}{35} \rightarrow \frac{1}{2} + 0 + 1 = 1\frac{1}{2}$

Round to the nearest whole number.

1. 9.23 **9**

2. 3.045 **3**

3. 17.792 **18**

4. 634.572 **635**

5. $37\frac{5}{29}$ **37**

6. $6\frac{5}{6}$ **7**

7. $13\frac{1}{7}$ **13**

8. $4\frac{8}{9}$ **5**

Round each fraction to 0, $\frac{1}{2}$, or 1.

9. $\frac{17}{35}$ **$\frac{1}{2}$**

10. $\frac{5}{9}$ **$\frac{1}{2}$**

11. $\frac{2}{11}$ **0**

12. $\frac{15}{16}$ **1**

Estimate each sum or difference. Sample answers are given.

13. $24.02 + 17.46$ **40**

14. $74.63 - 65.89$ **9**

15. $10\frac{17}{20} - 8\frac{2}{9}$ **3**

16. $28\frac{1}{6} - 4\frac{9}{17}$ **23**

17. $2\frac{4}{11} + \frac{6}{31}$ **2**

18. $21\frac{6}{7} + 5\frac{8}{27}$ **27**

5-3 Study Guide

Adding and Subtracting Decimals

Student Edition
Pages 234–238

To add or subtract decimals, first align the decimal points and place zeros where necessary. Then add or subtract as with whole numbers.

$$\text{Solve } m = 38.5 + 52.12 \rightarrow \begin{array}{r} 38.50 \\ + 52.12 \\ \hline m = 90.62 \end{array}$$

$$\text{Solve } d = 235 - 13.8 \rightarrow \begin{array}{r} 235.0 \\ - 13.8 \\ \hline d = 221.1 \end{array}$$

Solve each equation.

1. $x = 3.2 + 4.7$

2. $-2.06 + 3.15 = m$

3. $y = -36.09 - (-7.01)$

4. $47.9 + 3.24 = w$

5. $g = 0.5623 - 0.3541$

6. $52.5 + 8.62 = k$

7. $h = -27.8 + (-14.32)$

8. $3.09 - 0.05 = b$

9. $m = 16.2 - 5.59$

10. $58 - 0.232 = z$

11. $j = 23 + (-1.59)$

12. $15.6 - 0.423 = g$

13. $r = -8.52 + 2.43$

14. $150 - 25.6 = f$

15. $v = -3.56 - 0.49$

Simplify each expression.

16. $0.5y + 0.7y$

17. $9x - 2.5x$

18. $3.81n + 0.092n + 4.6n$

19. $3.56t - 0.59t + 46.08t$

20. $3.0w - 24.15w + 56.052w$

21. $215.5v - 36v - 4.63v$

5-3 Study Guide
Adding and Subtracting Decimals

To add or subtract decimals, first align the decimal points and place zeros where necessary. Then add or subtract as with whole numbers.

Solve $m = 38.5 + 52.12 \rightarrow$
$$\begin{array}{r} 38.50 \\ + 52.12 \\ \hline m = 90.62 \end{array}$$

Solve $d = 235 - 13.8 \rightarrow$
$$\begin{array}{r} 235.0 \\ - 13.8 \\ \hline d = 221.1 \end{array}$$

Solve each equation.

1. $x = 3.2 + 4.7$ **7.9**

2. $-2.06 + 3.15 = m$
1.09

3. $y = -36.09 - (-7.01)$
−29.08

4. $47.9 + 3.24 = w$
51.14

5. $g = 0.5623 - 0.3541$
0.2082

6. $52.5 + 8.62 = k$ **61.12**

7. $h = -27.8 + (-14.32)$
−42.12

8. $3.09 - 0.05 = b$
3.04

9. $m = 16.2 - 5.59$ **10.61**

10. $58 - 0.232 = z$
57.768

11. $j = 23 + (-1.59)$
21.41

12. $15.6 - 0.423 = g$
15.177

13. $r = -8.52 + 2.43$
−6.09

14. $150 - 25.6 = f$ **124.4**

15. $v = -3.56 - 0.49$
−4.05

Simplify each expression.

16. $0.5y + 0.7y$ **1.2y**

17. $9x - 2.5x$ **6.5x**

18. $3.81n + 0.092n + 4.6n$ **8.502n**

19. $3.56t - 0.59t + 46.08t$ **49.05t**

20. $3.0w - 24.15w + 56.052w$ **34.902w**

21. $215.5v - 36v - 4.63v$ **174.87v**

5-4 Study Guide

Adding and Subtracting Like Fractions

To add fractions with like denominators, add the numerators. Write the sum over the common denominator. When the sum of the two fractions is greater than 1, the sum is written as a mixed number.

$$w = \frac{4}{12} + \frac{10}{12}$$
$$= \frac{14}{12}$$
$$= 1\frac{2}{12} \text{ or } 1\frac{1}{6}$$

$$n = 2\frac{2}{5} + 1\frac{1}{5}$$
$$= 3\frac{3}{5}$$

To subtract fractions with like denominators, subtract the numerators. Write the difference over the common denominator.

$$x = \frac{7}{15} - \frac{1}{15}$$
$$x = \frac{6}{15} \text{ or } \frac{2}{5}$$

$$y = 4\frac{3}{4} - 2\frac{1}{4}$$
$$y = 2\frac{2}{4} - 2\frac{1}{2}$$

Solve each equation. Write the solution in simplest form.

1. $\frac{4}{7} + \frac{2}{7} = a$

2. $m = 1\frac{6}{9} + 2\frac{3}{9}$

3. $s = 1\frac{12}{20} + \frac{7}{20}$

4. $\frac{15}{16} + \frac{7}{16} = n$

5. $\frac{13}{20} - \frac{3}{20} = v$

6. $d = \frac{23}{18} - \frac{15}{18}$

7. $-\frac{12}{50} + \left(-\frac{2}{50}\right) = h$

8. $j = 1\frac{13}{16} - \frac{7}{16}$

9. $\frac{62}{52} - \frac{12}{52} = f$

10. $\frac{11}{8} - \frac{17}{8} = g$

11. $\frac{17}{32} - \frac{5}{32} = d$

12. $b = 1\frac{15}{42} + \left(-\frac{11}{42}\right)$

13. $2\frac{2}{30} - \frac{12}{30} = y$

14. $c = 6\frac{6}{7} + \frac{6}{7}$

15. $p = \frac{7}{8} - \frac{3}{8}$

Evaluate each expression if $x = \frac{1}{15}$, $y = \frac{8}{15}$, and $z = \frac{4}{15}$. Write in simplest form.

16. $x - y$

17. $z - x$

18. $x + z$

19. $x + y$

20. $y - z$

21. $y + z$

5-4 Study Guide

Adding and Subtracting Like Fractions

Student Edition
Pages 239–243

To add fractions with like denominators, add the numerators. Write the sum over the common denominator. When the sum of the two fractions is greater than 1, the sum is written as a mixed number.

$$w = \frac{4}{12} + \frac{10}{12}$$
$$= \frac{14}{12}$$
$$= 1\frac{2}{12} \text{ or } 1\frac{1}{6}$$

$$n = 2\frac{2}{5} + 1\frac{1}{5}$$
$$= 3\frac{3}{5}$$

To subtract fractions with like denominators, subtract the numerators. Write the difference over the common denominator.

$$x = \frac{7}{15} - \frac{1}{15}$$
$$x = \frac{6}{15} \text{ or } \frac{2}{5}$$

$$y = 4\frac{3}{4} - 2\frac{1}{4}$$
$$y = 2\frac{2}{4} - 2\frac{1}{2}$$

Solve each equation. Write the solution in simplest form.

1. $\frac{4}{7} + \frac{2}{7} = a$ $\frac{6}{7}$

2. $m = 1\frac{6}{9} + 2\frac{3}{9}$ **4**

3. $s = 1\frac{12}{20} + \frac{7}{20}$ $1\frac{19}{20}$

4. $\frac{15}{16} + \frac{7}{16} = n$ $1\frac{3}{8}$

5. $\frac{13}{20} - \frac{3}{20} = v$ $\frac{1}{2}$

6. $d = \frac{23}{18} - \frac{15}{18}$ $\frac{4}{9}$

7. $-\frac{12}{50} + \left(-\frac{2}{50}\right) = h$ $-\frac{7}{25}$

8. $j = 1\frac{13}{16} - \frac{7}{16}$ $1\frac{3}{8}$

9. $\frac{62}{52} - \frac{12}{52} = f$ $\frac{25}{26}$

10. $\frac{11}{8} - \frac{17}{8} = g$ $-\frac{3}{4}$

11. $\frac{17}{32} - \frac{5}{32} = d$ $\frac{3}{8}$

12. $b = 1\frac{15}{42} + \left(-\frac{11}{42}\right)$ $1\frac{2}{21}$

13. $2\frac{2}{30} - \frac{12}{30} = y$ $1\frac{2}{3}$

14. $c = 6\frac{6}{7} + \frac{6}{7}$ $7\frac{5}{7}$

15. $p = \frac{7}{8} - \frac{3}{8}$ $\frac{1}{2}$

Evaluate each expression if $x = \frac{1}{15}$, $y = \frac{8}{15}$, and $z = \frac{4}{15}$. Write in simplest form.

16. $x - y$ $-\frac{7}{15}$

17. $z - x$ $\frac{1}{5}$

18. $x + z$ $\frac{1}{3}$

19. $x + y$ $\frac{3}{5}$

20. $y - z$ $\frac{4}{15}$

21. $y + z$ $\frac{12}{15}$

5-5 Study Guide

Adding and Subtracting Unlike Fractions

To find the sum or difference of two fractions with unlike denominators, rename each fraction with a common denominator. The common denominator will be the least common multiple of the given denominators. This is called the **least common denominator (LCD)**.

List the multiples to find the LCD.	Rename each fraction with the LCD.	Add or subtract. Simplify if necessary.
$\frac{1}{9}$ 9: 9, 18, 27, . . . $\rightarrow$	$\frac{1}{9} = \frac{2}{18}$ $\rightarrow$	$\frac{2}{18}$
$+\frac{2}{6}$ 6: 6, 12, 18, . . . $\rightarrow$	$+\frac{2}{6} = \frac{6}{18}$ $\rightarrow$	$+\frac{6}{18}$
LCM: 18		$\frac{8}{18}$ or $\frac{4}{9}$

Solve each equation. Write the solution in simplest form.

1. $\frac{1}{3} - \frac{1}{6} = c$

2. $\frac{1}{5} + \frac{1}{7} = k$

3. $b = \frac{1}{8} + \frac{1}{9}$

4. $\frac{7}{16} - \frac{3}{8} = a$

5. $g = \frac{7}{10} + \frac{2}{5}$

6. $\frac{3}{14} - \frac{1}{7} = h$

7. $2\frac{5}{12} + 1\frac{1}{3} = d$

8. $6\frac{5}{4} + 3\frac{1}{2} = b$

9. $4\frac{1}{6} - 3\frac{1}{8} = s$

10. $a = 9\frac{1}{6} + 7\frac{4}{9}$

11. $11\frac{3}{16} - 5\frac{1}{12} = m$

12. $18\frac{7}{30} - 3\frac{1}{6} = y$

Evaluate each expression if $c = -\frac{2}{3}$, $d = \frac{3}{4}$, and $f = 2\frac{5}{6}$. Write the solution in simplest form.

13. $f + c$

14. $d + f$

15. $c - d$

16. $f - c$

17. $c + d$

18. $d + f + c$

19. $f - d + c$

20. $f + d - c$

21. $c + f - d$

5-5 Study Guide

Adding and Subtracting Unlike Fractions

To find the sum or difference of two fractions with unlike denominators, rename each fraction with a common denominator. The common denominator will be the least common multiple of the given denominators. This is called the **least common denominator (LCD)**.

List the multiples to find the LCD.	Rename each fraction with the LCD.	Add or subtract. Simplify if necessary.

$\dfrac{1}{9}$ 9: 9, 18, 27, . . . → $\dfrac{1}{9} = \dfrac{2}{18}$ → $\dfrac{2}{18}$

$+\dfrac{2}{6}$ 6: 6, 12, 18, . . . → $+\dfrac{2}{6} = \dfrac{6}{18}$ → $+\dfrac{6}{18}$

LCM: 18

$\dfrac{8}{18}$ or $\dfrac{4}{9}$

Solve each equation. Write the solution in simplest form.

1. $\dfrac{1}{3} - \dfrac{1}{6} = c$ $\dfrac{1}{6}$

2. $\dfrac{1}{5} + \dfrac{1}{7} = k$ $\dfrac{12}{35}$

3. $b = \dfrac{1}{8} + \dfrac{1}{9}$ $\dfrac{17}{72}$

4. $\dfrac{7}{16} - \dfrac{3}{8} = a$ $\dfrac{1}{16}$

5. $g = \dfrac{7}{10} + \dfrac{2}{5}$ $1\dfrac{1}{10}$

6. $\dfrac{3}{14} - \dfrac{1}{7} = h$ $\dfrac{1}{14}$

7. $2\dfrac{5}{12} + 1\dfrac{1}{3} = d$ $3\dfrac{3}{4}$

8. $6\dfrac{5}{4} + 3\dfrac{1}{2} = b$ $10\dfrac{3}{4}$

9. $4\dfrac{1}{6} - 3\dfrac{1}{8} = s$ $1\dfrac{1}{24}$

10. $a = 9\dfrac{1}{6} + 7\dfrac{4}{9}$ $16\dfrac{11}{18}$

11. $11\dfrac{3}{16} - 5\dfrac{1}{12} = m$ $6\dfrac{5}{48}$

12. $18\dfrac{7}{30} - 3\dfrac{1}{6} = y$ $15\dfrac{1}{15}$

Evaluate each expression if $c = -\dfrac{2}{3}$, $d = \dfrac{3}{4}$, and $f = 2\dfrac{5}{6}$. Write the solution in simplest form.

13. $f + c$ $2\dfrac{1}{6}$

14. $d + f$ $3\dfrac{7}{12}$

15. $c - d$ $-1\dfrac{5}{12}$

16. $f - c$ $3\dfrac{1}{2}$

17. $c + d$ $\dfrac{1}{12}$

18. $d + f + c$ $2\dfrac{11}{12}$

19. $f - d + c$ $1\dfrac{5}{12}$

20. $f + d - c$ $4\dfrac{1}{4}$

21. $c + f - d$ $1\dfrac{5}{12}$

     Pre-Algebra

5-6 Study Guide
Solving Equations

An equation like $x - 6.2 = 13.4$ can be solved using addition.

$$x - 6.2 = 13.4$$

$$x - 6.2 + 6.2 = 13.4 + 6.2 \quad \textbf{Add 6.2 to each side.}$$

$$x = 19.6$$

To check the solution, replace x with 19.6

$$x - 6.2 = 13.4$$

$$19.6 - 6.2 \stackrel{?}{=} 13.4$$

$$13.4 = 13.4 \; ✔ \quad \textbf{The solution is 19.6.}$$

An equation like $s + \frac{2}{3} = \frac{5}{2}$ can be solved using subtraction.

$$s + \frac{2}{3} = \frac{5}{2}$$

$$s + \frac{2}{3} - \frac{2}{3} = \frac{5}{2} - \frac{2}{3} \quad \textbf{Subtract } \frac{2}{3} \textbf{ from each side.}$$

$$s = \frac{11}{6}$$

To check the solution, replace s with $\frac{11}{6}$.

$$s + \frac{2}{3} = \frac{5}{2} \rightarrow \frac{11}{6} + \frac{2}{3} = \frac{5}{2}$$

$$\frac{15}{6} \stackrel{?}{=} \frac{5}{2}$$

$$\frac{5}{2} = \frac{5}{2} \; ✔ \quad \textbf{The solution is } \frac{11}{16}.$$

Solve each equation. Check your solution.

1. $x + 5.3 = 19.6$

2. $q - 1.8 = 4.25$

3. $x + 9.16 = {}^-10.16$

4. $^-35.2 = n - 16$

5. $m - 4.3 = {}^-7.5$

6. $0.45 + p = 1.35$

7. $\frac{6}{5} = n + \frac{4}{10}$

8. $\frac{1}{3} + w = \frac{2}{5}$

9. $5\frac{1}{2} = a - 3\frac{2}{3}$

10. $h - 10.6 = 7.3$

11. $d + 5.8 = 4.17$

12. $a - 2\frac{1}{4} = 6\frac{1}{8}$

13. $q - 0.24 = 32.15$

14. $c + \frac{5}{12} = \frac{5}{6}$

15. $62.03 + j = 78.2$

16. $b - 7\frac{1}{2} = 1\frac{1}{2}$

17. $14.7 = k - 17.3$

18. $0.75 + c = 2.81$

5-6 Study Guide
Solving Equations

An equation like $x - 6.2 = 13.4$ can be solved using addition.

$$x - 6.2 = 13.4$$

$$x - 6.2 + 6.2 = 13.4 + 6.2 \quad \textbf{Add 6.2 to each side.}$$

$$x = 19.6$$

To check the solution, replace x with 19.6

$$x - 6.2 = 13.4$$

$$19.6 - 6.2 \stackrel{?}{=} 13.4$$

$$13.4 = 13.4 \ \checkmark \quad \textbf{The solution is 19.6.}$$

An equation like $s + \dfrac{2}{3} = \dfrac{5}{2}$ can be solved using subtraction.

$$s + \frac{2}{3} = \frac{5}{2}$$

$$s + \frac{2}{3} - \frac{2}{3} = \frac{5}{2} - \frac{2}{3} \quad \textbf{Subtract } \frac{2}{3} \textbf{ from each side.}$$

$$s = \frac{11}{6}$$

To check the solution, replace s with $\dfrac{11}{6}$.

$$s + \frac{2}{3} = \frac{5}{2} \rightarrow \frac{11}{6} + \frac{2}{3} = \frac{5}{2}$$

$$\frac{15}{6} \stackrel{?}{=} \frac{5}{2}$$

$$\frac{5}{2} = \frac{5}{2} \ \checkmark \quad \textbf{The solution is } \frac{11}{16}.$$

Solve each equation. Check your solution.

1. $x + 5.3 = 19.6$ **14.3**

2. $q - 1.8 = 4.25$ **6.05**

3. $x + 9.16 = {}^-10.16$
 ⁻19.32

4. $^-35.2 = n - 16$ **⁻19.2**

5. $m - 4.3 = {}^-7.5$ **⁻3.2**

6. $0.45 + p = 1.35$ **0.9**

7. $\dfrac{6}{5} = n + \dfrac{4}{10}$ **$\dfrac{4}{5}$**

8. $\dfrac{1}{3} + w = \dfrac{2}{5}$ **$\dfrac{1}{15}$**

9. $5\dfrac{1}{2} = a - 3\dfrac{2}{3}$ **$9\dfrac{1}{6}$**

10. $h - 10.6 = 7.3$ **17.9**

11. $d + 5.8 = 4.17$ **⁻1.63**

12. $a - 2\dfrac{1}{4} = 6\dfrac{1}{8}$ **$8\dfrac{3}{8}$**

13. $q - 0.24 = 32.15$
 32.39

14. $c + \dfrac{5}{12} = \dfrac{5}{6}$ **$\dfrac{5}{12}$**

15. $62.03 + j = 78.2$
 16.17

16. $b - 7\dfrac{1}{2} = 1\dfrac{1}{2}$ **9**

17. $14.7 = k - 17.3$ **32**

18. $0.75 + c = 2.81$ **2.06**

5-7 Study Guide
Solving Inequalities

An equation like $b + \frac{3}{7} \geq 2$ can be solved using subtraction.

$$b + \frac{3}{7} \geq 2$$

$$b + \frac{3}{7} - \frac{3}{7} \geq 2 - \frac{3}{7} \quad \text{Subtract } \frac{3}{7} \text{ from each side.}$$

$$b \geq \frac{14}{7} - \frac{3}{7} \quad \text{Rename 2 as } \frac{14}{7}.$$

$$b \geq \frac{11}{7} \text{ or } 1\frac{4}{7}$$

Check the solution, replacing b with a number greater than $1\frac{4}{7}$. Try 2.

$$b + \frac{3}{7} \geq 2$$

$$2 + \frac{3}{7} \stackrel{?}{\geq} 2$$

$$2\frac{3}{7} \geq 2 \checkmark \quad \text{The solution is } b \geq 1\frac{4}{7}.$$

An equation like $d - 2.4 \leq 5.3$ can be solved using addition.

$$d - 2.4 \leq 5.3$$

$$d - 2.4 + 2.4 \leq 5.3 + 2.4 \quad \text{Add 2.4 to each side.}$$

$$d \leq 7.7$$

Check the solution, replacing d with number less than or equal to 7.7 Try 7.4.

$$d - 2.4 \leq 5.3$$

$$7.4 - 2.4 \stackrel{?}{\leq} 5.3$$

$$5 \leq 5.3 \checkmark \quad \text{The solution is } d \leq 7.7.$$

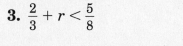

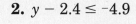

Solve each inequality and check your solution. Then graph the solution on the number line.

1. $w - 1\frac{3}{4} \geq \frac{5}{12}$

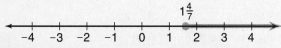

2. $y - 2.4 \leq {}^-4.9$

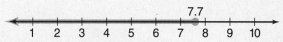

3. $\frac{2}{3} + r < \frac{5}{8}$

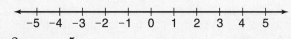

4. $b + 7\frac{1}{2} < 3\frac{1}{2}$

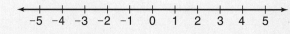

5. $53.60 + m > 49.10$

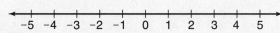

6. $x + \frac{1}{6} \leq 3\frac{3}{5}$

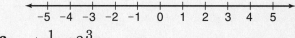

7. $^-5.8 \leq n - 2.3$

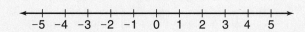

8. $0.75 + c > 2.81$

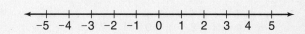

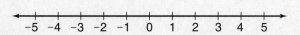

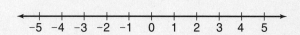

5-7 Study Guide
Solving Inequalities

Student Edition
Pages 251–254

An equation like $b + \frac{3}{7} \geq 2$ can be solved using subtraction.

$$b + \frac{3}{7} \geq 2$$

$$b + \frac{3}{7} - \frac{3}{7} \geq 2 - \frac{3}{7} \quad \textbf{Subtract } \frac{3}{7} \textbf{ from each side.}$$

$$b \geq \frac{14}{7} - \frac{3}{7} \quad \textbf{Rename 2 as } \frac{14}{7}.$$

$$b \geq \frac{11}{7} \text{ or } 1\frac{4}{7}$$

Check the solution, replacing b with a number greater than $1\frac{4}{7}$. Try 2.

$$b + \frac{3}{7} \geq 2$$

$$2 + \frac{3}{7} \overset{?}{\geq} 2$$

$$2\frac{3}{7} \geq 2 \;✔ \quad \textbf{The solution is } b \geq 1\frac{4}{7}.$$

An equation like $d - 2.4 \leq 5.3$ can be solved using addition.

$$d - 2.4 \leq 5.3$$

$$d - 2.4 + 2.4 \leq 5.3 + 2.4 \quad \textbf{Add 2.4 to each side.}$$

$$d \leq 7.7$$

Check the solution, replacing d with number less than or equal to 7.7 Try 7.4.

$$d - 2.4 \leq 5.3$$

$$7.4 - 2.4 \overset{?}{\leq} 5.3$$

$$5 \leq 5.3 \;✔ \quad \textbf{The solution is } d \leq 7.7.$$

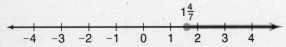

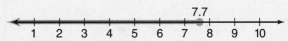

Solve each inequality and check your solution. Then graph the solution on the number line.

1. $w - 1\frac{3}{4} \geq \frac{5}{12}$ $\boldsymbol{w \geq 2\frac{1}{6}}$

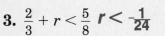

2. $y - 2.4 \leq {}^{-}4.9$ $\boldsymbol{y \leq {}^{-}2.5}$

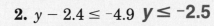

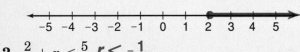

3. $\frac{2}{3} + r < \frac{5}{8}$ $\boldsymbol{r < {}^{-}\frac{1}{24}}$

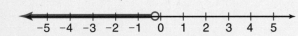

4. $b + 7\frac{1}{2} < 3\frac{1}{2}$ $\boldsymbol{b < {}^{-}4}$

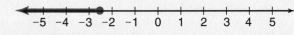

5. $53.60 + m > 49.10$ $\boldsymbol{m > {}^{-}4.5}$

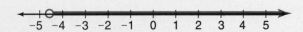

6. $x + \frac{1}{6} \leq 3\frac{3}{5}$ $\boldsymbol{x \leq 3\frac{13}{30}}$

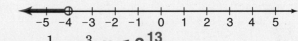

7. ${}^{-}5.8 \leq n - 2.3$ $\boldsymbol{n \geq {}^{-}3.5}$

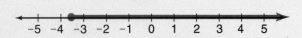

8. $0.75 + c > 2.81$ $\boldsymbol{c > 2.06}$

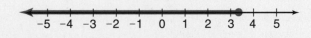

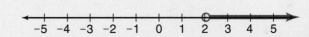

Pre-Algebra

5-8 Study Guide
Problem-Solving Strategy: Using Logical Reasoning

To make a conclusion based on what has happened in the past is called **inductive reasoning**.

Example: Carla noticed that for the last four Wednesdays her teacher has given a pop quiz. So, Carla assumed that on Wednesday there will be a pop quiz.

Deductive reasoning uses a rule to make a conclusion or a decision.

Example: The radius of a circle is half its diameter. Circle G has a diameter 12 meters long. Therefore, the measure of the radius must be 6 meters.

State whether each is an example of inductive or deductive reasoning. Explain your answer.

1. The school cafeteria has served pizza every Tuesday for five weeks. Jessica says, "Tomorrow is Tuesday. We will probably have pizza."

2. Teams that win seven games will make the playoffs. Carter Junior High won seven games, so they will go to the playoffs.

3. It has rained on the first day of school for the past three years. Kimo thinks that it will rain on the first day of school this year.

4. Any number multiplied by zero is equal to zero. $408,249 \times 0 = 0$

5. If a student earns an 90% or higher on his or her term paper, then the paper will be entered in the literature contest. Andre earned an 98%, so his paper will be entered in the literature contest.

6. Every customer who came into Balmer's Clothing was carrying an umbrella. Mrs. Balmer decided that it was probably raining.

43

5-8 Study Guide

Problem-Solving Strategy: Using Logical Reasoning

To make a conclusion based on what has happened in the past is called **inductive reasoning**.

Example: Carla noticed that for the last four Wednesdays her teacher has given a pop quiz. So, Carla assumed that on Wednesday there will be a pop quiz.

Deductive reasoning uses a rule to make a conclusion or a decision.

Example: The radius of a circle is half its diameter. Circle *G* has a diameter 12 meters long. Therefore, the measure of the radius must be 6 meters.

State whether each is an example of inductive or deductive reasoning. Explain your answer. **See students' explanations.**

1. The school cafeteria has served pizza every Tuesday for five weeks. Jessica says, "Tomorrow is Tuesday. We will probably have pizza." **inductive**

2. Teams that win seven games will make the playoffs. Carter Junior High won seven games, so they will go to the playoffs. **deductive**

3. It has rained on the first day of school for the past three years. Kimo thinks that it will rain on the first day of school this year. **inductive**

4. Any number multiplied by zero is equal to zero. $408,249 \times 0 = 0$ **deductive**

5. If a student earns an 90% or higher on his or her term paper, then the paper will be entered in the literature contest. Andre earned an 98%, so his paper will be entered in the literature contest. **deductive**

6. Every customer who came into Balmer's Clothing was carrying an umbrella. Mrs. Balmer decided that it was probably raining. **inductive**

T 43

5-9 Study Guide

Integration: Discrete Mathematics
Arithmetic Sequences

The list of numbers 4, 11, 18, 25, 32, 39, $\cdots$ is called a **sequence**.

Each term is 7 more than the previous term. That is, there is a **common difference** of 7.

$11 - 4 = 7, \ 18 - 11 = 7, \ 25 - 18 = 7, \cdots$

Since the difference between any two consecutive terms is the same, the sequence is called an **arithmetic sequence**.

State whether each sequence is an arithmetic sequence. Then write the next three terms of each sequence.

1. 5, 14, 23, 32, 41, $\cdots$

2. 24, 39, 54, 69, 84, $\cdots$

3. 16.5, 18.3, 21.1, 24.9, 29.7, $\cdots$

4. 0.50, 0.54, 0.58, 0.62, 0.66, $\cdots$

5. $4\frac{1}{3}, 5\frac{2}{3}, 7, 8\frac{1}{3}, 9\frac{2}{3}, \cdots$

6. $\frac{2}{3}, \frac{3}{4}, \frac{4}{5}, \frac{5}{6}, \frac{6}{7}, \cdots$

7. 112, 125, 139, 154, $\cdots$

8. 0.3, 0.6, 0.9, $\cdots$

9. 4, 4, 4, 4, $\cdots$

10. 2.06, 2.12, 2.18, 2.24, $\cdots$

11. $53\frac{3}{10}, 55\frac{4}{5}, 58\frac{3}{10}, \cdots$

12. $6\frac{1}{2}, 7\frac{1}{12}, 7\frac{2}{3}, \cdots$

5-9 Study Guide

Integration: Discrete Mathematics
Arithmetic Sequences

The list of numbers 4, 11, 18, 25, 32, 39, · · · is called a **sequence**.

Each term is 7 more than the previous term. That is, there is a **common difference** of 7.

$11 - 4 = 7, \ 18 - 11 = 7, \ 25 - 18 = 7, \cdots$

Since the difference between any two consecutive terms is the same, the sequence is called an **arithmetic sequence**.

State whether each sequence is an arithmetic sequence. Then write the next three terms of each sequence.

1. 5, 14, 23, 32, 41, · · · **yes; 50, 59, 68**

2. 24, 39, 54, 69, 84, · · · **yes; 99, 114, 129**

3. 16.5, 18.3, 21.1, 24.9, 29.7, · · · **no; 35.5, 42.3, 50.1**

4. 0.50, 0.54, 0.58, 0.62, 0.66, · · · **yes; 0.7, 0.74, 0.78**

5. $4\frac{1}{3}, 5\frac{2}{3}, 7, 8\frac{1}{3}, 9\frac{2}{3}, \cdots$ **yes; 11, $12\frac{1}{3}$, $13\frac{2}{3}$**

6. $\frac{2}{3}, \frac{3}{4}, \frac{4}{5}, \frac{5}{6}, \frac{6}{7}, \cdots$ **no; $\frac{7}{8}, \frac{8}{9}, \frac{9}{10}$**

7. 112, 125, 139, 154, · · · **no; 170, 187, 205**

8. 0.3, 0.6, 0.9, · · · **yes; 1.2, 1.5, 1.8**

9. 4, 4, 4, 4, · · · **yes; 4, 4, 4**

10. 2.06, 2.12, 2.18, 2.24, · · · **yes; 2.3, 2.36, 2.42**

11. $53\frac{3}{10}, 55\frac{4}{5}, 58\frac{3}{10}, \cdots$ **no; $60\frac{4}{5}, 63\frac{3}{10}, 65\frac{4}{5}$**

12. $6\frac{1}{2}, 7\frac{1}{12}, 7\frac{2}{3}, \cdots$ **yes; $8\frac{1}{4}, 8\frac{5}{6}, 9\frac{5}{12}$**

6-1 Study Guide

Writing Fractions as Decimals

To change a fraction to a decimal, divide the numerator by the denominator. Stop when a remainder of zero is obtained or a pattern develops in the quotient.

Examples: Change each fraction to a decimal.

a. $\dfrac{13}{20}$

$$
\begin{array}{r}
0.65 \\
20\overline{)13.00} \\
-120 \\
\hline
100 \\
-100 \\
\hline
0
\end{array}
$$

b. $\dfrac{1}{6}$

$$
\begin{array}{r}
0.166 \\
6\overline{)1.000} \\
-6 \\
\hline
40 \\
-36 \\
\hline
40 \\
-36
\end{array}
$$

$\dfrac{1}{6} = 0.166\ldots$

$= 0.1\overline{6}$ **This bar shows which digit(s) repeats.**

$\dfrac{13}{20}$ is equivalent to the terminating decimal 0.65.

$\dfrac{1}{6}$ is equivalent to the repeating decimal $0.1\overline{6}$.

On a number line, numbers are in order of size (magnitude).

$$-\frac{4}{5} < \frac{5}{6}$$

Write each fraction as a decimal. Use a bar to show a repeating decimal.

1. $\dfrac{1}{4}$

2. $\dfrac{17}{20}$

3. $-\dfrac{3}{8}$

4. $\dfrac{2}{9}$

5. $\dfrac{19}{25}$

6. $-\dfrac{5}{6}$

7. $-\dfrac{4}{5}$

8. $\dfrac{5}{8}$

9. $\dfrac{33}{40}$

10. $\dfrac{7}{16}$

11. $-\dfrac{11}{15}$

12. $-\dfrac{5}{12}$

Write > or < in each blank to make a true sentence.

13. $4\dfrac{1}{4}$ ____ 4.13

14. $\dfrac{2}{3}$ ____ $\dfrac{3}{5}$

15. $3\dfrac{2}{7}$ ____ $-2\dfrac{1}{4}$

16. $\dfrac{4}{11}$ ____ $\dfrac{7}{12}$

17. $-7\dfrac{1}{8}$ ____ -7.34

18. $1\dfrac{6}{7}$ ____ 1.893

Student Edition
Pages 274–279

6-1 Study Guide
Writing Fractions as Decimals

To change a fraction to a decimal, divide the numerator by the denominator. Stop when a remainder of zero is obtained or a pattern develops in the quotient.

Examples: Change each fraction to a decimal.

a. $\dfrac{13}{20}$

$$
\begin{array}{r}
0.65 \\
20\overline{)13.00} \\
-120 \\
\hline
100 \\
-100 \\
\hline
0
\end{array}
$$

b. $\dfrac{1}{6}$

$$
\begin{array}{r}
0.166 \\
6\overline{)1.000} \\
-\ 6 \\
\hline
40 \\
-36 \\
\hline
40 \\
-36
\end{array}
$$

$\dfrac{1}{6} = 0.166\ldots$

$\phantom{\dfrac{1}{6}} = 0.1\overline{6}$ **This bar shows which digit(s) repeats.**

$\dfrac{13}{20}$ is equivalent to the terminating decimal 0.65.

$\dfrac{1}{6}$ is equivalent to the repeating decimal $0.1\overline{6}$.

On a number line, numbers are in order of size (magnitude).

$$-\dfrac{4}{5} < \dfrac{5}{6}$$

←Lesser $-\frac{4}{5}$ $\frac{5}{6}$ Greater→

Write each fraction as a decimal. Use a bar to show a repeating decimal.

1. $\dfrac{1}{4}$ **0.25**

2. $\dfrac{17}{20}$ **0.85**

3. $-\dfrac{3}{8}$ **−0.375**

4. $\dfrac{2}{9}$ **$0.\overline{2}$**

5. $\dfrac{19}{25}$ **0.76**

6. $-\dfrac{5}{6}$ **$-0.8\overline{3}$**

7. $-\dfrac{4}{5}$ **−0.8**

8. $\dfrac{5}{8}$ **0.625**

9. $\dfrac{33}{40}$ **0.825**

10. $\dfrac{7}{16}$ **0.4375**

11. $-\dfrac{11}{15}$ **$-0.7\overline{3}$**

12. $-\dfrac{5}{12}$ **$-0.41\overline{6}$**

Write > or < in each blank to make a true sentence.

13. $4\dfrac{1}{4}$ **>** 4.13

14. $\dfrac{2}{3}$ **>** $\dfrac{3}{5}$

15. $3\dfrac{2}{7}$ **>** $-2\dfrac{1}{4}$

16. $\dfrac{4}{11}$ **<** $\dfrac{7}{12}$

17. $-7\dfrac{1}{8}$ **>** −7.34

18. $1\dfrac{6}{7}$ **<** 1.893

Pre-Algebra

6-2 Study Guide
Estimating Products and Quotients

Student Edition
Pages 280–283

Estimate the products and quotients of rational numbers by using rounding and compatible numbers.

$26.5 \div 4.16 \rightarrow 28 \div 4$ or 7   **Even though 26.5 rounds to 27, 28 is a compatible number because 28 is divisible by 4.**

$3 \times 47.98 \rightarrow 3 \times 50$ or 150

$\frac{4}{9} \times 20 \rightarrow \frac{1}{2} \times 20$ or 10   **$\frac{4}{9}$ is close to $\frac{1}{2}$.**

$25 \div 4\frac{5}{6} \rightarrow 25 \div 5$ or 5   **$4\frac{5}{6}$ is close to 5.**

Estimate each product or quotient.

1. 27.2×8.1

2. 9.32×6.5

3. $19.1 \div 3.6$

4. $(8.53)(4.86)$

5. $75.61 \div 1.9$

6. $24.6 \div 4.8$

7. $\frac{1}{3} \times 23$

8. $\left(\frac{1}{9}\right)(35)$

9. $\frac{3}{7} \times 12$

10. $\frac{7}{16} \times 240$

11. $\frac{6}{10} \times 28$

12. $16 \times \frac{21}{48}$

13. $45 \div 8\frac{6}{7}$

14. $315 \div 4\frac{11}{12}$

15. $\frac{29}{54} \times 304$

16. $400 \times \frac{11}{21}$

17. $156 \div 12\frac{14}{15}$

18. $46 \div 1\frac{32}{37}$

19. $14.7 \div 5.03$

20. $48.9 \div 24.8$

21. $68.04 \div 0.96$

6-2 Study Guide

Estimating Products and Quotients

Estimate the products and quotients of rational numbers by using rounding and compatible numbers.

$26.5 \div 4.16 \;\rightarrow\; 28 \div 4$ or 7 **Even though 26.5 rounds to 27, 28 is a compatible number because 28 is divisible by 4.**

$3 \times 47.98 \;\rightarrow\; 3 \times 50$ or 150

$\dfrac{4}{9} \times 20 \;\rightarrow\; \dfrac{1}{2} \times 20$ or 10 $\dfrac{4}{9}$ **is close to** $\dfrac{1}{2}$.

$25 \div 4\dfrac{5}{6} \;\rightarrow\; 25 \div 5$ or 5 $4\dfrac{5}{6}$ **is close to 5.**

Estimate each product or quotient. Sample answers are given.

1. 27.2×8.1 **240**

2. 9.32×6.5 **63**

3. $19.1 \div 3.6$ **5**

4. $(8.53)(4.86)$ **45**

5. $75.61 \div 1.9$ **38**

6. $24.6 \div 4.8$ **5**

7. $\dfrac{1}{3} \times 23$ **8**

8. $\left(\dfrac{1}{9}\right)(35)$ **4**

9. $\dfrac{3}{7} \times 12$ **6**

10. $\dfrac{7}{16} \times 240$ **120**

11. $\dfrac{6}{10} \times 28$ **14**

12. $16 \times \dfrac{21}{48}$ **8**

13. $45 \div 8\dfrac{6}{7}$ **5**

14. $315 \div 4\dfrac{11}{12}$ **63**

15. $\dfrac{29}{54} \times 304$ **152**

16. $400 \times \dfrac{11}{21}$ **52**

17. $156 \div 12\dfrac{14}{15}$ **12**

18. $46 \div 1\dfrac{32}{37}$ **23**

19. $14.7 \div 5.03$ **3**

20. $48.9 \div 24.8$ **2**

21. $68.04 \div 0.96$ **68**

6-3 Study Guide
Multiplying Fractions

Student Edition
Pages 284–288

To multiply two fractions, first multiply the numerators. Then, multiply the denominators. Write the product in simplest form.

$\frac{1}{2} \times \frac{3}{5} = \frac{1 \times 3}{2 \times 5} = \frac{3}{10}$

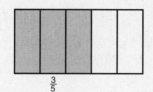 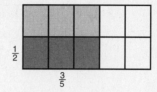

To multiply with mixed numbers, first change the mixed numbers to improper fractions. Then multiply the fraction.

Solve each equation. Write the solution in simplest form.

1. $t = \frac{1}{2} \times \left(-\frac{1}{3}\right)$

2. $\frac{3}{4} \times \frac{1}{2} = f$

3. $c = -\frac{2}{3} \times \left(-\frac{1}{5}\right)$

4. $\frac{1}{3} \times \frac{2}{7} = d$

5. $n = \frac{1}{10} \times \left(-\frac{3}{6}\right)$

6. $-\frac{4}{9} \times \frac{6}{7} = b$

7. $\frac{6}{7} \times \frac{1}{12} = w$

8. $\frac{2}{9} \times \frac{4}{5} = q$

9. $m = 3\frac{1}{3} \times 2\frac{1}{4}$

10. $y = -\frac{3}{4} \times \left(-1\frac{1}{2}\right)$

11. $t = 5\frac{5}{6} \times \left(-\frac{1}{14}\right)$

12. $4\frac{3}{4} \times 2\frac{2}{3} = r$

Evaluate each expression if $a = \frac{3}{4}$, $x = \frac{1}{2}$, **and** $y = \frac{3}{7}$.

13. a^2

14. $2ax$

15. ay

16. xy

17. $\frac{1}{2}a$

18. $3y$

6-3 Study Guide
Multiplying Fractions

To multiply two fractions, first multiply the numerators. Then, multiply the denominators. Write the product in simplest form.

$$\frac{1}{2} \times \frac{3}{5} = \frac{1 \times 3}{2 \times 5} = \frac{3}{10}$$

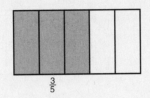 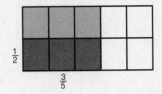

To multiply with mixed numbers, first change the mixed numbers to improper fractions. Then multiply the fraction.

Solve each equation. Write the solution in simplest form.

1. $t = \frac{1}{2} \times \left(-\frac{1}{3}\right)$ $-\frac{1}{6}$

2. $\frac{3}{4} \times \frac{1}{2} = f$ $\frac{3}{8}$

3. $c = -\frac{2}{3} \times \left(-\frac{1}{5}\right)$ $\frac{2}{15}$

4. $\frac{1}{3} \times \frac{2}{7} = d$ $\frac{2}{21}$

5. $n = \frac{1}{10} \times \left(-\frac{3}{6}\right)$ $-\frac{1}{20}$

6. $-\frac{4}{9} \times \frac{6}{7} = b$ $-\frac{8}{21}$

7. $\frac{6}{7} \times \frac{1}{12} = w$ $\frac{1}{14}$

8. $\frac{2}{9} \times \frac{4}{5} = q$ $\frac{8}{45}$

9. $m = 3\frac{1}{3} \times 2\frac{1}{4}$ $7\frac{1}{2}$

10. $y = -\frac{3}{4} \times \left(-1\frac{1}{2}\right)$ $1\frac{1}{8}$

11. $t = 5\frac{5}{6} \times \left(-\frac{1}{14}\right)$ $-\frac{5}{12}$

12. $4\frac{3}{4} \times 2\frac{2}{3} = r$ $12\frac{2}{3}$

Evaluate each expression if $a = \frac{3}{4}$, $x = \frac{1}{2}$, and $y = \frac{3}{7}$.

13. a^2 $\frac{9}{16}$

14. $2ax$ $\frac{3}{4}$

15. ay $\frac{9}{28}$

16. xy $\frac{3}{14}$

17. $\frac{1}{2}a$ $\frac{3}{8}$

18. $3y$ $\frac{9}{7}$ or $1\frac{2}{7}$

6-4 Study Guide
Dividing Fractions

Student Edition
Pages 289–293

When dividing with fractions, you will use the reciprocal of a number. Two numbers whose product is 1 are called **reciprocals**. The reciprocal is also called the **multiplicative inverse**.

The reciprocal of 4 is $\frac{1}{4}$ because $4 \times \frac{1}{4} = 1$.

The reciprocal of $-\frac{4}{5}$ is $-\frac{5}{4}$ because $-\frac{4}{5} \times -\frac{5}{4} = 1$.

To divide by a rational number, multiply by its multiplicative inverse (its reciprocal).	If dividing mixed numbers, first rename the mixed numbers as fractions. Then, divide.

$$4 \div \frac{1}{2} = 4 \times \frac{2}{1} = 8 \qquad\qquad -1\frac{1}{5} \div 2\frac{2}{5} = -\frac{6}{5} \div \frac{12}{5} = -\frac{6}{5} \times \frac{5}{12} = -\frac{30}{60} = -\frac{1}{2}$$

Name the multiplicative inverse for each rational number.

1. $\frac{4}{5}$ 2. $\frac{8}{3}$ 3. $-\frac{2}{7}$ 4. $\frac{5}{6}$

5. 3 6. -7 7. $-\frac{1}{8}$ 8. $\frac{1}{10}$

Solve each equation. Write the solution in simplest form.

9. $\frac{1}{4} \div \left(-\frac{2}{5}\right) = r$ 10. $\frac{5}{8} \div \frac{4}{5} = j$ 11. $y = -\frac{2}{9} \div \frac{3}{5}$

12. $m = 10 \div \frac{2}{3}$ 13. $t = -\frac{1}{3} \div (-4)$ 14. $n = \frac{2}{3} \div \left(-\frac{1}{2}\right)$

15. $-1\frac{3}{5} \div \frac{1}{2} = q$ 16. $4\frac{1}{9} \div \frac{5}{6} = x$ 17. $\frac{3}{5} \div 1\frac{1}{2} = d$

18. $p = 1\frac{3}{4} \div 2\frac{2}{3}$ 19. $f = -2\frac{1}{2} \div \left(-1\frac{4}{5}\right)$ 20. $1\frac{1}{4} \div 4\frac{1}{8} = w$

       Pre-Algebra

6-4 Study Guide
Dividing Fractions

When dividing with fractions, you will use the reciprocal of a number. Two numbers whose product is 1 are called **reciprocals**. The reciprocal is also called the **multiplicative inverse**.

The reciprocal of 4 is $\frac{1}{4}$ because $4 \times \frac{1}{4} = 1$.

The reciprocal of $-\frac{4}{5}$ is $-\frac{5}{4}$ because $-\frac{4}{5} \times -\frac{5}{4} = 1$.

To divide by a rational number, multiply by its multiplicative inverse (its reciprocal).	If dividing mixed numbers, first rename the mixed numbers as fractions. Then, divide.

$4 \div \frac{1}{2} = 4 \times \frac{2}{1} = 8$

$-1\frac{1}{5} \div 2\frac{2}{5} = -\frac{6}{5} \div \frac{12}{5} = -\frac{6}{5} \times \frac{5}{12} = -\frac{30}{60} = -\frac{1}{2}$

Name the multiplicative inverse for each rational number.

1. $\frac{4}{5}$ $\frac{5}{4}$

2. $\frac{8}{3}$ $\frac{3}{8}$

3. $-\frac{2}{7}$ $-\frac{7}{2}$

4. $\frac{5}{6}$ $\frac{6}{5}$

5. 3 $\frac{1}{3}$

6. -7 $-\frac{1}{7}$

7. $-\frac{1}{8}$ -8

8. $\frac{1}{10}$ 10

Solve each equation. Write the solution in simplest form.

9. $\frac{1}{4} \div \left(-\frac{2}{5}\right) = r$ $-\frac{5}{8}$

10. $\frac{5}{8} \div \frac{4}{5} = j$ $\frac{25}{32}$

11. $y = -\frac{2}{9} \div \frac{3}{5}$ $-\frac{10}{27}$

12. $m = 10 \div \frac{2}{3}$ 15

13. $t = -\frac{1}{3} \div (-4)$ $\frac{1}{12}$

14. $n = \frac{2}{3} \div \left(-\frac{1}{2}\right)$ $-1\frac{1}{3}$

15. $-1\frac{3}{5} \div \frac{1}{2} = q$ $-3\frac{1}{5}$

16. $4\frac{1}{9} \div \frac{5}{6} = x$ $4\frac{14}{15}$

17. $\frac{3}{5} \div 1\frac{1}{2} = d$ $\frac{2}{5}$

18. $p = 1\frac{3}{4} \div 2\frac{2}{3}$ $\frac{21}{32}$

19. $f = -2\frac{1}{2} \div \left(-1\frac{4}{5}\right)$ $1\frac{7}{18}$

20. $1\frac{1}{4} \div 4\frac{1}{8} = w$ $\frac{10}{33}$

6-5 Study Guide

Multiplying and Dividing Decimals

When multiplying decimals, the number of decimal places in the product is the same as the sum of the decimal places in the factors.

Example: $c = (-8.4)(0.62)$

$$
\begin{array}{r}
-8.4 \\
\times\ 0.62 \\
\hline
168 \\
+504 \\
\hline
-5.208
\end{array}
$$

-8.4 ⟵ 1 decimal place
$\times\ 0.62$ ⟵ 2 decimal places
-5.208 ⟵ 3 decimal places

The sum of the decimal places in the factors is 3, so the product has 3 decimal places.

$c = -5.208$

To divide by a decimal, first multiply both the divisor and dividend by a power of ten so that the divisor is a whole number. Then divide as with whole numbers.

Example: $0.8\overline{)12.96}$ → Since 0.8 has 1 decimal place, multiply 0.8 and 12.96 by 10.

$0.8\overline{)12.96}$ → $8\overline{)129.6}$ quotient 16.2

Solve each equation.

1. $(66.3)(0.04) = k$

2. $(4.1)(-12.2) = p$

3. $x = (-84)(-2.4)$

4. $(-34.7)(-3) = m$

5. $c = (80.4)(0.02)$

6. $(-7.19)(3.9) = t$

7. $d = (1.94)(18)$

8. $(23.5)(-0.7) = f$

9. $n = (4283)(-1.4)$

10. $0.184 \div 8 = b$

11. $d = 0.18 \div 0.9$

12. $c = 3.066 \div (-0.3)$

13. $-0.045 \div 0.5 = f$

14. $w = 40.05 \div (-4.5)$

15. $135 \div (-0.15) = q$

16. $-30.91 \div (-11) = x$

17. $27.606 \div 0.086 = f$

18. $t = -0.992 \div 8$

Pre-Algebra

NAME _____ DATE _____

6-5 Study Guide

Multplying and Dividing Decimals

Student Edition
Pages 295–299

When multiplying decimals, the number of decimal places in the product is the same as the sum of the decimal places in the factors.

Example: $c = (-8.4)(0.62)$

$$
\begin{array}{rl}
-8.4 & \longleftarrow \text{1 decimal place} \\
\times\ 0.62 & \longleftarrow \text{2 decimal places} \\
\hline
168 & \\
+504 & \\
\hline
-5.208 & \longleftarrow \text{3 decimal places}
\end{array}
$$

The sum of the decimal places in the factors is 3, so the product has 3 decimal places.

$c = -5.208$

To divide by a decimal, first multiply both the divisor and dividend by a power of ten so that the divisor is a whole number. Then divide as with whole numbers.

Example: $0.8\overline{)12.96}$ → Since 0.8 has 1 decimal place, multiply 0.8 and 12.96 by 10. $0.8\overline{)12.96}$ → $8.\overline{)129.6}$ quotient 16.2

Solve each equation.

1. $(66.3)(0.04) = k$ **2.652**

2. $(4.1)(-12.2) = p$ **−50.02**

3. $x = (-84)(-2.4)$ **201.6**

4. $(-34.7)(-3) = m$ **104.1**

5. $c = (80.4)(0.02)$ **1.608**

6. $(-7.19)(3.9) = t$ **−28.041**

7. $d = (1.94)(18)$ **34.92**

8. $(23.5)(-0.7) = f$ **−16.45**

9. $n = (4283)(-1.4)$ **−5996.2**

10. $0.184 \div 8 = b$ **0.023**

11. $d = 0.18 \div 0.9$ **0.2**

12. $c = 3.066 \div (-0.3)$ **−10.22**

13. $-0.045 \div 0.5 = f$ **−0.09**

14. $w = 40.05 \div (-4.5)$ **−8.9**

15. $135 \div (-0.15) = q$ **−900**

16. $-30.91 \div (-11) = x$ **2.81**

17. $27.606 \div 0.086 = f$ **321**

18. $t = -0.992 \div 8$ **−0.124**

6-6 Study Guide

Integration: Statistics
Measures of Central Tendency

Student Edition
Pages 301–306

Member	Height in Inches
JC	57
KL	60
MW	61
NL	62
PK	62
LV	70

The heights of the school ensemble members are listed at the left.

The **mean** height is the sum of all the heights divided by the number of addends.

$$\frac{57 + 60 + 61 + 62 + 62 + 70}{6} = \frac{372}{6} \text{ or } 62$$

The mean is 62.

The **median** height is the middle number when the data are listed in order. Since there are two middle numbers, 61 and 62, the median is the mean of these two. The median is 61.5.

The **mode** is the height that appears most often. The mode is 62.

List each set of data from least to greatest. Then find the mean, median, and mode. When necessary, round to the nearest tenth.

1. 98, 63, 51, 52, 99, 57, 54, 99

2. 69, 68, 65, 64, 68, 69, 68, 67

3. 73, 75, 71, 69, 72, 71, 73, 71

4. 14, 11, 12, 13, 14, 15, 16, 13, 12, 13

Solve.

5. Jim's math quiz scores were 87, 79, 100, 83, and 88. Find the mean of his scores.

6. The high temperatures for a week in May were 68, 70, 68, 66, 70, 74, and 72. Find the median, mean, and mode.

6-6 Study Guide

Integration: Statistics
Measures of Central Tendency

Member	Height in Inches
JC	57
KL	60
MW	61
NL	62
PK	62
LV	70

The heights of the school ensemble members are listed at the left.

The **mean** height is the sum of all the heights divided by the number of addends.

$$\frac{57 + 60 + 61 + 62 + 62 + 70}{6} = \frac{372}{6} \text{ or } 62$$

The mean is 62.

The **median** height is the middle number when the data are listed in order. Since there are two middle numbers, 61 and 62, the median is the mean of these two. The median is 61.5.

The **mode** is the height that appears most often. The mode is 62.

List each set of data from least to greatest. Then find the mean, median, and mode. When necessary, round to the nearest tenth.

1. 98, 63, 51, 52, 99, 57, 54, 99 **51, 52, 54, 57, 63, 98, 99, 99; 60, 71.6, 99**

2. 69, 68, 65, 64, 68, 69, 68, 67 **64, 65, 67, 68, 68, 68, 69, 69; 68, 67.3, 68**

3. 73, 75, 71, 69, 72, 71, 73, 71 **69, 71, 71, 71, 72, 73, 73, 75; 71.5, 71.9, 71**

4. 14, 11, 12, 13, 14, 15, 16, 13, 12, 13 **11, 12, 12, 13, 13, 13, 14, 14, 15, 16; 13, 13.3, 13**

Solve.

5. Jim's math quiz scores were 87, 79, 100, 83, and 88. Find the mean of his scores. **87.4**

6. The high temperatures for a week in May were 68, 70, 68, 66, 70, 74, and 72. Find the median, mean, and mode. **70, ≈ 69.7, 68 and 70**

Pre-Algebra

6-7 Study Guide

Solving Equations and Inequalities

To solve equations containing rational numbers, multiply each side by the same number to get the variable by itself.

The number you multiply each side by is the reciprocal of the number that is multiplied times the variable.

$$-\frac{y}{5} = 8$$

$$-\frac{1}{5} \cdot y = 8$$

$$-\frac{5}{1} \cdot \left(-\frac{1}{5}\right) \cdot y = -\frac{5}{1} \cdot 8$$

$$y = -40$$

Use the same method to solve inequalities containing rational numbers.

When you multiply or divide each side of an inequality by a negative number, you must reverse the inequality sign.

$$-\frac{2}{3}x \leq \frac{1}{2}$$

$$-\frac{3}{2} \cdot -\frac{2}{3} \cdot x \leq \frac{1}{2} \cdot -\frac{3}{2}$$

$$x \geq -\frac{3}{4}$$

Write the number you would multiply each side by in order to get the variable by itself.

1. $4n = 12$ **2.** $\frac{a}{2} = 50$ **3.** $-7t = 21$ **4.** $-\frac{m}{6} = 2$

5. $-35 < \frac{h}{7}$ **6.** $0.25b < 5$ **7.** $2.4 \leq -6x$ **8.** $-\frac{c}{3} \geq -12$

Solve each equation or inequality. Check your solution.

9. $4n = 12$ **10.** $\frac{a}{2} = 50$ **11.** $-7t = 21$ **12.** $-\frac{m}{6} = 2$

13. $4n \leq 12$ **14.** $\frac{a}{2} > 50$ **15.** $-7t > 21$ **16.** $-\frac{m}{6} \leq 2$

17. $-35 = \frac{h}{7}$ **18.** $0.25b = 5$ **19.** $2.4 = -6x$ **20.** $-\frac{c}{3} = -12$

21. $-35 \geq \frac{h}{7}$ **22.** $0.25b < 5$ **23.** $2.4 < -6x$ **24.** $-\frac{c}{3} > -12$

6-7 Study Guide
Solving Equations and Inequalities

Student Edition
Pages 308–311

To solve equations containing rational numbers, multiply each side by the same number to get the variable by itself.

$$-\frac{y}{5} = 8$$

$$-\frac{1}{5} \cdot y = 8$$

$$-\frac{5}{1} \cdot \left(-\frac{1}{5}\right) \cdot y = -\frac{5}{1} \cdot 8$$

$$y = -40$$

The number you multiply each side by is the reciprocal of the number that is multiplied times the variable.

Use the same method to solve inequalities containing rational numbers.

$$-\frac{2}{3}x \le \frac{1}{2}$$

$$-\frac{3}{2} \cdot -\frac{2}{3} \cdot x \le \frac{1}{2} \cdot -\frac{3}{2}$$

$$x \ge -\frac{3}{4}$$

When you multiply or divide each side of an inequality by a negative number, you must reverse the inequality sign.

Write the number you would multiply each side by in order to get the variable by itself.

1. $4n = 12$ $\dfrac{1}{4}$

2. $\dfrac{a}{2} = 50$ $\dfrac{2}{1}$

3. $-7t = 21$ $-\dfrac{1}{7}$

4. $-\dfrac{m}{6} = 2$ **−6**

5. $-35 < \dfrac{h}{7}$ $\dfrac{7}{1}$

6. $0.25b < 5$ $\dfrac{1}{0.25}$ **or 4**

7. $2.4 \le -6x$ $-\dfrac{1}{6}$

8. $-\dfrac{c}{3} \ge -12$ **−3**

Solve each equation or inequality. Check your solution.

9. $4n = 12$ **3**

10. $\dfrac{a}{2} = 50$ **100**

11. $-7t = 21$ **−3**

12. $-\dfrac{m}{6} = 2$ **−12**

13. $4n \le 12$ $n \le 3$

14. $\dfrac{a}{2} > 50$ $a > 100$

15. $-7t > 21$ $t < -3$

16. $-\dfrac{m}{6} \le 2$ $m \ge -12$

17. $-35 = \dfrac{h}{7}$ **−245**

18. $0.25b = 5$ **20**

19. $2.4 = -6x$ **−0.4**

20. $-\dfrac{c}{3} = -12$ **36**

21. $-35 \ge \dfrac{h}{7}$ $h \le -245$

22. $0.25b < 5$ $b < 20$

23. $2.4 < -6x$ $x < -0.4$

24. $-\dfrac{c}{3} > -12$ $c < 36$

6-8 Study Guide

Integration: Discrete Mathematics
Geometric Sequences

Two lists of numbers, or sequences, are shown below.

$3, 6, 12, 24, 48, \cdots$ Each number in the pattern is
2 times the number before it.

$162, 54, 18, 6, 2, \cdots$ Each number in the pattern is
$\frac{1}{3}$ times the number before it.

In each sequence above, each number after the first can be obtained from the previous one by multiplying it by a fixed number called the **common ratio**. Such a sequence is called a **geometric sequence**. The common ratios above are 2 and $\frac{1}{3}$, respectively.

$$\frac{6}{3} = 2 \qquad\qquad \frac{12}{6} = 2 \qquad\qquad \frac{24}{12} = 2 \qquad\qquad \frac{48}{24} = 2$$
$$\frac{54}{162} = \frac{1}{3} \qquad\qquad \frac{18}{54} = \frac{1}{3} \qquad\qquad \frac{6}{18} = \frac{1}{3} \qquad\qquad \frac{2}{6} = \frac{1}{3}$$

State whether each sequence is a geometric sequence. If so, state the common ratio and list the next three terms.

1. $1, 2, 4, 8, 16, \cdots$

2. $\frac{1}{3}, \frac{1}{9}, \frac{1}{27}, \frac{1}{81}, \frac{1}{243}, \cdots$

3. $\frac{1}{2}, \frac{1}{3}, \frac{1}{4}, \frac{1}{5}, \frac{1}{6}, \cdots$

Complete each geometric sequence.

4. $8, 4, 2, \underline{\ ?\ }, \underline{\ ?\ }, \underline{\ ?\ }$

5. $\underline{\ ?\ }, 7, 14, 28, \underline{\ ?\ }, \underline{\ ?\ }$

6. $\underline{\ ?\ }, \frac{1}{24}, \frac{1}{12}, \frac{1}{6}, \underline{\ ?\ }, \underline{\ ?\ }$

7. $\underline{\ ?\ }, 10^{98}, 10^{96}, \underline{\ ?\ }, \underline{\ ?\ }, 10^{90}$

Write the first five terms of each geometric sequence described below.

8. first term, 5; ratio, 2

9. first term, 8; ratio, $\frac{1}{2}$

10. first term, 81; ratio, $\frac{1}{3}$

11. first term, $\frac{8}{9}$; ratio, $\frac{3}{2}$

6-8 Study Guide

Integration: Discrete Mathematics
Geometric Sequences

Two lists of numbers, or sequences, are shown below.

3, 6, 12, 24, 48, $\cdots$ Each number in the pattern is 2 times the number before it.

162, 54, 18, 6, 2, $\cdots$ Each number in the pattern is $\frac{1}{3}$ times the number before it.

In each sequence above, each number after the first can be obtained from the previous one by multiplying it by a fixed number called the **common ratio**. Such a sequence is called a **geometric sequence**. The common ratios above are 2 and $\frac{1}{3}$, respectively.

$$\frac{6}{3} = 2 \qquad \frac{12}{6} = 2 \qquad \frac{24}{12} = 2 \qquad \frac{48}{24} = 2$$

$$\frac{54}{162} = \frac{1}{3} \qquad \frac{18}{54} = \frac{1}{3} \qquad \frac{6}{18} = \frac{1}{3} \qquad \frac{2}{6} = \frac{1}{3}$$

State whether each sequence is a geometric sequence. If so, state the common ratio and list the next three terms.

1. 1, 2, 4, 8, 16, $\cdots$ **yes; 2; 32, 64, 128**

2. $\frac{1}{3}, \frac{1}{9}, \frac{1}{27}, \frac{1}{81}, \frac{1}{243}, \cdots$ **yes; $\frac{1}{3}$; $\frac{1}{729}, \frac{1}{2187}, \frac{1}{6561}$**

3. $\frac{1}{2}, \frac{1}{3}, \frac{1}{4}, \frac{1}{5}, \frac{1}{6}, \cdots$ **no**

Complete each geometric sequence.

4. 8, 4, 2, __?__, __?__, __?__   **1; $\frac{1}{2}$; $\frac{1}{4}$**

5. __?__, 7, 14, 28, __?__, __?__   **$3\frac{1}{2}$; 56; 112**

6. __?__, $\frac{1}{24}, \frac{1}{12}, \frac{1}{6}$, __?__, __?__   **$\frac{1}{48}$; $\frac{1}{3}$; $\frac{2}{3}$**

7. __?__, $10^{98}, 10^{96}$, __?__, __?__, 10^{90} **10^{100}; 10^{94}; 10^{92}**

Write the first five terms of each geometric sequence described below.

8. first term, 5; ratio, 2 **5, 10, 20, 40, 80**

9. first term, 8; ratio, $\frac{1}{2}$ **8, 4, 2, 1, $\frac{1}{2}$**

10. first term, 81; ratio, $\frac{1}{3}$ **81, 27, 9, 3, 1**

11. first term, $\frac{8}{9}$; ratio, $\frac{3}{2}$ **$\frac{8}{9}, \frac{24}{18}, \frac{72}{36}, \frac{216}{72}, \frac{648}{144}$**

6-9 Study Guide
Scientific Notation

A convenient form for writing very large and very small numbers is called **scientific notation**. All numbers expressed in scientific notation are given as the product of a number between 1 and 10 and a power of 10.

Write 2.31×10^{-4} in standard form as follows:

$$2.31 \times 10^{-4} \longrightarrow 0.000231$$

To multiply by 10^{-4}, move the decimal point 4 places to the left.

Write 2.31×10^4 in standard form as follows:

$$2.31 \times 10^4 \longrightarrow 23,100$$

To multiply by 10^4, move the decimal point 4 places to the right.

Write 4000 in scientific notation as follows:

$$4000 = 4 \times 10^3$$

Move the decimal point 3 places to the left. Multiply by 10^3.

Write 0.00712 in scientific notation as follows:

$$0.00712 = 7.12 \times 10^{-3}$$

Move the decimal point 3 places to the right. Multiply by 10^{-3}.

Write each number in standard form.

1. 7×10^5

2. 3.2×10^3

3. 1.7×10^{-6}

4. 6.366×10^{-4}

5. 2.979×10^4

6. 5.09×10^{-7}

Write each number in scientific notation.

7. 50,000

8. 3700

9. 0.000249

10. 2030

11. 0.0000755

12. 51,000

13. 0.0046

14. 12,800

15. 724

16. 0.176

17. 2156

18. 0.03278

6-9 Study Guide
Scientific Notation

Student Edition
Pages 317–320

A convenient form for writing very large and very small numbers is called **scientific notation**. All numbers expressed in scientific notation are given as the product of a number between 1 and 10 and a power of 10.

Write 2.31×10^{-4} in standard form as follows:

$$2.31 \times 10^{-4} \longrightarrow 0.000231$$

To multiply by 10^{-4}, move the decimal point 4 places to the left.

Write 2.31×10^4 in standard form as follows:

$$2.31 \times 10^4 \longrightarrow 23,100$$

To multiply by 10^4, move the decimal point 4 places to the right.

Write 4000 in scientific notation as follows:

$$4000 = 4 \times 10^3$$

Move the decimal point 3 places to the left. Multiply by 10^3.

Write 0.00712 in scientific notation as follows:

$$0.00712 = 7.12 \times 10^{-3}$$

Move the decimal point 3 places to the right. Multiply by 10^{-3}.

Write each number in standard form.

1. 7×10^5 **700,000**

2. 3.2×10^3 **3200**

3. 1.7×10^{-6} **0.0000017**

4. 6.366×10^{-4} **0.0006366**

5. 2.979×10^4 **29,790**

6. 5.09×10^{-7} **0.000000509**

Write each number in scientific notation.

7. 50,000 **5×10^4**

8. 3700 **3.7×10^3**

9. 0.000249 **2.49×10^{-4}**

10. 2030 **2.03×10^3**

11. 0.0000755 **7.55×10^{-5}**

12. 51,000 **5.1×10^4**

13. 0.0046 **4.6×10^{-3}**

14. 12,800 **1.28×10^4**

15. 724 **7.24×10^2**

16. 0.176 **1.76×10^{-1}**

17. 2156 **2.156×10^3**

18. 0.03278 **3.278×10^{-2}**

7-1 Study Guide
Problem-Solving Strategy: Work Backward

To solve problems by **working backward**, start with the end result and *undo* each step.

A certain number is added to 7, and the result is multiplied by 17. The final answer is 136. Find the number.

Explore	The final answer is 136. You want to find the original number.
Plan	Since this problem gives the end result and asks for something that happened earlier, start with the end result and work backward.
Solve	The final answer → 136
	Undo multiplication by 17. → $136 \div 17 = 8$
	Undo addition of 7. → $8 - 7 = 1$
	The original number is 1.
Examine	Suppose that you start with the number 1. After adding 7, the result is 8. Multiplying 8 by 17 the result is 136.

Solve by working backward.

1. A certain number is multiplied by 4, and then 12 is added to the result. The final answer is 36. Find the number.

2. A certain number is divided by 8, and then 4 is subtracted from the result. The final answer is 76. Find the number.

3. Vladimir won some money on a radio contest. He gave half of the money to Julianne and $20 to Hector. Vladimir ended up with $84. How much did he originally win?

4. Pennie received her tax refund. She put $150 of her refund into savings and paid $200 for her car insurance. Then she spent one-half of what was left on a gift and $48 on a sweatshirt. How much was Pennie's tax refund if she had $56 left?

7-1 Study Guide

Problem-Solving Strategy: Work Backward

To solve problems by **working backward**, start with the end result and *undo* each step.

A certain number is added to 7, and the result is multiplied by 17. The final answer is 136. Find the number.

Explore   The final answer is 136. You want to find the original number.

Plan   Since this problem gives the end result and asks for something that happened earlier, start with the end result and work backward.

Solve   The final answer $\rightarrow$ 136
Undo multiplication by 17. $\rightarrow$ $136 \div 17 = 8$
Undo addition of 7. $\rightarrow$ $8 - 7 = 1$

The original number is 1.

Examine   Suppose that you start with the number 1. After adding 7, the result is 8. Multiplying 8 by 17 the result is 136.

Solve by working backward.

1. A certain number is multiplied by 4, and then 12 is added to the result. The final answer is 36. Find the number. **6**

2. A certain number is divided by 8, and then 4 is subtracted from the result. The final answer is 76. Find the number. **640**

3. Vladimir won some money on a radio contest. He gave half of the money to Julianne and $20 to Hector. Vladimir ended up with $84. How much did he originally win? **$208**

4. Pennie received her tax refund. She put $150 of her refund into savings and paid $200 for her car insurance. Then she spent one-half of what was left on a gift and $48 on a sweatshirt. How much was Pennie's tax refund if she had $56 left? **$558**

7-2 Study Guide

Solving Two-Step Equations

Some equations contain more than one operation. To solve an equation with more than one operation, use the work-backward strategy and undo each operation.

Example: Solve $\frac{c}{2} - 13 = 7$.

$\frac{c}{2} - 13 + 13 = 7 + 13$ **Add to undo subtraction.**

Check the solution.

$\frac{c}{2} = 20$

$\frac{c}{2} - 13 = 7$ **Replace c with 40.**

$2 \cdot \frac{c}{2} = 20 \cdot 2$ **Multiply to undo division.**

$\frac{40}{2} - 13 \stackrel{?}{=} 7$

$c = 40$

$20 - 13 \stackrel{?}{=} 7$

$7 = 7$ ✔ **The solution is 40.**

Solve each equation. Check your solution.

1. $4a - 10 = 42$

2. $12 - 3m = 18$

3. $-10 = -5w - 25$

4. $\frac{m}{4} + 6 = 70$

5. $-3 + \frac{c}{2} = 12$

6. $\frac{-v}{3} + 8 = 22$

7. $5.8t + 15 = -14$

8. $8 - 6.2u = -23$

9. $-4 - 2.4w = -16$

10. $4(x + 6) = 12$

11. $-13 = \frac{4 - b}{3}$

12. $-16 = 4(2 - 2x)$

13. $-1.4(a + 2) = 4.2$

14. $7.7 = 2.1 - 7m$

15. $\frac{a + 4}{2} = 10.8$

55

7-2 Study Guide

Student Edition
Pages 334–337

Solving Two-Step Equations

Some equations contain more than one operation. To solve an equation with more than one operation, use the work-backward strategy and undo each operation.

Example: Solve $\frac{c}{2} - 13 = 7$.

$\frac{c}{2} - 13 + 13 = 7 + 13$ **Add to undo subtraction.**

$\frac{c}{2} = 20$

$2 \cdot \frac{c}{2} = 20 \cdot 2$ **Multiply to undo division.**

$c = 40$

Check the solution.

$\frac{c}{2} - 13 = 7$ **Replace c with 40.**

$\frac{40}{2} - 13 \overset{?}{=} 7$

$20 - 13 \overset{?}{=} 7$

$7 = 7$ ✔ **The solution is 40.**

Solve each equation. Check your solution.

1. $4a - 10 = 42$ **13**

2. $12 - 3m = 18$ **-2**

3. $-10 = -5w - 25$ **-3**

4. $\frac{m}{4} + 6 = 70$ **256**

5. $-3 + \frac{c}{2} = 12$ **30**

6. $\frac{-v}{3} + 8 = 22$ **-42**

7. $5.8t + 15 = -14$ **-5**

8. $8 - 6.2u = -23$ **5**

9. $-4 - 2.4w = -16$ **5**

10. $4(x + 6) = 12$ **-3**

11. $-13 = \frac{4 - b}{3}$ **43**

12. $-16 = 4(2 - 2x)$ **3**

13. $-1.4(a + 2) = 4.2$ **-5**

14. $7.7 = 2.1 - 7m$ **-0.8**

15. $\frac{a + 4}{2} = 10.8$ **17.6**

7-3 Study Guide
Writing Two-Step Equations

Example: The World Trade Center in New York City is 1350 feet tall. Suppose each floor is about 12.3 feet high. You ride the elevator from the top floor downward. How many floors have you passed when you drop to 120 feet?

Explore   You know the height of the building and the height of each floor. You are looking for the number of floors passed when you drop to 120 feet.

Plan   Let f = the number of floors. Write an equation.

1350	descend	12.3 feet for f floors	is 120 feet
1350	$-$	$12.3f$	$= 120$

Solve $1350 - 12.3f = 120$

$-12.3f = 120 - 1350$

$-12.3f = -1230$

$$\frac{-12.3f}{-12.3} = \frac{-1230}{-12.3}$$

$f = 100$

Examine   After 100 floors, you have dropped 1230 feet. Since $1350 - 1230$ is 120, the answer is correct.

Define a variable and write an equation for each situation. Then solve.

1. During one day in 1918, the temperature in Granville, North Dakota, began at ⁻33° and rose for 12 hours. The high temperature was 49.8°. How many degrees per hour did the temperature rise?

2. During one day in 1943, the temperature in Sparkfish, South Dakota, began at ⁻4° and rose an average of 0.41 degrees per minute until it was 45.2°. How long did this temperature increase take?

3. A skydiver jumps from an airplane at an altitude of 12,000 feet. After 42 seconds, she reaches 11,370 feet and opens her parachute. How many feet per second did she descend before opening her parachute?

4. A skydiver jumps from an airplane at an altitude of 12,775 feet. He descends 15 feet per second. In how many seconds will his altitude be 10,000 feet?

7-3 Study Guide
Writing Two-Step Equations

Example: The World Trade Center in New York City is 1350 feet tall. Suppose each floor is about 12.3 feet high. You ride the elevator from the top floor downward. How many floors have you passed when you drop to 120 feet?

Explore   You know the height of the building and the height of each floor. You are looking for the number of floors passed when you drop to 120 feet.

Plan   Let f = the number of floors. Write an equation.

1350	descend	12.3 feet for f floors	is 120 feet
1350	−	12.3f	= 120

Solve $1350 - 12.3f = 120$

$$-12.3f = 120 - 1350$$
$$-12.3f = -1230$$
$$\frac{-12.3f}{-12.3} = \frac{-1230}{-12.3}$$
$$f = 100$$

Examine   After 100 floors, you have dropped 1230 feet. Since 1350 − 1230 is 120, the answer is correct.

Define a variable and write an equation for each situation. Then solve.

1. During one day in 1918, the temperature in Granville, North Dakota, began at ‾33° and rose for 12 hours. The high temperature was 49.8°. How many degrees per hour did the temperature rise? **Let d = number of degrees; ‾33 + 12d = 49.8; d = 6.9, 6.9 degrees per hour**

2. During one day in 1943, the temperature in Sparkfish, South Dakota, began at ‾4° and rose an average of 0.41 degrees per minute until it was 45.2°. How long did this temperature increase take? **Let m = number of minutes; ‾4 + 0.41m = 45.2; m = 210, 120 minutes**

3. A skydiver jumps from an airplane at an altitude of 12,000 feet. After 42 seconds, she reaches 11,370 feet and opens her parachute. How many feet per second did she descend before opening her parachute? **Let f = number of feet; 12,000 − 42f = 11,370; f = 15, 15 feet**

4. A skydiver jumps from an airplane at an altitude of 12,775 feet. He descends 15 feet per second. In how many seconds will his altitude be 10,000 feet? **Let s = number of seconds; 12,775 − 15s = 10,000; s = 185, 185 seconds**

Pre-Algebra

7-4 Study Guide

Student Edition
Pages 341–344

Integration: Geometry
Circles and Circumference

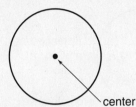 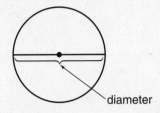 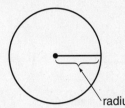 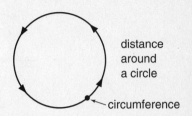

center   diameter   radius   distance around a circle   circumference

Examples: C = circumference; d = diameter; r = radius; use 3.14 for π.

$$C = \pi d$$

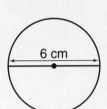

6 cm

$C = \pi d$
$C \approx 3.14(6)$
$C \approx 18.84$
$C \approx 19$ cm

$$C = 2\pi r \quad d = 2r$$

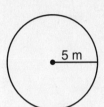

5 m

$C = 2\pi r$
$C \approx 2(3.14)(5)$
$C \approx 10(3.14)$
$C \approx 31.4$
$C \approx 31$ m

Find the *circumference* of each circle.

1.

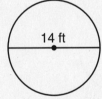

14 ft

2.

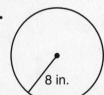

8 in.

3.

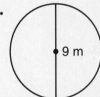

9 m

4. The radius is $6\frac{1}{5}$ feet.

5. The diameter is 4.7 yards.

Solve. Round to the nearest inch.

6. What is the circumference of the top of an ice cream cone if its diameter is about $1\frac{7}{8}$ inches? $\left(\frac{7}{8} = 0.875\right)$

7. The radius of the basketball rim is 9 inches. What is the circumference?

Pre-Algebra

7-4 Study Guide

Integration: Geometry
Circles and Circumference

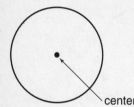 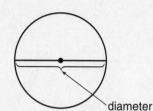 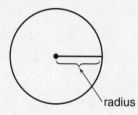 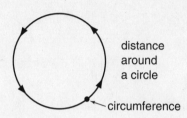

center   diameter   radius   distance around a circle   circumference

Examples: C = circumference; d = diameter; r = radius; use 3.14 for π.

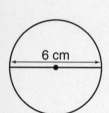

6 cm

$$C = \pi d$$

$C = \pi d$
$C \approx 3.14(6)$
$C \approx 18.84$
$C \approx 19$ cm

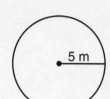

5 m

$$C = 2\pi r \quad d = 2r$$

$C = 2\pi r$
$C \approx 2(3.14)(5)$
$C \approx 10(3.14)$
$C \approx 31.4$
$C \approx 31$ m

Find the circumference of each circle.

1.

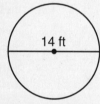

14 ft

$C \approx$ **44 ft**

2.

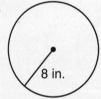

8 in.

$C \approx$ **50 in.**

3.

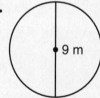

9 m

$C \approx$ **28 m**

4. The radius is $6\frac{1}{5}$ feet. $C \approx$ **39 m**

5. The diameter is 4.7 yards. $C \approx$ **15 yd**

Solve. Round to the nearest inch.

6. What is the circumference of the top of an ice cream cone if its diameter is about $1\frac{7}{8}$ inches? $\left(\frac{7}{8} = 0.875\right)$ $C \approx$ **6 in.**

7. The radius of the basketball rim is 9 inches. What is the circumference? $C \approx$ **57 in.**

7-5 Study Guide

Student Edition
Pages 346–350

Solving Equations with Variables on Each Side

When an equation has the variable on each side, the first step is to write an equivalent equation with the variable on just one side.

$$4a - 25 = 6a + 50$$

$$4a - 25 + (^-6a) = 6a + 50 + (^-6a) \quad \textbf{Add } ^-6a \textbf{ to each side.}$$

$$^-2a - 25 = 50$$

From this point, the equation is solved by first adding 25 to each side, and then dividing each side by $^-2$.

1. Complete the solution of the equation in the example above.

2. Solve the equation in the example again. This time, first isolate the variable on the right side.

Solve each equation. Check your solution.

3. $4a + 26 = 50 + 6a$

4. $2r + 36 = 6r - 12$

5. $4(b + 24) = 16b + 60$

6. $x + 21 = ^-x + 87$

7. $25c + 17 = ^-5c + 143$

8. $8v + 5 = 7v - 21$

9. $6n - 42 = 4n$

10. $2x = 3x + 2$

11. $5y = 2y - 12$

12. $a = 5a - 28$

13. $2w + 3 = 5w$

14. $^-45m + 68 = 84m - 61$

7-5 Study Guide
Solving Equations with Variables on Each Side

When an equation has the variable on each side, the first step is to write an equivalent equation with the variable on just one side.

$$4a - 25 = 6a + 50$$

$$4a - 25 + (-6a) = 6a + 50 + (-6a)$$ **Add -6a to each side.**

$$-2a - 25 = 50$$

From this point, the equation is solved by first adding 25 to each side, and then dividing each side by -2.

1. Complete the solution of the equation in the example above.
$$-2a = 75$$
$$a = -37.5$$

2. Solve the equation in the example again. This time, first isolate the variable on the right side.
$$4a - 25 = 6a + 50$$
$$-25 - 50 = 6a - 4a$$
$$-75 = 2a$$
$$-37.5 = a$$

Solve each equation. Check your solution.

3. $4a + 26 = 50 + 6a$
-12

4. $2r + 36 = 6r - 12$ **12**

5. $4(b + 24) = 16b + 60$
3

6. $x + 21 = -x + 87$ **33**

7. $25c + 17 = -5c + 143$
4.2

8. $8v + 5 = 7v - 21$ **-26**

9. $6n - 42 = 4n$ **21**

10. $2x = 3x + 2$ **-2**

11. $5y = 2y - 12$ **-4**

12. $a = 5a - 28$ **7**

13. $2w + 3 = 5w$ **1**

14. $-45m + 68 = 84m - 61$
1

7-6 Study Guide

Solving Multi-Step Inequalities

The inequality $13 - 6y > 49 - 2y$ can be solved by applying the same steps as solving equations.

$$13 - 6y > 49 - 2y$$
$$13 - 6y - 13 > 49 - 2y - 13 \qquad \text{Subtract 13 from each side}$$
$$-6y > 36 - 2y$$
$$-6y + 2y > 36 - 2y + 2y \qquad \text{Add 2y to each side.}$$
$$-4y > 36$$
$$\frac{-4y}{-4} < \frac{36}{-4} \qquad \text{Divide each side by -4.}$$
$$\text{Reverse the order symbol.}$$
$$y < -9 \qquad \text{Any number less than -9 is a solution.}$$

Check: Replace y with a number less than -9. Try -10.

$$13 - 6y \overset{?}{>} 49 - 2y$$
$$13 - 6(-10) \overset{?}{>} 49 - 2(-10)$$
$$13 + 60 \overset{?}{>} 49 + 20$$
$$73 > 69 \ ✔$$

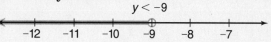
$y < -9$

Solve each inequality and check your solution. Graph the solution on the number line.

1. $6x + 14 \le 32$

2. $18 - 3w < 15$

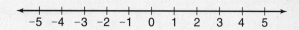

3. $5n + 8 > 20 - n$

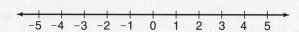

4. $2y + 2 \ge 6y + 6$

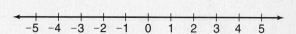

5. $\frac{1}{2}(10h - 6) > -23$

6. $4(7 - 3x) \le -20$

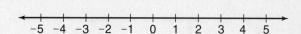

7. $-15 \le \frac{c}{-4} - 15$

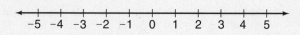

8. $\frac{-n}{3} - 5 < -4$

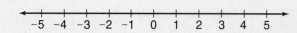

7-6 Study Guide
Solving Multi-Step Inequalities

The inequality $13 - 6y > 49 - 2y$ can be solved by applying the same steps as solving equations.

$$13 - 6y > 49 - 2y$$
$$13 - 6y - 13 > 49 - 2y - 13 \qquad \text{Subtract 13 from each side}$$
$$^-6y > 36 - 2y$$
$$^-6y + 2y > 36 - 2y + 2y \qquad \text{Add 2y to each side.}$$
$$^-4y > 36$$
$$\frac{^-4y}{^-4} < \frac{36}{^-4} \qquad \text{Divide each side by -4.}$$
$$\qquad\qquad\qquad\quad \text{Reverse the order symbol.}$$
$$y < ^-9 \qquad \text{Any number less than -9 is a solution.}$$

Check: Replace y with a number less than $^-9$. Try $^-10$.

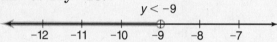

$$13 - 6y > 49 - 2y$$
$$13 - 6(^-10) \overset{?}{>} 49 - 2(^-10)$$
$$13 + 60 \overset{?}{>} 49 + 20$$
$$73 > 69 \; ✔$$

Solve each inequality and check your solution. Graph the solution on the number line.

1. $6x + 14 \le 32$ $\boldsymbol{x \le 3}$

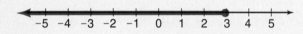

2. $18 - 3w < 15$ $\boldsymbol{w > 1}$

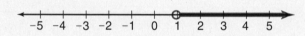

3. $5n + 8 > 20 - n$ $\boldsymbol{n > 2}$

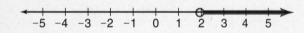

4. $2y + 2 \ge 6y + 6$ $\boldsymbol{y \le ^-1}$

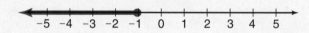

5. $\frac{1}{2}(10h - 6) > ^-23$ $\boldsymbol{h > ^-4}$

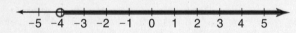

6. $4(7 - 3x) \le ^-20$ $\boldsymbol{x \ge 4}$

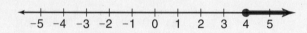

7. $^-15 \le \frac{c}{^-4} - 15$ $\boldsymbol{c \le 0}$

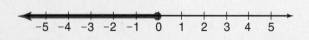

8. $\frac{^-n}{3} - 5 < ^-4$ $\boldsymbol{n > ^-3}$

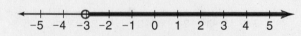

7-7 Study Guide
Writing Inequalities

You purchase three notebooks at 65¢ each and some pens at 35¢ each. How many pens can you buy if you have $3?

Explore   You want to find the amount of pens.

Plan   Let n represent the amount. Write and solve an inequality.

Solve

three times notebook cost	plus	pen cost times pen amount	is at most	$3
3(65)	+	35n	≤	300

$3(65) + 35n \leq 300$

$195 + 35n \leq 300$ **Subtract 195 from each side.**

$195 + 35n - 195 \leq 300 - 195$

$\dfrac{35n}{35} \leq \dfrac{105}{35}$ **Divide each side by 35.**

$n \leq 3$ **The number must be less than or equal to 3.**

Examine   Suppose you buy 2 pens, a number less than 3.
The total cost will be 3(65¢) + 2(35¢) or $2.65.
$2.65 ≤ $3.00, so you will have enough money.

**Define a variable and write an inequality for each situation.
Then solve.**

1. Twice a number decreased by six is at least 18. What is the number?

2. The sum of a positive even integer and the next greater even integer is at most 14. What are the integers?

3. Four times a number decreased by nine times the same number is greater than 35. What is the number?

4. Alicia spent at least $23.50 on calico and plaid fabric. She bought 5 yards of calico at $1.99 per yard. What is the most she spent on the plaid fabric?

7-7 Study Guide
Writing Inequalities

You purchase three notebooks at 65¢ each and some pens at 35¢ each. How many pens can you buy if you have $3?

Explore   You want to find the amount of pens.

Plan   Let n represent the amount. Write and solve an inequality.

Solve

three times notebook cost	plus	pen cost times pen amount	is at most	$3
$3(65)$	$+$	$35n$	$\leq$	300

$$3(65) + 35n \leq 300$$
$$195 + 35n \leq 300 \qquad \text{Subtract 195 from each side.}$$
$$195 + 35n - 195 \leq 300 - 195$$
$$\frac{35n}{35} \leq \frac{105}{35} \qquad \text{Divide each side by 35.}$$
$$n \leq 3 \qquad \text{The number must be less than or equal to 3.}$$

Examine   Suppose you buy 2 pens, a number less than 3.
The total cost will be $3(65¢) + 2(35¢)$ or $2.65.
$2.65 \leq $3.00, so you will have enough money.

Define a variable and write an inequality for each situation. Then solve.

1. Twice a number decreased by six is at least 18. What is the number? **Let n = the number; $2n - 6 \geq 18$; The number is any number greater than or equal to 12.**

2. The sum of a positive even integer and the next greater even integer is at most 14. What are the integers? **Let n = the lesser number, then $n + 2$ = the greater number; $n + n + 2 \leq 14$; The number is any number less than or equal to 6.**

3. Four times a number decreased by nine times the same number is greater than 35. What is the number? **Let n = the number; $4n - 9n > 35$; The number is any number less than -7.**

4. Alicia spent at least $23.50 on calico and plaid fabric. She bought 5 yards of calico at $1.99 per yard. What is the most she spent on the plaid fabric? **Let n = the cost of plaid fabric; $5(1.99) + n \geq 23.50$; $13.55**

7-8 Study Guide

Integration: Measurement
Using the Metric System

To convert units within the metric system, multiply or divide by powers of ten.

Larger units to smaller units: MULTIPLY→

Unit of length

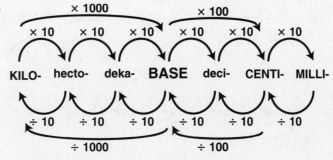

Smaller units to larger units: ←DIVIDE

Examples:

2.3 mm = $\underline{\ ?\ }$ cm
Smaller to larger means fewer units. Divide by 10.
$2.3 \div 10 = 0.23$
2.3 mm $= 0.23$ cm

6 kg = $\underline{\ ?\ }$ g
Larger to smaller means more units. Multiply by 1000.
$6 \times 1000 = 6000$
6 kg $= 6000$ g

35 mL = $\underline{\ ?\ }$ L
Smaller to larger means fewer units. Divide by 1000.
$35 \div 1000 = 0.035$
35 mL $= 0.035$ L

Complete each sentence.

1. 2.5 m = _____ cm

2. 0.35 m = _____ mm

3. 565 m = _____ km

4. 17 cm = _____ m

5. 0.3 cm = _____ mm

6. 2100 cm = _____ km

7. 3.4 km = _____ m

8. 53 cm = _____ m

9. 2 m = _____ cm

10. 800 m = _____ km

11. 42 mm = _____ cm

12. 4600 mL = _____ L

13. 8 L = _____ mL

14. 786 cm = _____ m

15. 3571 mg = _____ g

16. 3 kg = _____ g

17. 58 g = _____ mg

18. 0.045 m = _____ mm

7-8 Study Guide

Integration: Measurement
Using the Metric System

To convert units within the metric system, multiply or divide by powers of ten.

Larger units to smaller units: MULTIPLY→

Unit of length

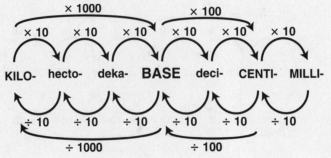

Smaller units to larger units: ←DIVIDE

Examples:

2.3 mm = __?__ cm
Smaller to larger means fewer units. Divide by 10.
$2.3 \div 10 = 0.23$
2.3 mm = 0.23 cm

6 kg = __?__ g
Larger to smaller means more units. Multiply by 1000.
$6 \times 1000 = 6000$
6 kg = 6000 g

35 mL = __?__ L
Smaller to larger means fewer units. Divide by 1000.
$35 \div 1000 = 0.035$
35 mL = 0.035 L

Complete each sentence.

1. 2.5 m = ____ cm **250**

2. 0.35 m = ____ mm
   350

3. 565 m = ____ km
   0.565

4. 17 cm = ____ m **0.17**

5. 0.3 cm = ____ mm **3**

6. 2100 cm = ____ km
   0.021

7. 3.4 km = ____ m
   3400

8. 53 cm = ____ m **0.53**

9. 2 m = ____ cm **200**

10. 800 m = ____ km **0.8**

11. 42 mm = ____ cm **4.2**

12. 4600 mL = ____ L **4.6**

13. 8 L = ____ mL **8000**

14. 786 cm = ____ m **7.86**

15. 3571 mg = ____ g
    3.571

16. 3 kg = ____ g **3000**

17. 58 g = ____ mg
    58,000

18. 0.045 m = ____ mm
    45

8-1 Study Guide
Relations and Functions

A **relation** is a set of ordered pairs. The set of first coordinates is called the **domain**. The second set of coordinates is called the **range**.

{(0, 1), (3, 4), (5, 6)}

x	1	1	4
y	−1	3	7

x	y
2	3
6	−1
2	−1

The domain is {0, 3, 5}.
The range is {1, 4, 6}.

The domain is {1, 4}.
The range is {−1, 3, 7}.

The domain is {2, 6}.
The range is {−1, 3}.

A **function** is a relation in which each element of the domain is paired with exactly one element in the range.

x	3	2	−6	−1
y	5	1	2	0

This relation is a function.

{(4, 1), (−2, 6), (4, 3), (1, 0)}

This relation is not a function.

Each element of the domain is paired with exactly one element in the range.

The element 4 in the domain is paired with two elements, 3 and 1, in the range.

Write the domain and range of each relation.

1. {(0, 7), (5, 3), (3, 7), (2, 7)}

2. $\left\{\left(-\frac{1}{4}, \frac{1}{3}\right), \left(2\frac{2}{3}, -10\right), \left(-6\frac{1}{2}, 42\right)\right\}$

Express the relation shown in each table or graph as a set of ordered pairs. Then state the domain and range of the relation.

3.

x	y
2	−3
−4	−2
1	5
3	5
2	−1

4.

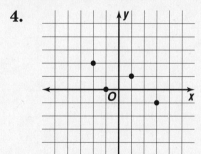

5.

x	y
−1	0
−1	4
3	0
−1	3
2	4

Determine whether each relation is a function.

6.

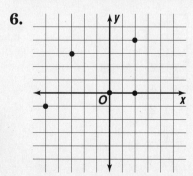

7. {(8, 7), (4, −2), (0, 0), (8, 7)}

8.

x	y
1	−3
0	2
−2	4
3	2
−1	5

NAME _____ DATE _____

8-1 Study Guide

Relations and Functions

Student Edition
Pages 372–377

A **relation** is a set of ordered pairs. The set of first coordinates is called the **domain**. The second set of coordinates is called the **range**.

{(0, 1), (3, 4), (5, 6)}

x	1	1	4
y	-1	3	7

x	y
2	3
6	-1
2	-1

The domain is {0, 3, 5}.
The range is {1, 4, 6}.

The domain is {1, 4}.
The range is {-1, 3, 7}.

The domain is {2, 6}.
The range is {-1, 3}.

A **function** is a relation in which each element of the domain is paired with exactly one element in the range.

x	3	2	-6	-1
y	5	1	2	0

This relation is a function.

{(4, 1), (-2, 6), (4, 3), (1, 0)}

This relation is not a function.

Each element of the domain is paired with exactly one element in the range.

The element 4 in the domain is paired with two elements, 3 and 1, in the range.

Write the domain and range of each relation.

1. {(0, 7), (5, 3), (3, 7), (2, 7)}

D = {0, 5, 3, 2}; R = {7, 3}

2. $D = \left\{-\frac{1}{4}, 2\frac{2}{3}, -6\frac{1}{2}\right\}; R = \left\{\frac{1}{3}, -10, 42\right\}$

2. $\left\{\left(-\frac{1}{4}, \frac{1}{3}\right), \left(2\frac{2}{3}, -10\right), \left(-6\frac{1}{2}, 42\right)\right\}$

Express the relation shown in each table or graph as a set of ordered pairs. Then state the domain and range of the relation.

3.

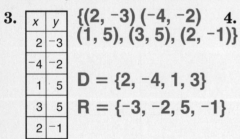

x	y
2	-3
-4	-2
1	5
3	5
2	-1

{(2, -3) (-4, -2) (1, 5), (3, 5), (2, -1)}

D = {2, -4, 1, 3}
R = {-3, -2, 5, -1}

4.

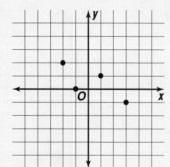

4. {(-1, 0), (-2, 2), (1, 1), (3, -1)}
D = {-1, -2, 1, 3}
R = {0, 2, 1, -1}

5.

x	y
-1	0
-1	4
3	0
-1	3
2	4

5. {(-1, 0), (-1, 4), (3, 0), (-1, 3), (2, -4)}
D = {-1, 3, 2}
R = {0, 4, 3, -4}

Determine whether each relation is a function.

6.

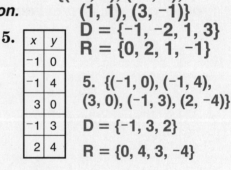

no

7. {(8, 7), (4, -2), (0, 0), (8, 7)}

yes

8.

x	y
1	-3
0	2
-2	4
3	2
-1	5

yes

8-2 Study Guide

Integration: Statistics
Scatter Plots

A **scatter plot** is a graph of ordered pairs that shows the relationship between two sets of data.

If the points on a graph seem to slant upward to the right, there is a *positive* relationship.

If the points appear to slant downward to the right, there is a *negative* relationship.

If the points seem random, there is *no* relationship.

Example: The scatter plot on the right shows the relationship between the heights of a group of people and their shoe sizes. In this graph, the points go upward to the right. Therefore, there is a positive relationship. In general, the scatter plot seems to show that the taller a person is, the greater the shoe size.

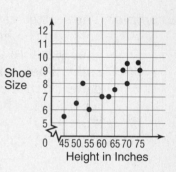

What type of relationship, positive, negative, or none, is shown by each scatter plot?

1.

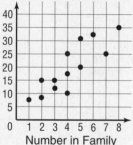

2.

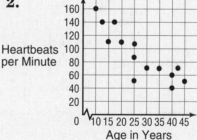

3.

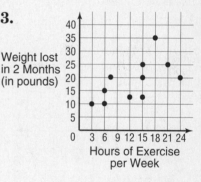

Determine whether a scatter plot of the data for the following might show a positive, a negative, or no relationship. Explain your answer.

4. study time, higher grades

5. height, intelligence

6. shoe size, salary

7. age of car, value of car

8. miles per gallon, gas expense

9. education, salary

10. wrist circumference, appetite

11. birthdate, ring size

12. windchill, ice cream sales

13. age of tree, number of rings

14. amount of snowfall, shovel sales

15. hair length, hat size

63

8-2 Study Guide

Student Edition
Pages 379–384

Integration: Statistics
Scatter Plots

A **scatter plot** is a graph of ordered pairs that shows the relationship between two sets of data.

If the points on a graph seem to slant upward to the right, there is a *positive* relationship.

If the points appear to slant downward to the right, there is a *negative* relationship.

If the points seem random, there is *no* relationship.

Example: The scatter plot on the right shows the relationship between the heights of a group of people and their shoe sizes. In this graph, the points go upward to the right. Therefore, there is a positive relationship. In general, the scatter plot seems to show that the taller a person is, the greater the shoe size.

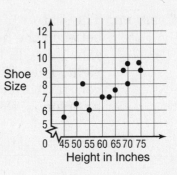

What type of relationship, positive, negative, or none, is shown by each scatter plot?

1.

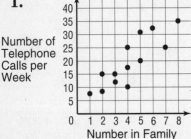

Positive

2.

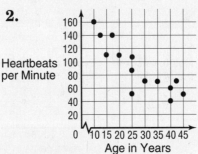

Negative

3.

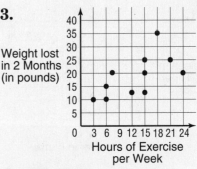

Positive

Determine whether a scatter plot of the data for the following might show a positive, a negative, or no relationship. Explain your answer. **Sample answers given. See students' explanations.**

4. study time, higher grades **positive**

5. height, intelligence **none**

6. shoe size, salary **none**

7. age of car, value of car **negative**

8. miles per gallon, gas expense **negative**

9. education, salary **positive**

10. wrist circumference, appetite **none**

11. birthdate, ring size **none**

12. windchill, ice cream sales **negative**

13. age of tree, number of rings **positive**

14. amount of snowfall, shovel sales **positive**

15. hair length, hat size **none**

Pre-Algebra

8-3 Study Guide
Graphing Linear Relations

To find a solution of an equation that has two variables, choose any value for x, substitute that value into the equation and find the corresponding value for y.

$y = 7 + x$ **Suppose $x = 4$**
$y = 7 + 4$ **Replace x with 4.**
$y = 11$

When $x = 4$, $y = 11$. So the ordered pair $(4, 11)$ is a solution of the equation $y = 7 + x$.

An equation has many ordered pairs that are solutions. For example, four ordered pairs for the equation $y = x - 1$ are $(3, 2)$, $(0, -1)$, $(2, 1)$, and $(-1, -2)$. To graph an equation, graph the ordered pairs and then draw the line that contains the points. An equation is called a **linear equation** if its graph is a straight line.

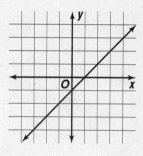

Find four solutions for each equation. Write the solutions as ordered pairs.

1. $y = x$

2. $y = x + 1$

3. $y = x - 2$

4. $2x - y = 3$

5. $y = -4x + 1$

6. $y = \frac{1}{2}x + 3$

Determine whether each relation is linear.

7. $-3x + 2y = 1$

8. $y = x^2 - 1$

9. $y = -x - 3$

Graph each equation.

10. $y = 2x - 4$

11. $-3x + y = -5$

12. $y = -\frac{1}{2}x$

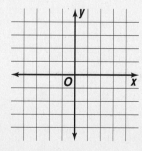
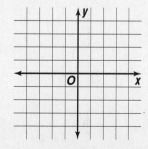
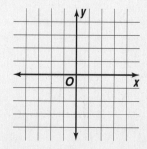

8-3 Study Guide
Graphing Linear Relations

Student Edition
Pages 385–390

To find a solution of an equation that has two variables, choose any value for x, substitute that value into the equation and find the corresponding value for y.

$y = 7 + x$ **Suppose $x = 4$**
$y = 7 + 4$ **Replace x with 4.**
$y = 11$

When $x = 4$, $y = 11$. So the ordered pair (4, 11) is a solution of the equation $y = 7 + x$.

An equation has many ordered pairs that are solutions. For example, four ordered pairs for the equation $y = x - 1$ are (3, 2), (0, −1), (2, 1), and (−1, −2). To graph an equation, graph the ordered pairs and then draw the line that contains the points. An equation is called a **linear equation** if its graph is a straight line.

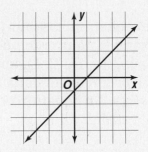

Find four solutions for each equation. Write the solutions as ordered pairs. **Answers may vary. Four possible solutions are given.**

1. $y = x$ **(3,3), (0, 0), (−3, −3), (−1, −1)**

2. $y = x + 1$ **(0, 1), (3, 4), (−1, 0), (−2, −1)**

3. $y = x - 2$ **(0, −2), (1,−1), (−2,−4), (2, 0)**

4. $2x - y = 3$ **(−2, −7), (0, −3), (2, 1), (3, 0)**

5. $y = -4x + 1$ **(1, −3), (0, 1), (−1, 5), (2, −7)**

6. $y = \frac{1}{2}x + 3$ **(2, 4), (0, 3), (−2, 2), (4, 5)**

Determine whether each relation is linear.

7. $-3x + 2y = 1$ **yes**

8. $y = x^2 - 1$ **no**

9. $y = -x - 3$ **yes**

Graph each equation.

10. $y = 2x - 4$

11. $-3x + y = -5$

12. $y = -\frac{1}{2}x$

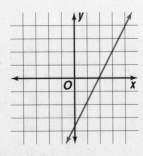

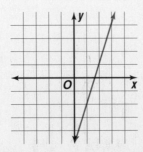

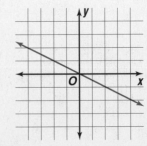

8-4 Study Guide
Equations as Functions

Suppose $y = 3x + 2$ and the domain is $\{-2, 0, 1\}$. Make a table of the domain and corresponding range values.

x	y
-2	-4
0	2
1	5

Graph $y = 3x + 2$ using the ordered pairs.

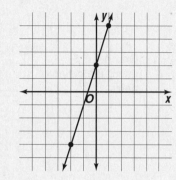

Using the vertical line test, we find that $y = 3x + 2$ is a function.

Equations that represent functions can be written in **functional notation, $f(x)$**. The symbol $f(x)$ represents the value in the range that corresponds to the value of x in the domain. The equation $y = 3x + 2$ can be written as $f(x) = 3x + 2$.

To determine a functional value, substitute the given value for x in the equation. For example, if $f(x) = 3x + 2$ and $x = -3$, then $f(-3) = 3(-3) + 2$ or -7.

For each equation,
a. solve for the domain = $\{-4, 0, 1\}$, and
b. determine whether the equation is a function.

1. $x + y = 12$ **2.** $x = 3 - y$ **3.** $y = 8 + x^2$

Given $h(x) = 2x - 9$ and $g(x) = x^2 + 4$, find each value.

4. $h(-3)$ **5.** $g(-5)$ **6.** $5[h(0)]$

7. $g\left(-\dfrac{1}{4}\right)$ **8.** $g(2.2b)$ **9.** $g(3a)$

10. $h(-0.48)$ **11.** $2[g(2)]$ **12.** $h\left(\dfrac{1}{2}\right)$

NAME _____ DATE _____

8-4 Study Guide

Equations as Functions

Suppose $y = 3x + 2$ and the domain is $\{-2, 0, 1\}$. Make a table of the domain and corresponding range values.

x	y
-2	-4
0	2
1	5

Graph $y = 3x + 2$ using the ordered pairs.

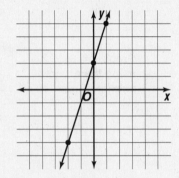

Using the vertical line test, we find that $y = 3x + 2$ is a function.

Equations that represent functions can be written in **functional notation, $f(x)$**. The symbol $f(x)$ represents the value in the range that corresponds to the value of x in the domain. The equation $y = 3x + 2$ can be written as $f(x) = 3x + 2$.

To determine a functional value, substitute the given value for x in the equation. For example, if $f(x) = 3x + 2$ and $x = -3$, then $f(-3) = 3(-3) + 2$ or -7.

For each equation,
a. solve for the domain = $\{-4, 0, 1\}$, and
b. determine whether the equation is a function.

1. $x + y = 12$ **16, 12, 11; yes**   2. $x = 3 - y$ **7, 3, 2; yes**   3. $y = 8 + x^2$ **24, 8, 9; yes**

Given $h(x) = 2x - 9$ and $g(x) = x^2 + 4$, find each value.

4. $h(-3)$ **-3**

5. $g(-5)$ **29**

6. $5[h(0)]$ **-45**

7. $g\left(-\frac{1}{4}\right)$ **$4\frac{1}{16}$**

8. $g(2.2b)$ **$4.84b^2 + 4$**

9. $g(3a)$ **$9a^2 + 4$**

10. $h(-0.48)$ **-9.96**

11. $2[g(2)]$ **16**

12. $h\left(\frac{1}{2}\right)$ **-8**

8-5 Study Guide
Problem-Solving Strategy:
Draw a Graph

Student Edition
Pages 396–399

The interest Leon earned on $160 was $8. If he had deposited $200, he would have earned $10. How much money would he need to deposit to earn $12?

Explore Given the interest earned for $160 and $200, you need to determine how much money to deposit to earn $12.

Plan Graph the given information. Then read the graph to find how much money to deposit to earn $12.

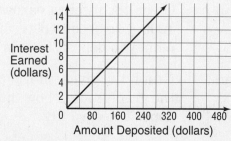

Solve Let the horizontal axis represent the amount deposited. Let the vertical axis represent the amount earned. Graph the ordered pairs (160, 8) and (200, 10). Draw a line that contains these points. He will need to deposit $240.

Examine Recall that Leon earned $8 for $160. Since $12 = 8 \times 1.5$, the deposit should be 1.5×160 or $240 to earn $12 in interest.

Use a graph to solve each problem. Assume that the rate is constant in each problem.

1. Scoopers ice cream shop sells one scoop of ice cream for $1.60. They sell three scoops for $4.80. How much money is needed to buy two scoops of ice cream?

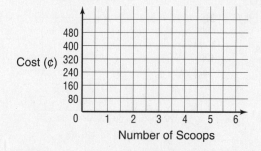

2. Kevin earned $90 for baby-sitting 15 hours. He would have earned $120 for five more hours. How much does he charge per hour? How much will Kevin earn if he works 10 hours?

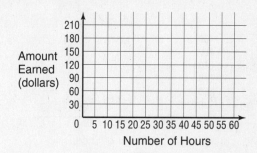

3. Sami measures the heights of the steps going into her house. The 2nd step is 1 foot above ground. The 5th step is $2\frac{1}{2}$ feet above ground. What is the height of the 11th step?

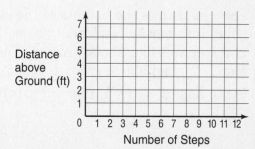

8-5 Study Guide
Problem-Solving Strategy: Draw a Graph

The interest Leon earned on $160 was $8. If he had deposited $200, he would have earned $10. How much money would he need to deposit to earn $12?

Explore   Given the interest earned for $160 and $200, you need to determine how much money to deposit to earn $12.

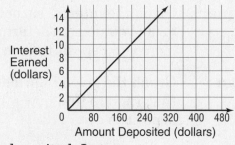

Interest Earned (dollars) / Amount Deposited (dollars)

Plan   Graph the given information. Then read the graph to find how much money to deposit to earn $12.

Solve   Let the horizontal axis represent the amount deposited. Let the vertical axis represent the amount earned. Graph the ordered pairs (160, 8) and (200, 10). Draw a line that contains these points. He will need to deposit $240.

Examine   Recall that Leon earned $8 for $160. Since 12 = 8 × 1.5, the deposit should be 1.5 × 160 or $240 to earn $12 in interest.

Use a graph to solve each problem. Assume that the rate is constant in each problem.

1. Scoopers ice cream shop sells one scoop of ice cream for $1.60. They sell three scoops for $4.80. How much money is needed to buy two scoops of ice cream? **$3.20**

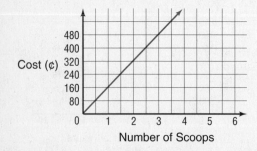

Cost (¢) / Number of Scoops

2. Kevin earned $90 for baby-sitting 15 hours. He would have earned $120 for five more hours. How much does he charge per hour? How much will Kevin earn if he works 10 hours? **$6.00; $60.00**

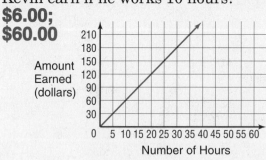

Amount Earned (dollars) / Number of Hours

3. Sami measures the heights of the steps going into her house. The 2nd step is 1 foot above ground. The 5th step is $2\frac{1}{2}$ feet above ground. What is the height of the 11th step? $5\frac{1}{2}$ **feet**

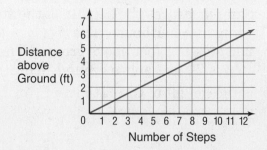

Distance above Ground (ft) / Number of Steps

8-6 Study Guide
Slope

The steepness of a line is called its **slope**. The vertical change is called the **change in y**, and the horizontal change is called the **change in x**.

$$\text{slope} = \frac{\text{change in } y}{\text{change in } x}$$

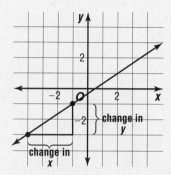

Example: In the graph above, the change in y is 2, and the change in x is 3. Therefore, the slope of the line is $\frac{2}{3}$.

The slope of a line can also be found by using the coordinates of any two points on the line.

$$\text{slope} = \frac{\text{change in } y}{\text{change in } x} \text{ or } \frac{\text{difference in } y\text{-coordinates}}{\text{difference in } x\text{-coordinates}}$$

Example: Find the slope of the line that contains the points $A(-1, -2)$ and $B(-4, -3)$.

$$\text{slope} = \frac{-2 - (-3)}{-1 - (-4)}$$
$$= \frac{-2 + 3}{-1 + 4} \text{ or } \frac{1}{3}$$

Find the slope of each line.

1.
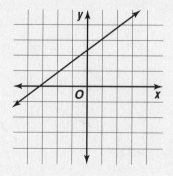

2.
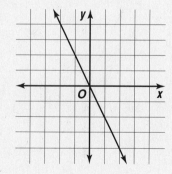

3.
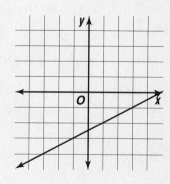

Find the slope of the line that contains each pair of points.

4. $R(-2, -3), S(-1, -1)$

5. $T(-4, -2), U(-2, -1)$

6. $V(-4, 1), W(2, 0)$

7. $P(1, -2), Q(-5, -2)$

8. $L(1, 4), M(1, -3)$

9. $M(-2, -4), N(-1, -1)$

8-6 Study Guide

Slope

Student Edition
Pages 400–404

The steepness of a line is called its **slope**. The vertical change is called the **change in y**, and the horizontal change is called the **change in x**.

$$\text{slope} = \frac{\text{change in } y}{\text{change in } x}$$

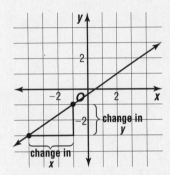

Example: In the graph above, the change in y is 2, and the change in x is 3. Therefore, the slope of the line is $\frac{2}{3}$.

The slope of a line can also be found by using the coordinates of any two points on the line.

$$\text{slope} = \frac{\text{change in } y}{\text{change in } x} \text{ or } \frac{\text{difference in } y\text{-coordinates}}{\text{difference in } x\text{-coordinates}}$$

Example: Find the slope of the line that contains the points $A(-1, -2)$ and $B(-4, -3)$.

$$\text{slope} = \frac{-2 - (-3)}{-1 - (-4)}$$
$$= \frac{-2 + 3}{-1 + 4} \text{ or } \frac{1}{3}$$

Find the slope of each line.

1.

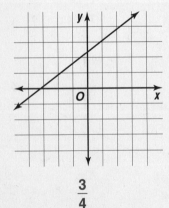

$\frac{3}{4}$

2.

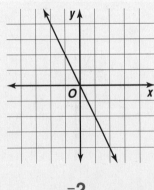

-2

3.

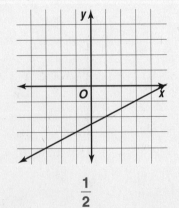

$\frac{1}{2}$

Find the slope of the line that contains each pair of points.

4. $R(-2, -3), S(-1, -1)$ **2**

5. $T(-4, -2), U(-2, -1)$ $\frac{1}{2}$

6. $V(-4, 1), W(2, 0)$ $-\frac{1}{6}$

7. $P(1, -2), Q(-5, -2)$ **0**

8. $L(1, 4), M(1, -3)$ **no slope**

9. $M(-2, -4), N(-1, -1)$ **3**

8-7 Study Guide
Intercepts

Student Edition
Pages 406–410

The point where a graph intersects an axis is called an **intercept** of the graph.

The lines at the right cross both axes. Line a crosses they y-axis at $(0, 2)$. Therefore, the y-intercept is 2. Notice that the x value of the y-intercept is 0.

The **y-intercept** is the value of an equation when $x = 0$. The **x-intercept** is the value when $y = 0$. To graph a linear equation using the x- and y-intercepts, find the intercepts. Graph them and then draw the line that contains them.

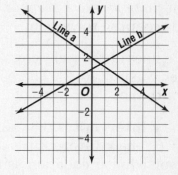

Example: Graph $y = x + 3$ using the x- and y-intercepts.

To find the x-intercept, let $y = 0$.	To find the y-intercept, let $x = 0$.
$y = x + 3$	$y = x + 3$
$0 = x + 3$	$y = 0 + 3$
$-3 = x$	$y = 3$
The x-intercept is -3.	The y-intercept is 3.
The ordered pair is $(-3, 0)$.	The ordered pair is $(0, 3)$.

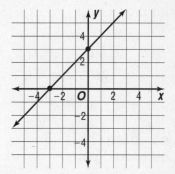

State the x-intercept and the y-intercept for each line.

1. a

2. b

3. c

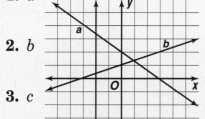

4. d

5. e

6. f

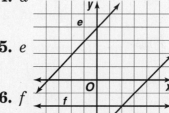

Use the x-intercept and y-intercept to graph each equation.

7. $y = 1 - 2x$

8. $y = \frac{1}{2}x + 1$

9. $-x - 3y = 3$

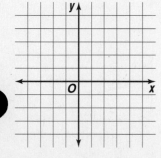

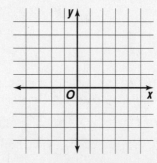

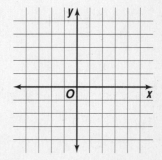

8-7 Study Guide
Intercepts

The point where a graph intersects an axis is called an **intercept** of the graph.

The lines at the right cross both axes. Line *a* crosses they *y*-axis at (0, 2). Therefore, the *y*-intercept is 2. Notice that the *x* value of the *y*-intercept is 0.

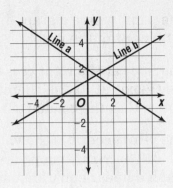

The **y-intercept** is the value of an equation when $x = 0$. The **x-intercept** is the value when $y = 0$. To graph a linear equation using the *x*- and *y*-intercepts, find the intercepts. Graph them and then draw the line that contains them.

Example: Graph $y = x + 3$ using the *x*- and *y*-intercepts.

To find the *x*-intercept, let $y = 0$.
$$y = x + 3$$
$$0 = x + 3$$
$$-3 = x$$
The *x*-intercept is -3.
The ordered pair is $(-3, 0)$.

To find the *y*-intercept, let $x = 0$.
$$y = x + 3$$
$$y = 0 + 3$$
$$y = 3$$
The *y*-intercept is 3.
The ordered pair is $(0, 3)$.

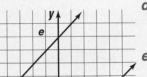

State the x-intercept and the y-intercept for each line.

1. *a*

2. *b*

3. *c*

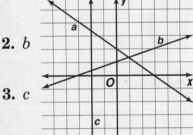

a: x-intercept: 3
y-intercept: 2

b: x-intercept: -3
y-intercept: 1

c: x-intercept: -2
y-intercept: none

4. *d*

5. *e*

6. *f*

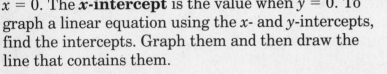

d: x-intercept: 4
y-intercept: -4

e: x-intercept: -4
y-intercept: 4

f: x-intercept: none
y-intercept: -2

Use the x-intercept and y-intercept to graph each equation.

7. $y = 1 - 2x$

8. $y = \frac{1}{2}x + 1$

9. $-x - 3y = 3$

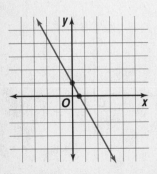

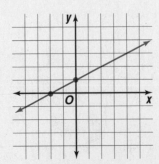

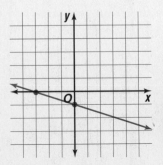

Pre-Algebra

8-8 Study Guide
Systems of Equations

The equations $y = -\frac{1}{2}x + 2$ and $y = 3x - 5$ together are called a **system of equations**.

The **solution** to this system is the ordered pair that is the solution of both equations. To solve a system of equations, graph each equation on the same coordinate plane. The point where both graphs intersect is the solution of the system of equations.

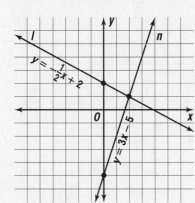

Line l is the graph of $y = -\frac{1}{2}x + 2$.

Line n is the graph of $y = 3x - 5$.

The lines intersect at (2, 1). Therefore, the solution to the system of equations is (2, 1).

Use a graph to solve each system of equations.

1. $y = x - 3$
  $y = -3x + 1$

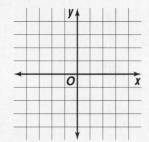

2. $y = 2x$
  $y = x + 1$

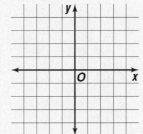

3. $y = 4x + 5$
  $y = 4x - 1$

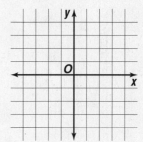

4. $y = x$
  $y = -2$

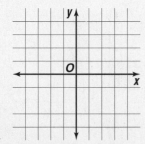

5. $y = -x - 1$
  $y = -3x - 3$

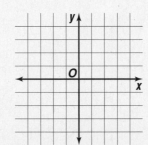

6. $y = 6x - 12$
  $y = 2x - 4$

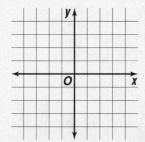

8-8 Study Guide

Systems of Equations

Student Edition
Pages 412–416

The equations $y = -\frac{1}{2}x + 2$ and $y = 3x - 5$ together are called a **system of equations**.

The **solution** to this system is the ordered pair that is the solution of both equations. To solve a system of equations, graph each equation on the same coordinate plane. The point where both graphs intersect is the solution of the system of equations.

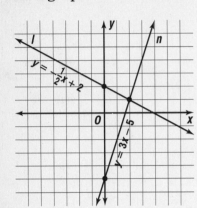

Line l is the graph of $y = -\frac{1}{2}x + 2$.

Line n is the graph of $y = 3x - 5$.

The lines intersect at (2, 1). Therefore, the solution to the system of equations is (2, 1).

Use a graph to solve each system of equations.

1. $y = x - 3$
$y = -3x + 1$ **(1, −2)**

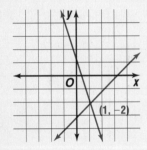

2. $y = 2x$
$y = x + 1$ **(1, 2)**

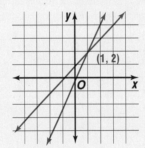

3. $y = 4x + 5$ **no**
$y = 4x - 1$ **solution**

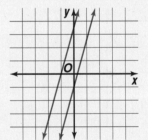

4. $y = x$
$y = -2$ **(−2, −2)**

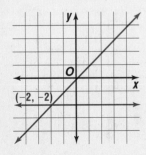

5. $y = -x - 1$
$y = -3x - 3$ **(−1, 0)**

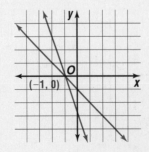

6. $y = 6x - 12$
$y = 2x - 4$ **(2, 0)**

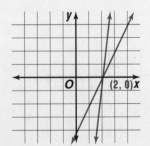

Pre-Algebra

8-9 Study Guide

Graphing Inequalities

1. Graph the following ordered pairs on the coordinate system at the right.

    (2, 3)   (3, 5)   (-2, -1)

    (-3, 2)   (3, 4)   (-1, 0)

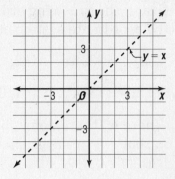

2. Where do these points lie in the plane in relation to the graph of $y = x$?

3. In each ordered pair in Exercise 1, is the x-coordinate less than, equal to, or greater than the y-coordinate?

4. Which of the following do the ordered pairs in Exercise 1 represent: $y = x$, $y > x$, or $y < x$?

5. Which of the following represents the points located below the graph of $y = x$: $y = x$, $y > x$, or $y < x$?

6. To represent all ordered pairs (x, y) where $y > x$, shade the portion of the coordinate plane above the graph of $y = x$. Note that the dashed line means that the graph of $y = x$ is not part of the graph of $y > x$.

7. Which of the following belong to the graph of $y > x$?

    $(10, 20)$ $\left(\dfrac{1}{4}, \dfrac{1}{2}\right)$ $\left(\dfrac{1}{2}, \dfrac{1}{4}\right)$ $(0, 0)$

Graph each inequality.

8. $y < 3x$

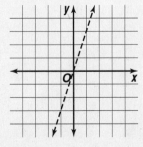

9. $y > 2x + 3$

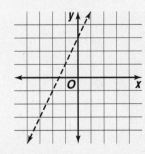

10. $x < 1 - y$

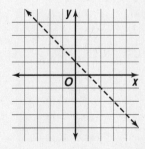

8-9 Study Guide

Graphing Inequalities

Student Edition
Pages 418–422

1. Graph the following ordered pairs on the coordinate system at the right.

   (2, 3)   (3, 5)   (−2, −1)

   (−3, 2)   (3, 4)   (−1, 0)

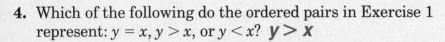

2. Where do these points lie in the plane in relation to the graph of $y = x$? **to the left of, or above, the line**

3. In each ordered pair in Exercise 1, is the x-coordinate less than, equal to, or greater than the y-coordinate? **less than**

4. Which of the following do the ordered pairs in Exercise 1 represent: $y = x$, $y > x$, or $y < x$? **$y > x$**

5. Which of the following represents the points located below the graph of $y = x$: $y = x$, $y > x$, or $y < x$? **$y < x$**

6. To represent all ordered pairs (x, y) where $y > x$, shade the portion of the coordinate plane above the graph of $y = x$. Note that the dashed line means that the graph of $y = x$ is not part of the graph of $y > x$.

7. Which of the following belong to the graph of $y > x$?

   (10, 20) $\left(\dfrac{1}{4}, \dfrac{1}{2}\right)$ $\left(\dfrac{1}{2}, \dfrac{1}{4}\right)$ (0, 0)

Graph each inequality.

8. $y < 3x$

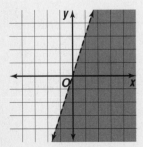

9. $y > 2x + 3$

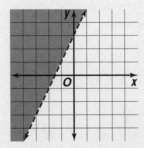

10. $x < 1 - y$

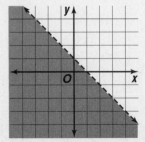

Pre-Algebra

9-1 Study Guide
Ratios and Rates

Student Edition
Pages 432–436

A **ratio** is a comparison of two numbers by division. If the two terms of a ratio have no common factors, the ratio is in simplest form.

$$\frac{4}{16} = \frac{1}{4} \qquad \text{The GCF of 4 and 16 is 4.}$$

(÷ 4)

One type of ratio is a **rate**. A rate compares two measurements with different units. Speeds, such as 50 miles per hour or 32 feet per second, are familiar examples of rates. To change a rate to a unit rate, divide both the numerator and denominator by the denominator.

$$\frac{5280 \text{ ft}}{4 \text{ min}} = \frac{1320 \text{ ft}}{1 \text{ min}}$$

Rate ÷ 4 → Unit Rate ÷ 4

A unit rate is a rate with a denominator of 1.

Write the ratio that compares each of the following.

1. number of *p*'s to number of *i*'s in *Mississippi*

2. number of *o*'s to total number of letters in *proportion*

3. number of months that have an *r* in their name to the number of months in a year

Express each ratio or rate as a fraction in simplest form.

4. 9 to 12

5. 12 to 9

6. 5:20

7. $2.50 for 5 notepads

8. 60¢ per dozen

9. $3.00 to rent 2 videotapes

Express each ratio as a unit rate.

10. 120 miles in 2 hours

11. 800 pounds for 40 square inches

12. $300 for 5 jackets

13. 45 meters in 3 minutes

14. 10 kilometers in 2 hours

15. 30 yards in 15 seconds

9-1 Study Guide

Student Edition
Pages 432–436

Ratios and Rates

A **ratio** is a comparison of two numbers by division. If the two terms of a ratio have no common factors, the ratio is in simplest form.

$$\frac{4}{16} = \frac{1}{4} \qquad \text{The GCF of 4 and 16 is 4.}$$

One type of ratio is a **rate**. A rate compares two measurements with different units. Speeds, such as 50 miles per hour or 32 feet per second, are familiar examples of rates. To change a rate to a unit rate, divide both the numerator and denominator by the denominator.

$$\frac{5280 \text{ ft}}{4 \text{ min}} = \frac{1320 \text{ ft}}{1 \text{ min}} \qquad \begin{array}{l}\text{A unit rate is a rate with} \\ \text{a denominator of 1.}\end{array}$$

Write the ratio that compares each of the following.

1. number of p's to number of i's in *Mississippi* $\frac{2}{4}$ or $\frac{1}{2}$

2. number of o's to total number of letters in *proportion* $\frac{3}{10}$

3. number of months that have an r in their name to the number of months in a year $\frac{8}{12}$ or $\frac{2}{3}$

Express each ratio or rate as a fraction in simplest form.

4. 9 to 12 $\frac{3}{4}$

5. 12 to 9 $\frac{4}{3}$

6. 5:20 $\frac{1}{4}$

7. $2.50 for 5 notepads $\frac{50¢}{1}$

8. 60¢ per dozen $\frac{5¢}{1}$

9. $3.00 to rent 2 videotapes $\frac{\$1.50}{1}$

Express each ratio as a unit rate.

10. 120 miles in 2 hours
60 miles per hour

11. 800 pounds for 40 square inches
20 pounds per square inch

12. $300 for 5 jackets
$60 per jacket

13. 45 meters in 3 minutes
15 meters per minute

14. 10 kilometers in 2 hours
5 kilometers per hour

15. 30 yards in 15 seconds
2 yards per second

Pre-Algebra

9-2 Study Guide
Problem-Solving Strategy: Make a Table

Student Edition
Pages 437–438

Example: Every week Evelyn and her sister Maria save some of their allowance to buy a present for their mother. Evelyn can save $0.90 a week and Maria can save $0.75. How many weeks will ti take them to save at least $11.00?

Explore   It would help in solving this problem to think of a way to keep track of how much money they have saved.

Plan   One way to keep track is to use a table.

Solve

Week	1	2					
Evelyn	$0.90	$1.80					
Maria	$0.75	$1.50					
Total							

1. Fill in the table above until you have found the solution to the problem in the example. Be sure to examine your solution.

2. Henrietta and Samuel start out driving separately from the same house on their way to their uncle's house. Henrietta drives 55 miles each hour and Samuel drives 50 miles each hour. How far will Samuel have traveled when Henrietta gets to her uncle's house, which is 385 miles away?

Henrietta	55									
Samuel	50									

3. Mario's dartboard has three scoring rings on it. The outer ring is only worth 1 point, the middle ring is worth 3 points, and the inner ring is worth 7 points. If he places the dart in the inner ring only once, and hits the outer ring twice as often as the middle ring, how many points has he scored in each of the three rings if his final score is 42 points? How many darts has he thrown for this score?

7									
3									
1									

9-2 Study Guide

Problem-Solving Strategy: Make a Table

Student Edition
Pages 437–438

Example: Every week Evelyn and her sister Maria save some of their allowance to buy a present for their mother. Evelyn can save $0.90 a week and Maria can save $0.75. How many weeks will ti take them to save at least $11.00?

Explore It would help in solving this problem to think of a way to keep track of how much money they have saved.

Plan One way to keep track is to use a table.

Solve

Week	1	2	3	4	5	6	7
Evelyn	$0.90	$1.80	$2.70	$3.60	$4.50	$5.40	$6.30
Maria	$0.75	$1.50	$2.25	$3.00	$3.75	$4.50	$5.25
Total	$1.65	$3.30	$4.95	$6.60	$8.25	$9.90	$11.55

1. Fill in the table above until you have found the solution to the problem in the example. Be sure to examine your solution.
See table; 7 weeks

2. Henrietta and Samuel start out driving separately from the same house on their way to their uncle's house. Henrietta drives 55 miles each hour and Samuel drives 50 miles each hour. How far will Samuel have traveled when Henrietta gets to her uncle's house, which is 385 miles away? **350 miles**

Henrietta	55	110	165	220	275	330	385			
Samuel	50	100	150	200	250	300	350			

3. Mario's dartboard has three scoring rings on it. The outer ring is only worth 1 point, the middle ring is worth 3 points, and the inner ring is worth 7 points. If he places the dart in the inner ring only once, and hits the outer ring twice as often as the middle ring, how many points has he scored in each of the three rings if his final score is 42 points? How many darts has he thrown for this score? **22 darts**

7	7	7	7	7	7	7	7			
3	3	6	9	12	15	18	21			
1	2	4	6	8	10	12	14			

9-3 Study Guide

Integration: Probability
Simple Probability

In mathematics, the study of chance is called **probability**.

$$\text{probability} = \frac{\text{number of ways a certain outcome can occur}}{\text{number of possible outcomes}}$$

When tossing a coin, there are two *outcomes*—heads or tails. Each outcome is equally likely. In other words, the probability of heads appearing is the same as that of tails appearing.

An outcome that definitely will happen has a probability of 1. An outcome that cannot happen has a probability of 0.

A cooler contains 2 cans of grape juice, 3 cans of grapefruit juice, and 7 cans of orange juice. A can of juice is chosen without looking. Find each probability.

1. P(grapefruit juice)

2. P(orange juice)

3. P(grape juice)

A die is rolled. Find each probability.

4. $P(5)$

5. $P(2)$

6. $P(2, 4, \text{ or } 6)$

7. $P(3 \text{ or } 4)$

8. $P(\text{not } 6)$

9. $P(1)$

There are 4 grape, 2 cherry, 3 lemon, and 7 raspberry gumballs in a bag. Suppose you select one gumball at random. Find each probability.

10. P(cherry gumball)

11. P(lemon or grape gumball)

12. P(raspberry or grape gumball)

13. P(lemon gumball)

14. P(peppermint gumball)

15. P(cherry or spearmint gumball)

16. P(grape, cherry, lemon, or raspberry gumball)

9-3 Study Guide
Integration: Probability
Simple Probability

In mathematics, the study of chance is called **probability**.

$$\text{probability} = \frac{\text{number of ways a certain outcome can occur}}{\text{number of possible outcomes}}$$

When tossing a coin, there are two *outcomes*—heads or tails. Each outcome is equally likely. In other words, the probability of heads appearing is the same as that of tails appearing.

An outcome that definitely will happen has a probability of 1. An outcome that cannot happen has a probability of 0.

A cooler contains 2 cans of grape juice, 3 cans of grapefruit juice, and 7 cans of orange juice. A can of juice is chosen without looking. Find each probability.

1. P(grapefruit juice) $\frac{1}{4}$

2. P(orange juice) $\frac{7}{12}$

3. P(grape juice) $\frac{1}{6}$

A die is rolled. Find each probability.

4. $P(5)$ $\frac{1}{6}$

5. $P(2)$ $\frac{1}{6}$

6. $P(2, 4, \text{ or } 6)$ $\frac{1}{2}$

7. $P(3 \text{ or } 4)$ $\frac{1}{3}$

8. $P(\text{not } 6)$ $\frac{5}{6}$

9. $P(1)$ $\frac{1}{6}$

There are 4 grape, 2 cherry, 3 lemon, and 7 raspberry gumballs in a bag. Suppose you select one gumball at random. Find each probability.

10. P(cherry gumball) $\frac{1}{8}$

11. P(lemon or grape gumball) $\frac{7}{16}$

12. P(raspberry or grape gumball) $\frac{11}{16}$

13. P(lemon gumball) $\frac{3}{16}$

14. P(peppermint gumball) **0**

15. P(cherry or spearmint gumball) $\frac{1}{8}$

16. P(grape, cherry, lemon, or raspberry gumball) **1**

9-4 Study Guide
Using Proportions

Student Edition
Pages 444–447

A proportion is a statement of equality of two or more ratios. To determine if two ratios form a proportion, check their cross products. If the cross products are equal, the rations form a proportion.

$$\frac{1}{2} \overset{?}{=} \frac{2}{4} \qquad\qquad \frac{2}{5} \overset{?}{=} \frac{6}{15} \qquad\qquad \frac{2}{3} \overset{?}{=} \frac{10}{12}$$

$$1 \times 4 \overset{?}{=} 2 \times 2 \qquad 2 \times 15 \overset{?}{=} 5 \times 6 \qquad 2 \times 12 \overset{?}{=} 3 \times 10$$

$4 = 4$ ✔ It is a proportion. $\qquad 30 = 30$ ✔ It is a proportion. $\qquad 24 \neq 30$ It is not a proportion.

Cross products can be used to solve proportions.

Example: Solve the proportion $\frac{3}{4} = \frac{x}{20}$.

$3 \cdot 20 = 4 \cdot x$ **Write the cross products.**

$60 = 4x$ **Multiply.**

$15 = x$ **Divide each side by 4.**

Write = or ≠ in each blank to make a true statement.

1. $\frac{3}{8}$ —— $\frac{12}{32}$

2. $\frac{15}{20}$ —— $\frac{3}{4}$

3. $\frac{4}{7}$ —— $\frac{16}{49}$

4. $\frac{1}{2}$ —— $\frac{1}{4}$

5. $\frac{35}{50}$ —— $\frac{7}{10}$

6. $\frac{40}{48}$ —— $\frac{5}{6}$

Solve each proportion.

7. $\frac{5}{8} = \frac{x}{40}$

8. $\frac{6}{3} = \frac{10}{t}$

9. $\frac{n}{5} = \frac{42}{7}$

10. $\frac{4}{11} = \frac{12}{x}$

11. $\frac{2}{3} = \frac{0.8}{n}$

12. $\frac{7}{12} = \frac{1.68}{b}$

Write a proportion that could be used to solve each problem. Then solve the proportion.

13. Cole can pick 2 rows of beans in 30 minutes. How long will it take him to pick 5 rows if he works at the same rate?

14. A tree casts a shadow 30 meters long. A 2.8-meter pole casts a shadow 2 meters long. How tall is the tree?

9-4 Study Guide
Using Proportions

A proportion is a statement of equality of two or more ratios. To determine if two ratios form a proportion, check their cross products. If the cross products are equal, the rations form a proportion.

$$\frac{1}{2} \overset{?}{=} \frac{2}{4} \qquad\qquad \frac{2}{5} \overset{?}{=} \frac{6}{15} \qquad\qquad \frac{2}{3} \overset{?}{=} \frac{10}{12}$$

$1 \times 4 \overset{?}{=} 2 \times 2$ $2 \times 15 \overset{?}{=} 5 \times 6$ $2 \times 12 \overset{?}{=} 3 \times 10$

$\quad 4 = 4$ ✔ It is a $30 = 30$ ✔ It is a $24 \neq 30$ It is not a
         proportion.   proportion.   proportion.

Cross products can be used to solve proportions.

Example: Solve the proportion $\frac{3}{4} = \frac{x}{20}$.

$\quad\quad 3 \cdot 20 = 4 \cdot x$ **Write the cross products.**
$\quad\quad\quad\quad 60 = 4x$ **Multiply.**
$\quad\quad\quad\quad 15 = x$ **Divide each side by 4.**

Write = or ≠ in each blank to make a true statement.

1. $\frac{3}{8} \;\neq\; \frac{12}{32}$ **2.** $\frac{15}{20} \;=\; \frac{3}{4}$ **3.** $\frac{4}{7} \;\neq\; \frac{16}{49}$

4. $\frac{1}{2} \;\neq\; \frac{1}{4}$ **5.** $\frac{35}{50} \;=\; \frac{7}{10}$ **6.** $\frac{40}{48} \;=\; \frac{5}{6}$

Solve each proportion.

7. $\frac{5}{8} = \frac{x}{40}$ **x = 25**   **8.** $\frac{6}{3} = \frac{10}{t}$ **t = 5**   **9.** $\frac{n}{5} = \frac{42}{7}$ **n = 30**

10. $\frac{4}{11} = \frac{12}{x}$ **x = 33**   **11.** $\frac{2}{3} = \frac{0.8}{n}$ **n = 1.2**   **12.** $\frac{7}{12} = \frac{1.68}{b}$ **b = 2.88**

Write a proportion that could be used to solve each problem. Then solve the proportion.

13. Cole can pick 2 rows of beans in 30 minutes. How long will it take him to pick 5 rows if he works at the same rate? $\frac{2}{30} = \frac{5}{x}$; **x = 75, 75 minutes**

14. A tree casts a shadow 30 meters long. A 2.8-meter pole casts a shadow 2 meters long. How tall is the tree? $\frac{x}{30} = \frac{2.8}{2}$; **x = 42, 42 meters**

9-5 Study Guide

Using the Percent Proportion

The proportion shown at the right is called the **percent proportion**. It can be used to solve problems involving percent.

$$\frac{\text{Percentage}}{\text{Base}} = \text{Rate or } \frac{P}{B} = \frac{r}{100}$$

The **percentage (P)** is a number that is compared to another number called the **base (B)**. The **rate** is a percent. Always compare r to 100.

Example: Of the 800 tomatoes in a crop, 60% will be used to make ketchup. How many tomatoes will be made into ketchup?

Use the proportion $\frac{P}{B} = \frac{r}{100}$.

$$\frac{P}{800} = \frac{60}{100}$$

$$P \cdot 100 = 800 \cdot 60$$

$$100P = 48{,}000$$

$$P = 480$$

There will be 480 tomatoes made into ketchup.

Use the percent proportion to solve each problem.

1. Find 70% of 90.

2. Find 15% of 400.

3. What number is 75% of 600?

4. What number is 50% of 96?

5. 20% of 140 is what number?

6. 45% of 32 is what number?

7. Find 60% of 60.

8. Find 24% of 10.5.

9. 100% of 8.73 is what number?

10. What number is 98% of 230?

11. Joan's income is $190 per week. She saves 20% of her weekly salary. How much does she save each week?

12. Ninety percent of the seats of a flight are filled. There are 240 seats. How many seats are filled?

9-5 Study Guide
Using the Percent Proportion

The proportion shown at the right is called the **percent proportion**. It can be used to solve problems involving percent.

$$\frac{\text{Percentage}}{\text{Base}} = \text{Rate or } \frac{P}{B} = \frac{r}{100}$$

The **percentage (P)** is a number that is compared to another number called the **base (B)**. The **rate** is a percent. Always compare r to 100.

Example: Of the 800 tomatoes in a crop, 60% will be used to make ketchup. How many tomatoes will be made into ketchup?

Use the proportion $\frac{P}{B} = \frac{r}{100}$.

$$\frac{P}{800} = \frac{60}{100}$$

$$P \cdot 100 = 800 \cdot 60$$

$$100P = 48,000$$

$$P = 480$$

There will be 480 tomatoes made into ketchup.

Use the percent proportion to solve each problem.

1. Find 70% of 90. **63**

2. Find 15% of 400. **60**

3. What number is 75% of 600? **450**

4. What number is 50% of 96? **48**

5. 20% of 140 is what number? **28**

6. 45% of 32 is what number? **14.4**

7. Find 60% of 60. **36**

8. Find 24% of 10.5. **2.52**

9. 100% of 8.73 is what number? **8.73**

10. What number is 98% of 230? **225.4**

11. Joan's income is $190 per week. She saves 20% of her weekly salary. How much does she save each week? **$38**

12. Ninety percent of the seats of a flight are filled. There are 240 seats. How many seats are filled? **216 seats**

9-6 Study Guide

Integration: Statistics
Using Statistics to Predict

Mr. Niles takes a poll of 10 students in his class. Of the
10 students polled, 3 prefer to have the test today, and 7 prefer to
have the test tomorrow. The 10 students polled are a **sample** of
all the students in the class. The result of the poll can be used to
predict the number of students who prefer to have the test
tomorrow.

There are 30 students in Mr. Niles's class. How many of these
students would you expect to prefer to take the test tomorrow?

Explore   What is given? 10 students polled; 3 prefer to have
            the test today and 7 prefer tomorrow.
            What is asked? 30 students in the class; how many
            prefer the test tomorrow?

Plan   Assume that the sample is representative of the
            entire class. Set up a proportion to show two
            equivalent ratios. Let t represent the total number of
            students that prefer to have the test tomorrow.

Solve $\dfrac{7}{10} = \dfrac{t}{30}$ Solve for t. $7 \times 30 = 10t$

$$210 = 10t$$

$$21 = t \quad \text{The solution is 21.}$$

Mr. Niles predicts that 21 students would prefer to
have the test tomorrow.

Examine   Replacing t in the original equation with 21, we see
            that $\dfrac{7}{10} = \dfrac{21}{30}$. Therefore, the answer is correct.

Solve. Use the poll shown below.

How many days per week should you have physical education?	
one day	13
two days	20
three days	27
four days	20

1. How many people are in the sample?

2. What part of the sample chose two days?

3. What percentage of the sample chose four days?

4. What part of the sample chose three days?

5. Suppose there are 240 people in the school. How many do you
   predict would say three days?

9-6 Study Guide

Integration: Statistics
Using Statistics to Predict

Mr. Niles takes a poll of 10 students in his class. Of the 10 students polled, 3 prefer to have the test today, and 7 prefer to have the test tomorrow. The 10 students polled are a **sample** of all the students in the class. The result of the poll can be used to predict the number of students who prefer to have the test tomorrow.

There are 30 students in Mr. Niles's class. How many of these students would you expect to prefer to take the test tomorrow?

Explore   What is given? 10 students polled; 3 prefer to have the test today and 7 prefer tomorrow.
What is asked? 30 students in the class; how many prefer the test tomorrow?

Plan   Assume that the sample is representative of the entire class. Set up a proportion to show two equivalent ratios. Let t represent the total number of students that prefer to have the test tomorrow.

Solve $\frac{7}{10} = \frac{t}{30}$ Solve for t. $7 \times 30 = 10t$
$$210 = 10t$$
$$21 = t \quad \text{The solution is 21.}$$

Mr. Niles predicts that 21 students would prefer to have the test tomorrow.

Examine   Replacing t in the original equation with 21, we see that $\frac{7}{10} = \frac{21}{30}$. Therefore, the answer is correct.

Solve. Use the poll shown below.

How many days per week should you have physical education?	
one day	13
two days	20
three days	27
four days	20

1. How many people are in the sample? **80**

2. What part of the sample chose two days? $\frac{1}{4}$ **or 25%**

3. What percentage of the sample chose four days? **25%**

4. What part of the sample chose three days? $\frac{27}{80}$ **or** $33\frac{3}{4}\%$

5. Suppose there are 240 people in the school. How many do you predict would say three days? **81**

       Pre-Algebra

9-7 Study Guide

Fractions, Decimals, and Percents

Student Edition
Pages 458–461

Fractions, decimals, and percents can all be used to represent the same number.

Example: Express 2.45 as a mixed number and as a percent.

mixed number	percent
$2.45 \rightarrow 2\dfrac{\overset{9}{\cancel{45}}}{\underset{20}{\cancel{100}}} \rightarrow 2\dfrac{9}{20}$	$2.45 \rightarrow 2.\underset{\sim}{45} \rightarrow 245\%$

Example: Express $\dfrac{1}{4}$ as a decimal and as a percent.

decimal

$\dfrac{1}{4} \rightarrow 4\overline{)1.00}^{\,0.25} \qquad \dfrac{1}{4} = 0.25$

percent

$\dfrac{1}{4} = \dfrac{r}{100}$

$100 = 4r$

$25 = r \qquad \dfrac{1}{4} = 25\%$

Express each percent or fraction as a decimal.

1. 49%

2. 185%

3. 16.9%

4. $\dfrac{2}{5}$

5. $\dfrac{21}{40}$

6. $\dfrac{5}{8}$

7. $1\dfrac{1}{2}$

8. 4%

Express each decimal or fraction as a percent.

9. 5.62

10. 0.327

11. 0.007

12. $\dfrac{25}{100}$

13. $\dfrac{5}{6}$

14. $3\dfrac{2}{5}$

15. 0.6

16. $2\dfrac{3}{10}$

Express each percent or decimal as a fraction or a mixed number.

17. 45%

18. 150%

19. 0.3

20. 0.235

21. 4.5

22. 0.55

23. 0.005

24. 56%

NAME _____ DATE _____

9-7 Study Guide

Fractions, Decimals, and Percents

Fractions, decimals, and percents can all be used to represent the same number.

Example: Express 2.45 as a mixed number and as a percent.

mixed number	percent

$$2.45 \rightarrow 2\frac{\overset{9}{\cancel{45}}}{\underset{20}{\cancel{100}}} \rightarrow 2\frac{9}{20}$$

$$2.45 \rightarrow 2.\underset{\smile}{45} \rightarrow 245\%$$

Example: Express $\frac{1}{4}$ as a decimal and as a percent.

decimal

$$\frac{1}{4} \rightarrow 4\overline{)1.00} \quad (0.25) \qquad \frac{1}{4} = 0.25$$

percent

$$\frac{1}{4} = \frac{r}{100}$$
$$100 = 4r$$
$$25 = r \qquad \frac{1}{4} = 25\%$$

Express each percent or fraction as a decimal.

1. 49% **0.49**

2. 185% **1.85**

3. 16.9% **0.169**

4. $\frac{2}{5}$ **0.4**

5. $\frac{21}{40}$ **0.525**

6. $\frac{5}{8}$ **0.625**

7. $1\frac{1}{2}$ **1.5**

8. 4% **0.04**

Express each decimal or fraction as a percent.

9. 5.62 **562%**

10. 0.327 **32.7%**

11. 0.007 **0.7%**

12. $\frac{25}{100}$ **25%**

13. $\frac{5}{6}$ **83.$\overline{3}$%**

14. $3\frac{2}{5}$ **340%**

15. 0.6 **60%**

16. $2\frac{3}{10}$ **230%**

Express each percent or decimal as a fraction or a mixed number.

17. 45% $\frac{9}{20}$

18. 150% $1\frac{1}{2}$

19. 0.3 $\frac{3}{10}$

20. 0.235 $\frac{47}{200}$

21. 4.5 $4\frac{1}{2}$

22. 0.55 $\frac{11}{20}$

23. 0.005 $\frac{1}{200}$

24. 56% $\frac{28}{50}$

Pre-Algebra

9-8 Study Guide
Percent and Estimation

Actual	Rounded	Fractional Equivalent	Estimate will be a little . . .
52%	50%	$\frac{1}{2}$	less
78%	80%	$\frac{4}{5}$	more

$\frac{1}{2} = 50\%$

$\frac{1}{4} = 25\%$

$\frac{3}{4} = 75\%$

$\frac{1}{3} = 33\frac{1}{3}\%$

$\frac{2}{3} = 66\frac{2}{3}\%$

$\frac{1}{5} = 20\%$

$\frac{2}{5} = 40\%$

$\frac{3}{5} = 60\%$

$\frac{4}{5} = 80\%$

$\frac{1}{8} = 12\frac{1}{2}\%$

$\frac{3}{8} = 37\frac{1}{2}\%$

$\frac{5}{8} = 62\frac{1}{2}\%$

$\frac{7}{8} = 87\frac{1}{2}\%$

$\frac{1}{10} = 10\%$

$\frac{3}{10} = 30\%$

$\frac{7}{10} = 70\%$

$\frac{9}{10} = 90\%$

Complete the table below. Use the chart on the right to find the closest percent.

	Actual	Rounded	Fractional Equivalent	Estimate will be a little . . .
1.	24%			
2.	67%			
3.	89%			
4.	76%			
5.	13%			
6.	9%			
7.	21%			
8.	62%			
9.	35%			
10.	58%			

9-8 Study Guide
Percent and Estimation

Actual	Rounded	Fractional Equivalent	Estimate will be a little . . .
52%	50%	$\frac{1}{2}$	less
78%	80%	$\frac{4}{5}$	more

$\frac{1}{2} = 50\%$

$\frac{1}{4} = 25\%$

$\frac{3}{4} = 75\%$

$\frac{1}{3} = 33\frac{1}{3}\%$

$\frac{2}{3} = 66\frac{2}{3}\%$

$\frac{1}{5} = 20\%$

$\frac{2}{5} = 40\%$

$\frac{3}{5} = 60\%$

$\frac{4}{5} = 80\%$

$\frac{1}{8} = 12\frac{1}{2}\%$

$\frac{3}{8} = 37\frac{1}{2}\%$

$\frac{5}{8} = 62\frac{1}{2}\%$

$\frac{7}{8} = 87\frac{1}{2}\%$

$\frac{1}{10} = 10\%$

$\frac{3}{10} = 30\%$

$\frac{7}{10} = 70\%$

$\frac{9}{10} = 90\%$

Complete the table below. Use the chart on the right to find the closest percent.

	Actual	Rounded	Fractional Equivalent	Estimate will be a little . . .
1.	24%	**25%**	$\frac{1}{4}$	**more**
2.	67%	**$66\frac{2}{3}\%$**	$\frac{2}{3}$	**less**
3.	89%	**90%**	$\frac{9}{10}$	**more**
4.	76%	**75%**	$\frac{3}{4}$	**less**
5.	13%	**$12\frac{1}{2}\%$**	$\frac{1}{8}$	**less**
6.	9%	**10%**	$\frac{1}{10}$	**more**
7.	21%	**20%**	$\frac{1}{5}$	**less**
8.	62%	**$62\frac{1}{2}\%$**	$\frac{5}{8}$	**more**
9.	35%	**$33\frac{1}{3}\%$**	$\frac{1}{3}$	**less**
10.	58%	**60%**	$\frac{3}{5}$	**more**

 Pre-Algebra

9-9 Study Guide

Using Percent Equations

Student Edition
Pages 467–471

To solve percent problems, use the percent equation, $P = R \cdot B$.
R represents $\frac{r}{100}$.

Example 1: Find 45% of 36.

What number is 45% of 36?

$$P = 45\% \times 36$$
$$P = 0.45 \times 36$$
$$P = 16.2$$

45% of 36 is 16.2.

Example 2: 8 is what percent of 16?

$$8 = R \times 16$$
$$\frac{8}{16} = \frac{16R}{16} \qquad \textbf{Divide each side by 16.}$$
$$0.5 = R \qquad \textbf{Use a calculator.}$$

8 is 50% of 16.

The amount of **interest (I)** earned on an account depends upon the **principal (p)**, which is the money deposited, the **rate (r)**, and the **time (t)** given in years.

interest = principal × rate × time

$$I = p \times r \times t$$

Solve each problem by using the percent equation, $P = R \cdot B$.

1. Find 40% of 80.

2. Find 15% of 600.

3. What number is 30% of 120?

4. What number is 90% of 50?

5. What percent of 250 is 25?

6. What percent of 35 is 7?

7. 100% of 67 is what number?

8. 200% of 67 is what number?

Find the interest to the nearest cent.

9. $160 at 5.5% for 1.25 years

10. $1800 at 6.5% for 2 years

11. $350 at 6% for 6 months

12. $7050 at 6% for 3 months

13. $3500 at 10% for 5 years

14. $75 at 12% for 6 years

9-9 Study Guide

Using Percent Equations

To solve percent problems, use the percent equation, $P = R \cdot B$.
R represents $\frac{r}{100}$.

Example 1: Find 45% of 36.

What number is 45% of 36?

$$P \quad = 45\% \times 36$$
$$P = 0.45 \times 36$$
$$P = 16.2$$

45% of 36 is 16.2.

Example 2: 8 is what percent of 16?

$$8 = R \times 16$$
$$\frac{8}{16} = \frac{16R}{16} \qquad \textbf{Divide each side by 16.}$$
$$0.5 = R \qquad \textbf{Use a calculator.}$$

8 is 50% of 16.

The amount of **interest (I)** earned on an account depends upon the **principal (p)**, which is the money deposited, the **rate (r)**, and the **time (t)** given in years.

interest = principal × rate × time
$$I \quad = \quad p \quad \times \ r \ \times \ t$$

Solve each problem by using the percent equation, $P = R \cdot B$.

1. Find 40% of 80. **32**

2. Find 15% of 600. **90**

3. What number is 30% of 120? **36**

4. What number is 90% of 50? **45**

5. What percent of 250 is 25? **10%**

6. What percent of 35 is 7? **20%**

7. 100% of 67 is what number? **67**

8. 200% of 67 is what number? **134**

Find the interest to the nearest cent.

9. $160 at 5.5% for 1.25 years **$11.00**

10. $1800 at 6.5% for 2 years **$234.00**

11. $350 at 6% for 6 months **$10.50**

12. $7050 at 6% for 3 months **$105.75**

13. $3500 at 10% for 5 years **$1750.00**

14. $75 at 12% for 6 years **$54.00**

Pre-Algebra

9-10 Study Guide
Percent of Change

Example: Al's Sporting Goods Store raised the price of one of its best-selling bicycles from \$125 to \$140. Find the **percent of increase**.

Subtract to find the amount of change.	$140 - 125 = 15$
Solve the percent equation. Compare the amount of increase to the original amount.	$P = R \cdot B$
	$15 = R \cdot 125$
	$\dfrac{15}{125} = \dfrac{125R}{125}$
The percent of change is 12%.	$0.12 = R$

Example: Al's Sporting Goods Store reduced the price of one of its less-popular bicycles from \$80 to \$60. Find the **percent of decrease**.

Divide the new amount by the original amount.	$60 \div 80 = 0.75$
Subtract 1 from the result and write the decimal as a percent.	$0.75 - 1 = -0.25$ or -25%

The percent of change is -25%.
The percent of decrease is 25%.

State whether each percent of change is a percent of increase or a percent of decrease. Then find the percent of increase or decrease. Round to the nearest whole percent.

1. a \$120 turntable now costs \$150

2. a \$6 album is now \$4.20

2. a \$100 digital watch is now \$72

4. a \$32 sweater now costs \$36.80

5. Cheryl weighed 120 pounds. She dieted and lost 12 pounds in three weeks. Find the percent of change in Cheryl's weight.

6. The junior high school's enrollment changed from 1200 to 1350 students. Find the percent of change in enrollment.

7. Potatoes baked in the oven require 60 minutes to cook. A pressure cooker can do the same job in 20 minutes. Find the percent of change in cooking time.

8. A \$320 stereo amplifier is on sale for a limited time at \$264. Find the percent of change in price.

 Pre-Algebra

9-10 Study Guide
Percent of Change

Example: Al's Sporting Goods Store raised the price of one of its best-selling bicycles from $125 to $140. Find the **percent of increase**.

Subtract to find the amount of change.

$$140 - 125 = 15$$

Solve the percent equation. Compare the amount of increase to the original amount.

$$P = R \cdot B$$
$$15 = R \cdot 125$$
$$\frac{15}{125} = \frac{125R}{125}$$

The percent of change is 12%.

$$0.12 = R$$

Example: Al's Sporting Goods Store reduced the price of one of its less-popular bicycles from $80 to $60. Find the **percent of decrease**.

Divide the new amount by the original amount.

$$60 \div 80 = 0.75$$

Subtract 1 from the result and write the decimal as a percent.

$$0.75 - 1 = -0.25 \text{ or } -25\%$$

The percent of change is -25%.
The percent of decrease is 25%.

State whether each percent of change is a percent of increase or a percent of decrease. Then find the percent of increase or decrease. Round to the nearest whole percent. **I = increase; D = decrease**

1. a $120 turntable now costs $150 **I; 25%**

2. a $6 album is now $4.20 **D; -30%**

2. a $100 digital watch is now $72 **D; -28%**

4. a $32 sweater now costs $36.80 **I; 15%**

5. Cheryl weighed 120 pounds. She dieted and lost 12 pounds in three weeks. Find the percent of change in Cheryl's weight. **D; -10%**

6. The junior high school's enrollment changed from 1200 to 1350 students. Find the percent of change in enrollment. **I; 13%**

7. Potatoes baked in the oven require 60 minutes to cook. A pressure cooker can do the same job in 20 minutes. Find the percent of change in cooking time. **D; -67%**

8. A $320 stereo amplifier is on sale for a limited time at $264. Find the percent of change in price. **D; -18%**

Pre-Algebra

10-1 Study Guide
Stem-and-Leaf Plots

The diagram at the right called a **stem-and-leaf plot**. It is one way to organize a list of numbers. This plot shows some of the numbers between 0 and 40.

Stems	Leaves
0	3 5
1	2 2 7 8
2	0 1 6 6 9
3	4 5 5 5

3 | 4 = 34

The key indicates that 3 | 4 represents 34. So, the "stems" are the tens-place digits, and the "leaves" are the ones-place digits. The numbers shown by the plot are listed below.

3, 5, 12, 12, 17, 18, 20, 21, 26, 26, 29, 34, 35, 35, 35

Write the numbers shown by each stem-and-leaf plot.

1.
0	1 4 6 6
1	0 3 4 9 9
2	2 3 3 3 4 8
3	0 3 5 5

0 | 4 = 4

2.
5	0 0 2 4 8
6	1 3 6
7	2 5 5 8
8	3 7 8 8 9 9

6 | 1 = 61

3. Use the stem-and-leaf plot in Exercise 1.

   a. How many numbers are shown on the plot?

   b. Which number(s) appears most frequently?

   c. Which numbers appear least frequently?

4. Use the stem-and-leaf plot in Exercise 2.

   a. Which number(s) appear most frequently?

   b. Are there more numbers greater than 70, or less than 70?

   c. How many numbers are shown?

5. The following numbers are the results of a survey. A group of ninth-grade students were asked to report the number of hours they spent watching television in one week. Complete the stem-and-leaf plot at the right, using the results of the survey.

0	
1	
2	

   0, 12, 25, 19, 23, 7, 7, 5, 26, 16,

   28, 0, 1, 0, 12, 25, 10, 2, 25, 18,

   23, 1, 14, 0, 26, 19, 14, 21, 25

10-1 Study Guide
Stem-and-Leaf Plots

Student Edition
Pages 486–489

The diagram at the right called a **stem-and-leaf plot**. It is one way to organize a list of numbers. This plot shows some of the numbers between 0 and 40.

The key indicates that 3|4 represents 34. So, the "stems" are the tens-place digits, and the "leaves" are the ones-place digits. The numbers shown by the plot are listed below.

Stems	Leaves
0	3 5
1	2 2 7 8
2	0 1 6 6 9
3	4 5 5 5

3 | 4 = 34

3, 5, 12, 12, 17, 18, 20, 21, 26, 26, 29, 34, 35, 35, 35

Write the numbers shown by each stem-and-leaf plot.

1. 0 | 1 4 6 6   **1, 4, 6, 6,**
    1 | 0 3 4 9 9   **10, 13, 14, 19, 19,**
    2 | 2 3 3 3 4 8 **22, 23, 23, 23, 24,**
    3 | 0 3 5 5

    0|4 = 4

2. 5 | 0 0 2 4 8   **50, 50, 52, 54, 58,**
    6 | 1 3 6   **61, 63, 66,**
    7 | 2 5 5 8   **72, 75, 75, 78,**
    8 | 3 7 8 8 9 9 **83, 87, 88, 88, 89, 89**

    6|1 = 61

3. Use the stem-and-leaf plot in Exercise 1.
    a. How many numbers are shown on the plot? **19**

    b. Which number(s) appears most frequently? **23**

    c. Which numbers appear least frequently? **1, 4, 10, 13, 14, 22, 24, 28, 30, 33**

4. Use the stem-and-leaf plot in Exercise 2.
    a. Which number(s) appear most frequently? **50, 75, 88, 89**

    b. Are there more numbers greater than 70, or less than 70? **greater than 70**

    c. How many numbers are shown? **18**

5. The following numbers are the results of a survey. A group of ninth-grade students were asked to report the number of hours they spent watching television in one week. Complete the stem-and-leaf plot at the right, using the results of the survey.

    0, 12, 25, 19, 23, 7, 7, 5, 26, 16,

    28, 0, 1, 0, 12, 25, 10, 2, 25, 18,

    23, 1, 14, 0, 26, 19, 14, 21, 25

    0 | 0 0 0 0 1 1 2 5 7 7

    1 | 0 2 2 4 4 6 8 9 9

    2 | 1 3 3 5 5 5 5 6 6 8

    2|1 = 21

10-2 Study Guide
Measures of Variation

The list below shows the test scores for a sample of 11 high school students.

65   65   ⑥⑦   72   75   ☐75☐   75   80   ⑧⑦   92   93

The difference between the least and the greatest number in the set is called the **range**. The range above is 93–65 or 28.

When a list of data is arranged in order, the **median** is the middle number. The median above is enclosed in a box.

The circled numbers in the list above are used to analyze the data. The **lower quartile** is the median of the lower half of the data. The **upper quartile** is the median of the upper half.

The difference between the lower quartile and the upper quartile is called the **interquartile range**. The interquartile range above is 87–67 or 20.

Recall that when there are two middle numbers, the median is their mean. This is also true for the upper and lower quartiles.

Find the range, median, upper and lower quartiles, and the interquartile range for each set of data.

1. 48, 50, 53, 50, 44, 52, 45

2. 32, 0, 6, 20, 0, 12, 15, 25, 18, 15, 24

3.

Ages of Eastside Health Club Members	
Aimee	19
Lucille	35
Leonard	20
Tiago	52
Nakeisha	43
Hector	27
Robin	44
Haleem	20
Marrissa	32
Tad	27

4.

Movies That Jerome Attended Each Year	
1987	22
1988	12
1989	27
1990	34
1991	3
1992	18
1993	40
1994	14
1995	10

10-2 Study Guide
Measures of Variation

The list below shows the test scores for a sample of 11 high school students.

65   65   (67)   72   75   [75]   75   80   (87)   92   93

The difference between the least and the greatest number in the set is called the **range**. The range above is 93–65 or 28.

When a list of data is arranged in order, the **median** is the middle number. The median above is enclosed in a box.

The circled numbers in the list above are used to analyze the data. The **lower quartile** is the median of the lower half of the data. The **upper quartile** is the median of the upper half.

The difference between the lower quartile and the upper quartile is called the **interquartile range**. The interquartile range above is 87–67 or 20.

Recall that when there are two middle numbers, the median is their mean. This is also true for the upper and lower quartiles.

Find the range, median, upper and lower quartiles, and the interquartile range for each set of data.

1. 48, 50, 53, 50, 44, 52, 45   **9; 50; 52, 45; 7**

2. 32, 0, 6, 20, 0, 12, 15, 25, 18, 15, 24
  32; 15; 24, 6; 18

3.

Ages of Eastside Health Club Members	
Aimee	19
Lucille	35
Leonard	20
Tiago	52
Nakeisha	43
Hector	27
Robin	44
Haleem	20
Marrissa	32
Tad	27

**33; 29.5;
43, 20; 23**

4.

Movies That Jerome Attended Each Year	
1987	22
1988	12
1989	27
1990	34
1991	3
1992	18
1993	40
1994	14
1995	10

**37; 18;
30.5, 11; 19.5**

10-3 Study Guide
Displaying Data

George surveyed a group of students who walk to school. This list shows the number of minutes it takes each person to walk from his or her house to the school.

5   5   10   (15)   15   20   25   [30]   30   30   30   30   (35)   40   45   50

The median is in the box. The lower and upper quartiles are circled.

A **box-and-whisker plot** is shown at the right. A box is drawn to show the median (30), lower quartile (15), and upper quartile (35). Other key numbers from the data list are the lower extreme (5) and upper extreme (50).

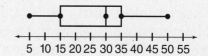

5 10 15 20 25 30 35 40 45 50 55

Use the box-and-whisker plots to answer each question below them.

1.

0 1 2 3 4 5 6 7 8 9 10

a. What is the median?

b. What are the lower quartile and the upper quartile?

c. What are the lower and upper extremes?

2.

0 10 20 30 40 50 60 70 80 90 100

a. What is the median?

b. What are the lower quartile and the upper quartile?

c. What are the lower and upper extremes?

3. Make a box-and-whisker plot at the right for this list of test scores.

60, 65, 65, 70, 75, 75, 75, 80, 85, 85, 85, 85, 85, 85, 90

4. Make a box-and-whisker plot at the right for this list of data. It shows the number of pets per family.

0, 0, 0, 1, 1, 1, 2, 2, 2, 2, 2, 3, 3, 3, 5

10-3 Study Guide
Displaying Data

George surveyed a group of students who walk to school. This list shows the number of minutes it takes each person to walk from his or her house to the school.

5   5   10 ⑮ 15 20 25 ☐30 30 30 30 30 ㉟ 40 45 50

The median is in the box. The lower and upper quartiles are circled.

A **box-and-whisker plot** is shown at the right. A box is drawn to show the median (30), lower quartile (15), and upper quartile (35). Other key numbers from the data list are the lower extreme (5) and upper extreme (50).

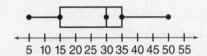

Use the box-and-whisker plots to answer each question below them.

1.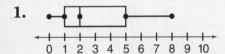

   a. What is the median? **2**

   b. What are the lower quartile and the upper quartile? **1, 5**

   c. What are the lower and upper extremes? **0, 8**

2.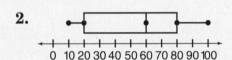

   a. What is the median? **60**

   b. What are the lower quartile and the upper quartile? **20, 80**

   c. What are the lower and upper extremes? **10, 100**

3. Make a box-and-whisker plot at the right for this list of test scores.

   60, 65, 65, 70, 75, 75, 75, 80, 85, 85, 85, 85, 85, 85, 90

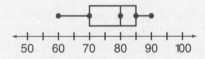

4. Make a box-and-whisker plot at the right for this list of data. It shows the number of pets per family.

   0, 0, 0, 1, 1, 1, 2, 2, 2, 2, 2, 3, 3, 3, 5

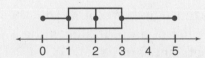

10-4 Study Guide
Misleading Statistics

The way in which data is displayed in a graph can cause the graph to be visually misleading. The two graphs below show the number of cookies sold each month by a gourmet cookie shop.

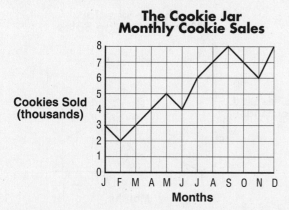

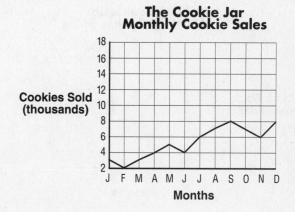

The graphs above contain the same data. However, the graph on the right suggests lower sales than the graph on the left. This is due to the shortened vertical axis. Also, notice that the vertical axis does not include zero.

The graph at the right displays data about money earned by high school students during summer vacation.

1. Is the graph misleading? Explain.

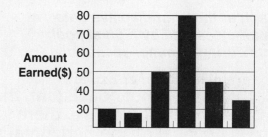

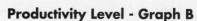

Kimiko made two different graphs showing employee productivity levels for each year in business.

Productivity Level - Graph A

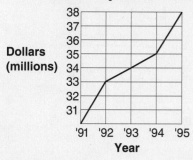

Productivity Level - Graph B

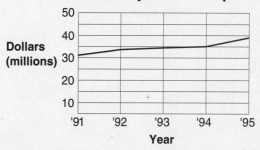

2. Which graph is misleading? Why?

3. If Kimiko wanted to ask the management to give the employees raises in 1996, which graph would be used? Explain your answer.

10-4 Study Guide

Misleading Statistics

The way in which data is displayed in a graph can cause the graph to be visually misleading. The two graphs below show the number of cookies sold each month by a gourmet cookie shop.

**The Cookie Jar
Monthly Cookie Sales**

Cookies Sold
(thousands)

J F M A M J J A S O N D
Months

**The Cookie Jar
Monthly Cookie Sales**

Cookies Sold
(thousands)

J F M A M J J A S O N D
Months

The graphs above contain the same data. However, the graph on the right suggests lower sales than the graph on the left. This is due to the shortened vertical axis. Also, notice that the vertical axis does not include zero.

The graph at the right displays data about money earned by high school students during summer vacation.

1. Is the graph misleading? Explain.
   yes; the scale is not consistent, the vertical axis does not include zero, there is no title, there is no label on the horizontal axis

Amount
Earned($)

Kimiko made two different graphs showing employee productivity levels for each year in business.

Productivity Level - Graph A

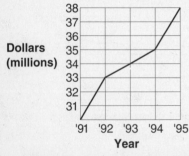

Dollars
(millions)

'91 '92 '93 '94 '95
Year

Productivity Level - Graph B

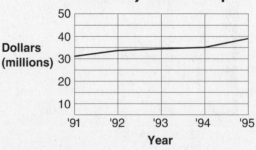

Dollars
(millions)

'91 '92 '93 '94 '95
Year

2. Which graph is misleading? Why?
   Graph A; the extended vertical axis, the shortened horizontal axis, and the vertical axis not to scale between zero and thirty-one all are misleading.

3. If Kimiko wanted to ask the management to give the employees raises in 1996, which graph would be used? Explain your answer. **Graph A; it appears to show a higher productivity level.**

10-5 Study Guide
Counting

Student Edition
Pages 509–513

Example: Cheryl has a choice of a pink, red, or yellow blouse with white or black slacks for an outfit. How many possible outfits are there?

Draw a **tree diagram** to determine the number of different outfits.

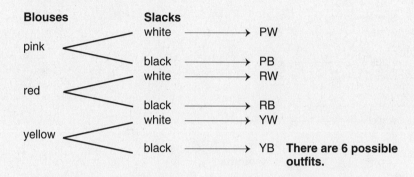

You can also find the number of possible outcomes by multiplying.

Number of different blouses		Number of different slacks		Total possible outfits
3	×	2	=	6

Draw a tree diagram to find the number of outcomes for each situation.

1. A bag contains one red marble and one white marble. A second bag contains two red marbles and a white one. How many different outcomes are possible if a marble is picked from each bag? The marbles are replaced each time.

2. How many different lunches can be made with a choice of hot dog, salad, or chili; pop, milk, or lemonade; and crackers, bread, or a roll?

Find the number of possible outcomes for each event.

3. At an ice cream shop, there are 31 flavors and 25 toppings. How many different ways are there to make a one-scoop ice cream sundae with one topping?

4. There are 4 quarterbacks and 6 centers on a football team that has 60 players. How many quarterback-center pairings are possible?

10-5 Study Guide
Counting

Student Edition
Pages 509–513

Example: Cheryl has a choice of a pink, red, or yellow blouse with white or black slacks for an outfit. How many possible outfits are there?

Draw a **tree diagram** to determine the number of different outfits.

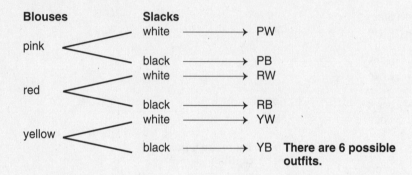

You can also find the number of possible outcomes by multiplying.

Number of different blouses		Number of different slacks		Total possible outfits
3	×	2	=	6

Draw a tree diagram to find the number of outcomes for each situation. **See student's diagrams.**

1. A bag contains one red marble and one white marble. A second bag contains two red marbles and a white one. How many different outcomes are possible if a marble is picked from each bag? The marbles are replaced each time. **6**

2. How many different lunches can be made with a choice of hot dog, salad, or chili; pop, milk, or lemonade; and crackers, bread, or a roll? **27**

Find the number of possible outcomes for each event.

3. At an ice cream shop, there are 31 flavors and 25 toppings. How many different ways are there to make a one-scoop ice cream sundae with one topping? **775**

4. There are 4 quarterbacks and 6 centers on a football team that has 60 players. How many quarterback-center pairings are possible? **24**

10-6 Study Guide

Permutations and Combinations

An arrangement where *order is important* is called a **permutation**.

Example: Mario, Sandy, Fred, and Shana are running for the offices of president, secretary, and treasurer. In how many ways can these offices be filled?

Any of the 4 people can fill the president's position. Once the president has been chosen, there are 3 people to fill the secretary's position. That leaves 2 people to fill the treasurer's position.

The symbol $P(4, 3)$ represents the number of permutations of 4 things taken 3 at a time.

$P(4, 3) = 4 \times 3 \times 2$, or 24. **The offices can be filled 24 ways.**

An arrangement where *order is not important* is called **combination**.

Example: Charles has four coins in his pocket and pulls out three at a time. How many different amounts can he get? The coins are a penny, a nickel, a dime, and a quarter.

There are $4 \times 3 \times 2$, or 24 different outcomes, but some are the same. To find the number of different combinations, divide the number of permutations $P(4, 3)$, by the number of different ways three items can be arranged.

$C(4, 3) = \dfrac{P(4, 3)}{3!} = \dfrac{4 \times 3 \times 2}{3 \times 2 \times 1}$ or 4. **4 different amounts can be chosen.**

⤷ *3! is read "three factorial."*

Find each value.

1. 5!

2. $P(4, 2)$

3. 8!

4. $C(15, 6)$

5. $P(3, 3)$

6. 13!

7. $C(5, 5)$

8. $P(10, 4)$

9. In how many ways can five books be arranged on a shelf? (Order is important.)

10. In how many ways can three students council members be elected from five candidates? (Order is not important.)

10-6 Study Guide
Permutations and Combinations

Student Edition
Pages 515–519

An arrangement where *order is important* is called a **permutation.**

Example: Mario, Sandy, Fred, and Shana are running for the offices of president, secretary, and treasurer. In how many ways can these offices be filled?

Any of the 4 people can fill the president's position. Once the president has been chosen, there are 3 people to fill the secretary's position. That leaves 2 people to fill the treasurer's position.

The symbol $P(4, 3)$ represents the number of permutations of 4 things taken 3 at a time.

$P(4, 3) = 4 \times 3 \times 2$, or 24. **The offices can be filled 24 ways.**

An arrangement where *order is not important* is called **combination**.

Example: Charles has four coins in his pocket and pulls out three at a time. How many different amounts can he get? The coins are a penny, a nickel, a dime, and a quarter.

There are $4 \times 3 \times 2$, or 24 different outcomes, but some are the same. To find the number of different combinations, divide the number of permutations $P(4, 3)$, by the number of different ways three items can be arranged.

$C(4, 3) = \dfrac{P(4, 3)}{3!} = \dfrac{4 \times 3 \times 2}{3 \times 2 \times 1}$ or 4.   **4 different amounts can be chosen.**

↑——3! is read "three factorial."

Find each value.

1. 5!
120

2. $P(4, 2)$
12

3. 8!
40,320

4. $C(15, 6)$
5005

5. $P(3, 3)$
6

6. 13!
6,227,020,800

7. $C(5, 5)$
1

8. $P(10, 4)$
5040

9. In how many ways can five books be arranged on a shelf? (Order is important.) **120**

10. In how many ways can three students council members be elected from five candidates? (Order is not important.) **20**

10-7 Study Guide
Odds

The **odds** in favor of an event is the ratio of the number of ways the outcome *can* occur to the number of ways the outcome *cannot* occur.

Example: Samantha has 2 quarters, 5 dimes, 4 nickels, and 10 pennies in her bank. If one coin is chosen, what are the odds that it is a penny or a quarter?

$$\begin{aligned}
\text{Odds of a penny} \atop \text{or a quarter} &= \underbrace{\text{ways to choose penny} \atop \text{or quarter}} : \underbrace{\text{ways to choose} \atop \text{other coins}} \\
&= \qquad 12 \qquad : \qquad 9 \\
&= 12{:}9 \\
&= 4{:}3 \qquad \text{This is read "4 to 3."}
\end{aligned}$$

Find the odds of each outcome if a card is drawn from the cards at the right.

1. an even number

2. a number less than 6

3. not 2 or 7

4. odd or even

5. 7 or a multiple of 2

6. a number greater than 6

Find the odds of each outcome if a laundry bag contains 3 dress shirts, 6 dish towels, 8 socks, 2 pairs of jeans, and 5 T-shirts.

7. a dish towel

8. a pair of jeans or a sock

9. not a T-shirt

10. *neither* dress shirt *nor* sock

11. sock, dish towel, or dress shirt

12. dish towel or T-shirt

Pre-Algebra

10-7 Study Guide
Odds

Student Edition
Pages 520–523

The **odds** in favor of an event is the ratio of the number of ways the outcome *can* occur to the number of ways the outcome *cannot* occur.

Example: Samantha has 2 quarters, 5 dimes, 4 nickels, and 10 pennies in her bank. If one coin is chosen, what are the odds that it is a penny or a quarter?

$$\begin{array}{ll}
\text{Odds of a penny} \\
\text{or a quarter}
\end{array} = \underbrace{\begin{array}{c}\text{ways to choose penny}\\\text{or quarter}\end{array}} : \underbrace{\begin{array}{c}\text{ways to choose}\\\text{other coins}\end{array}}$$

$$= \qquad 12 \qquad : \qquad 9$$
$$= 12{:}9$$
$$= \;\; 4{:}3 \qquad \textbf{This is read "4 to 3."}$$

Find the odds of each outcome if a card is drawn from the cards at the right.

Cards: 1 ACE, 2 TWO, 3 THREE, 4 FOUR, 5 FIVE, 6 SIX, 7 SEVEN (all hearts)

1. an even number **3:4**

2. a number less than 6 **5:2**

3. not 2 or 7 **5:2**

4. odd or even **1**

5. 7 or a multiple of 2 **4:3**

6. a number greater than 6 **1:6**

Find the odds of each outcome if a laundry bag contains 3 dress shirts, 6 dish towels, 8 socks, 2 pairs of jeans, and 5 T-shirts.

7. a dish towel **1:3**

8. a pair of jeans or a sock **5:7**

9. not a T-shirt **19:5**

10. *neither* dress shirt *nor* sock **13:11**

11. sock, dish towel, or dress shirt **17:7**

12. dish towel or T-shirt **11:13**

Pre-Algebra

10-8 Study Guide
Problem-Solving Strategy:
Use a Simulation

There are three gumball machines. Each machine contains an equal number of red, blue, and yellow gumballs. If Robin gets one gumball from each machine, what is the probability that two of the gumballs are red?

Explore   There are three gumball machines. There are three different colors of gumballs available. We need to find the probability that two out of three gumballs will be red.

Plan   Since three colors are available in equal amounts, a spinner like the one at the right can be used to simulate the situation. Spin the spinner and record the results. Repeat the simulation ten times.

Solve

Gumball Machine	Number 1	Number 2	Number 3
Simulation #1	Y	B	B
Simulation #2	Y	B	Y
Simulation #3	Y	B	Y
Simulation #4	B	Y	Y
Simulation #5	R	B	R
Simulation #6	R	B	B
Simulation #7	Y	Y	R
Simulation #8	B	Y	B
Simulation #9	Y	B	Y
Simulation #10	Y	R	B

One of the simulations results in two red gumballs. You can estimate the probability of getting two red gumballs will be $\frac{1}{10}$.

Examine   The actual probability that two of the three gumballs are red is $\frac{1}{3} \times \frac{1}{3}$ or $\frac{1}{9}$. The estimate is reasonable.

Solve. Use a simulation.

1. The aquarium at the pet store contains an equal amount of goldfish that have either orange or white fins. Linda chooses six fish at random. What is the probability that three of the six fish have white fins?

2. The M & W Bakery makes homemade white, wheat, rye, pumpernickel, garlic, and Italian bread. The baker chooses a type of bread at random to sell each day. What is the probability that the baker sells the same type of bread four days in one week?

3. What is the probability that a family of four children has three girls and one boy?

10-8 Study Guide
Problem-Solving Strategy:
Use a Simulation

There are three gumball machines. Each machine contains an equal number of red, blue, and yellow gumballs. If Robin gets one gumball from each machine, what is the probability that two of the gumballs are red?

Explore There are three gumball machines. There are three different colors of gumballs available. We need to find the probability that two out of three gumballs will be red.

Plan Since three colors are available in equal amounts, a spinner like the one at the right can be used to simulate the situation. Spin the spinner and record the results. Repeat the simulation ten times.

Solve

Gumball Machine	Number 1	Number 2	Number 3
Simulation #1	Y	B	B
Simulation #2	Y	B	Y
Simulation #3	Y	B	Y
Simulation #4	B	Y	Y
Simulation #5	R	B	R
Simulation #6	R	B	B
Simulation #7	Y	Y	R
Simulation #8	B	Y	B
Simulation #9	Y	B	Y
Simulation #10	Y	R	B

One of the simulations results in two red gumballs. You can estimate the probability of getting two red gumballs will be $\frac{1}{10}$.

Examine The actual probability that two of the three gumballs are red is $\frac{1}{3} \times \frac{1}{3}$ or $\frac{1}{9}$. The estimate is reasonable.

Solve. Use a simulation.

1. The aquarium at the pet store contains an equal amount of goldfish that have either orange or white fins. Linda chooses six fish at random. What is the probability that three of the six fish have white fins? **See students' work.**

2. The M & W Bakery makes homemade white, wheat, rye, pumpernickel, garlic, and Italian bread. The baker chooses a type of bread at random to sell each day. What is the probability that the baker sells the same type of bread four days in one week? **See students' work.**

3. What is the probability that a family of four children has three girls and one boy? **See students' work.**

T 88

10-9 Study Guide

Student Edition
Pages 530–534

Probability of Independent and Dependent Events

If the outcome of one event does *not* influence the outcome of a second event, the events are **independent**.

Example: A jar contains 12 red bells and 12 silver bells. Pick one, replace it, and pick another. The probability of picking a silver bell twice is

$$\frac{1}{2} \times \frac{1}{2} \text{ or } \frac{1}{4}.$$

If the outcome of the second event depends on the outcome of the first event, the events are **dependent**.

Example: A jar contains 12 red bells and 12 silver bells. Pick one, keep it and pick another. The probability of picking two red bells is

$$\frac{1}{2} \times \frac{11}{23} \text{ or } \frac{11}{46}.$$

Refer to the ten buttons on the left to find the probability of each outcome. Each button is replaced.

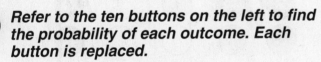

1. a white button twice

2. a gray button twice

3. a gray button, then a white button

4. a white button, then a black button

5. a black button twice

6. a black button, then a gray button

Refer to the ten buttons shown above to find the probability of each outcome. Each button is __not__ replaced.

7. a white button twice

8. a gray button twice

9. a gray button, then a white button

10. a white button, then a black button

11. a black button twice

12. a black button, then a gray button

Pre-Algebra

10-9 Study Guide
Probability of Independent and Dependent Events

If the outcome of one event does *not* influence the outcome of a second event, the events are **independent**.

Example: A jar contains 12 red bells and 12 silver bells. Pick one, replace it, and pick another. The probability of picking a silver bell twice is

$$\frac{1}{2} \times \frac{1}{2} \text{ or } \frac{1}{4}.$$

If the outcome of the second event depends on the outcome of the first event, the events are **dependent**.

Example: A jar contains 12 red bells and 12 silver bells. Pick one, keep it and pick another. The probability of picking two red bells is

$$\frac{1}{2} \times \frac{11}{23} \text{ or } \frac{11}{46}.$$

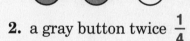

Refer to the ten buttons on the left to find the probability of each outcome. Each button is replaced.

1. a white button twice $\frac{9}{100}$

2. a gray button twice $\frac{1}{4}$

3. a gray button, then a white button $\frac{3}{20}$

4. a white button, then a black button $\frac{3}{50}$

5. a black button twice $\frac{1}{25}$

6. a black button, then a gray button $\frac{1}{10}$

Refer to the ten buttons shown above to find the probability of each outcome. Each button is _not_ replaced.

7. a white button twice $\frac{1}{15}$

8. a gray button twice $\frac{2}{9}$

9. a gray button, then a white button $\frac{1}{6}$

10. a white button, then a black button $\frac{1}{15}$

11. a black button twice $\frac{1}{45}$

12. a black button, then a gray button $\frac{1}{9}$

10-10 Study Guide
Probability of Compound Events

When two events *cannot* happen at the same time, they are **mutually exclusive**. For two events that are mutually exclusive, $P(A \text{ or } B) = P(A) + P(B)$.

Example: A die is tossed. Find $P(5 \text{ or } 6)$.

$$P(5 \text{ or } 6) = P(5) + P(6)$$
$$= \frac{1}{6} + \frac{1}{6}$$
$$= \frac{2}{6} \text{ or } \frac{1}{3}$$

The events are exclusive. The die cannot land on 5 and 6 at the same time.

When two events *can* occur at the same time, they are **inclusive**. For two events that are inclusive, $P(A \text{ or } B) = P(A) + P(B) - P(A \text{ and } B)$.

Example: A die is tossed. Find $P(\text{even or greater than } 4)$.

$$P(\text{even or} > 4) = P(\text{even}) + P(> 4) - P(\text{even and} > 4)$$
$$= \frac{3}{6} + \frac{2}{6} - \frac{1}{6}$$
$$= \frac{4}{6} \text{ or } \frac{2}{3}$$

The events are inclusive. It is possible to land on a number that is both even and greater than 4.

Determine whether each event is mutally exclusive or inclusive. Then find the probability.

1. The drawing at the right shows the 18 best seats at a concert hall. The tickets for these seats are given away during a raffle.

   a. a seat in row A or row C

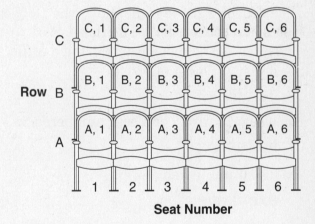

   b. a seat in row A or a seat numbered 3

   c. a seat numbered 2 or 5

   Seat Number

   d. a seat in row A, B, or C

   e. a seat numbered 1, 2, or 6

   f. an aisle seat or a seat in row C

   g. a seat in row C or a prime-numbered seat

   h. an odd-numbered seat or a seat in row C

   i. a seat *not* in row B or a seat numbered 2

10-10 Study Guide
Probability of Compound Events

When two events *cannot* happen at the same time, they are **mutually exclusive**. For two events that are mutually exclusive, $P(A \text{ or } B) = P(A) + P(B)$.

Example: A die is tossed. Find $P(5 \text{ or } 6)$.

$$P(5 \text{ or } 6) = P(5) + P(6)$$
$$= \frac{1}{6} + \frac{1}{6}$$
$$= \frac{2}{6} \text{ or } \frac{1}{3}$$

The events are exclusive. The die cannot land on 5 and 6 at the same time.

When two events *can* occur at the same time, they are **inclusive**. For two events that are inclusive, $P(A \text{ or } B) = P(A) + P(B) - P(A \text{ and } B)$.

Example: A die is tossed. Find $P(\text{even or greater than 4})$.

$$P(\text{even or} > 4) = P(\text{even}) + P(> 4) - P(\text{even and} > 4)$$
$$= \frac{3}{6} + \frac{2}{6} - \frac{1}{6}$$
$$= \frac{4}{6} \text{ or } \frac{2}{3}$$

The events are inclusive. It is possible to land on a number that is both even and greater than 4.

Determine whether each event is mutually exclusive or inclusive. Then find the probability.

1. The drawing at the right shows the 18 best seats at a concert hall. The tickets for these seats are given away during a raffle.

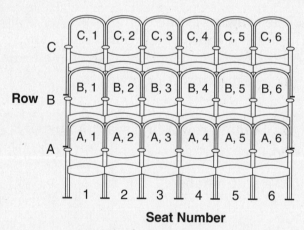

   a. a seat in row A or row C
   exclusive; $\frac{2}{3}$

   b. a seat in row A or a seat numbered 3
   inclusive; $\frac{4}{9}$

   c. a seat numbered 2 or 5
   exclusive; $\frac{1}{3}$

   d. a seat in row A, B, or C
   exclusive; 1

   e. a seat numbered 1, 2, or 6
   exclusive; $\frac{1}{2}$

   f. an aisle seat or a seat in row C
   exclusive; $\frac{5}{9}$

   g. a seat in row C or a prime-numbered seat **inclusive;** $\frac{2}{3}$

   h. an odd-numbered seat or a seat in row C **inclusive;** $\frac{2}{3}$

   i. a seat *not* in row B or a seat numbered 2 **inclusive;** $\frac{13}{18}$

11-1 Study Guide
The Language of Geometry

Student Edition
Pages 548–553

The **point** indicates a specific location. A straight path of points that extends infinitely in two directions is called a **line**. A **plane** is a flat surface with no boundaries, or edges. a **line segment** consists of two endpoints and all the points between them. A **ray** is part of a line that has one endpoint and extends from one point indefinitely in one direction. An **angle** is formed by two rays with a common endpoint called the **vertex**. Angles are measured in degrees.

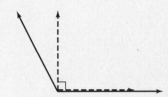

A **right angle** has a measure of 90°.

An **acute angle** has a measure between 0° and 90°.

An **obtuse angle** has a measure between 90° and 180°.

Use the figure at the right to name an example of each term.

1. ray

2. point

3. angle

4. line

5. line segment

6. vertex

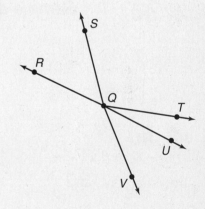

Classify each angle as acute, right, or obtuse.

7. ∠FBH   8. ∠CBD

9. ∠ABC   10. ∠ABG

11. ∠ABE   12. ∠EBH

13. ∠DBH   14. ∠FBG

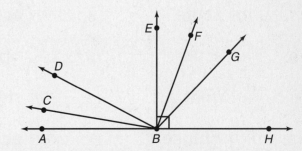

11-1 Study Guide

The Language of Geometry

Student Edition
Pages 548–553

The **point** indicates a specific location. A straight path of points that extends infinitely in two directions is called a **line**. A **plane** is a flat surface with no boundaries, or edges. a **line segment** consists of two endpoints and all the points between them. A **ray** is part of a line that has one endpoint and extends from one point indefinitely in one direction. An **angle** is formed by two rays with a common endpoint called the **vertex**. Angles are measured in degrees.

A **right angle** has a measure of 90°.

An **acute angle** has a measure between 0° and 90°.

An **obtuse angle** has a measure between 90° and 180°.

Use the figure at the right to name an example of each term.
Sample answers are given.

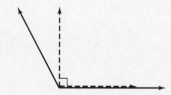

1. ray **QR**

2. point **T**

3. angle **∠TQS**

4. line **RU**

5. line segment **SQ**

6. vertex **Q**

Classify each angle as acute, right, or obtuse.

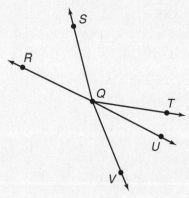

7. ∠FBH **acute**   8. ∠CBD **acute**

9. ∠ABC **acute**   10. ∠ABG **obtuse**

11. ∠ABE **right**   12. ∠EBH **right**

13. ∠DBH **obtuse**   14. ∠FBG **acute**

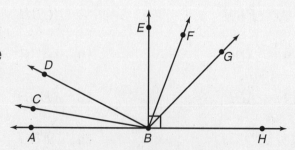

11-2 Study Guide

Integration: Statistics
Making Circle Graphs

Student Edition
Pages 556–560

A **circle graph** is used to illustrate data. In order to make a circle graph, the circle must be separated into sectors. Each circle is made up of 360°. Therefore, to separate the circle into sectors, multiply the percent needed by 360.

Example: 25% of a family's budget is spent for housing.

$$0.25 \times 360° = 90°$$

Use a protractor and measure 90°.
Then label the sector "Housing" as shown below.

1. The chart shows the percentages allotted for each item of the Johnson's family budget. Make a circle graph to display the data.

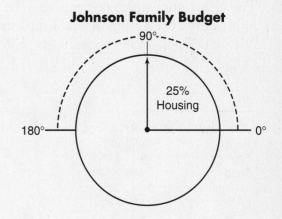

Johnson Family Budget

Family Budget	
Housing	25%
Savings	15%
Food	27%
Transportation	10%
Medical	10%
Other	13%

2. In a recent poll, a group of people were asked to name their favorite type of television show. Make a circle graph to display the data.

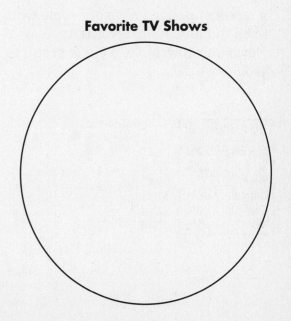

Favorite TV Shows

TV Preference	
Movies	12%
Sports	20%
News	4%
Drama	16%
Comedy	20%
Music	28%

11-2 Study Guide
Integration: Statistics
Making Circle Graphs

Student Edition
Pages 556–560

A **circle graph** is used to illustrate data. In order to make a circle graph, the circle must be separated into sectors. Each circle is made up of 360°. Therefore, to separate the circle into sectors, multiply the percent needed by 360.

Example: 25% of a family's budget is spent for housing.

$$0.25 \times 360° = 90°$$

Use a protractor and measure 90°.
Then label the sector "Housing" as shown below.

1. The chart shows the percentages allotted for each item of the Johnson's family budget. Make a circle graph to display the data.

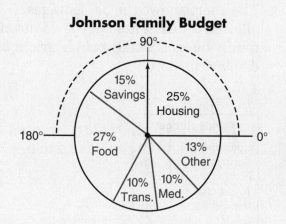
Johnson Family Budget

Family Budget		
Housing	25%	**90°**
Savings	15%	**54°**
Food	27%	**97.2°**
Transportation	10%	**36°**
Medical	10%	**36°**
Other	13%	**46.8°**

2. In a recent poll, a group of people were asked to name their favorite type of television show. Make a circle graph to display the data.

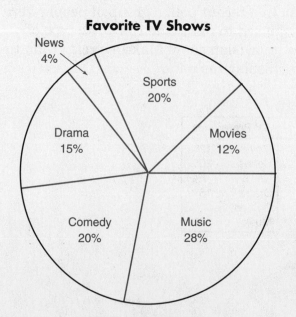
Favorite TV Shows

TV Preference		
Movies	12%	**43.2°**
Sports	20%	**72°**
News	4%	**14.4°**
Drama	16%	**57.6°**
Comedy	20%	**72°**
Music	28%	**100.8°**

11-3 Study Guide
Angle Relationships and Parallel Lines

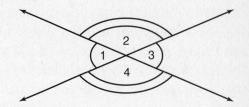

Opposite angles formed by intersecting lines are called **vertical angles**. Vertical angles are always congruent. ∠1 and ∠3, and ∠2 and ∠4 are pairs of vertical angles.

The sum of the measures of two **complementary angles** is 90°.

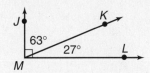

The sum of the measures of two **supplementary angles** is 180°.

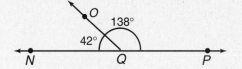

Line *n* is called a **transversal**. When two parallel lines, ℓ and *m*, are intersected by a transversal, certain pairs of angles are congruent.

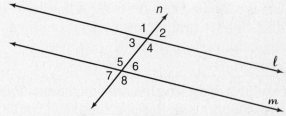

Corresponding angles are congruent. Pairs of corresponding angles are 2 and 6, 4 and 8, 1 and 5, and 3 and 7.
Alternate interior angles are congruent. Pairs of alternate interior angles are 3 and 6, and 4 and 5.
Alternate exterior angles are congruent. Pairs of alternate exterior angles are 1 and 8, and 2 and 7.

Each pair of angles is either complementary or supplementary. Find the value of x in each figure.

1.

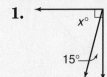

2.

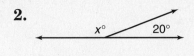

3.

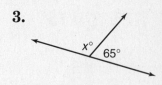

In the figure at the right, r ∥ s. If the measure of ∠4 is 38°, find the measure of each angle.

4. ∠1

5. ∠7

6. ∠2

7. ∠6

8. ∠8

9. ∠3

10. ∠5

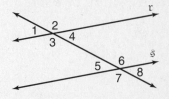

11-3 Study Guide

Student Edition
Pages 561–566

Angle Relationships and Parallel Lines

Opposite angles formed by intersecting lines are called **vertical angles**. Vertical angles are always congruent. ∠1 and ∠3, and ∠2 and ∠4 are pairs of vertical angles.

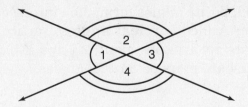

The sum of the measures of two **complementary angles** is 90°.

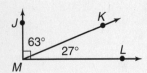

The sum of the measures of two **supplementary angles** is 180°.

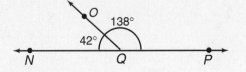

Line *n* is called a **transversal**. When two parallel lines, ℓ and *m*, are intersected by a transversal, certain pairs of angles are congruent.

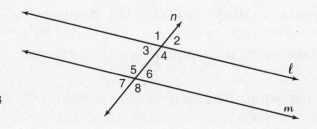

Corresponding angles are congruent. Pairs of corresponding angles are 2 and 6, 4 and 8, 1 and 5, and 3 and 7.

Alternate interior angles are congruent. Pairs of alternate interior angles are 3 and 6, and 4 and 5.

Alternate exterior angles are congruent. Pairs of alternate exterior angles are 1 and 8, and 2 and 7.

Each pair of angles is either complementary or supplementary.
Find the value of x in each figure.

1. 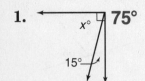 **75°**

2. 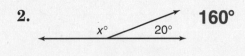 **160°**

3. 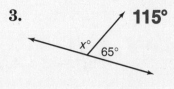 **115°**

In the figure at the right, r ∥ s. If the measure of ∠4 is 38°, find the measure of each angle.

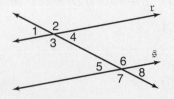

4. ∠1 **38°**

5. ∠7 **142°**

6. ∠2 **142°**

7. ∠6 **142°**

8. ∠8 **38°**

9. ∠3 **142°**

10. ∠5 **38°**

11-4 Study Guide
Triangles

A **right triangle** has one right angle. An **obtuse triangle** has one obtuse angle. All other triangles are **acute**. In an acute triangle, each of the three angles is acute.

For any triangle, the sum of the measures of the angles is 180°.

Example: In △AOD, the measure of ∠D is 35°, and the measure of ∠O is 107°. Find the measure of ∠A.

$$m\angle A + m\angle O + m\angle D = 180$$ The sum of the measures of the angles is 180.

$$m\angle A + 107 + 35 = 180$$ Replace $m\angle O$ with 107 and $m\angle D$ with 35.

$$m\angle A + 142 = 180$$ Add 107 and 35.

$$m\angle A = 38$$ Subtract 142 from each side.

Find the value of x. Then classify each triangle as acute, right, or obtuse.

1.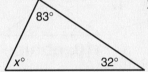

2.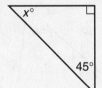

3.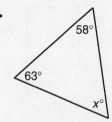

4.

Use the figure at the right to solve each of the following.

5. Find $m\angle 2$ if $m\angle 3 = 49°$ and $m\angle 1 = 63°$.

6. Find $m\angle 2$ if $m\angle 3 = 45°$ and $m\angle 1 = 50°$.

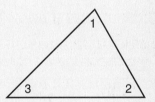

7. Find $m\angle 3$ if $m\angle 2 = 66°$ and $m\angle 1 = 64°$.

8. Find $m\angle 3$ if $m\angle 2 = 38°$ and $m\angle 1 = 70°$.

9. Find $m\angle 3$ if $m\angle 2 = 42°$ and $m\angle 1 = 58°$.

11-4 Study Guide
Triangles

A **right triangle** has one right angle. An **obtuse triangle** has one obtuse angle. All other triangles are **acute**. In an acute triangle, each of the three angles is acute.

For any triangle, the sum of the measures of the angles is 180°.

Example: In $\triangle AOD$, the measure of $\angle D$ is 35°, and the measure of $\angle O$ is 107°. Find the measure of $\angle A$.

$$m\angle A + m\angle O + m\angle D = 180 \qquad \text{The sum of the measures of the angles is 180.}$$
$$m\angle A + 107 + 35 = 180 \qquad \text{Replace } m\angle O \text{ with 107 and } m\angle D \text{ with 35.}$$
$$m\angle A + 142 = 180 \qquad \text{Add 107 and 35.}$$
$$m\angle A = 38 \qquad \text{Subtract 142 from each side.}$$

Find the value of x. Then classify each triangle as acute, right, or obtuse.

1.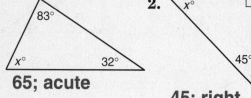

65; acute

2.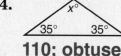

45; right

3.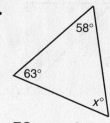

59; acute

4.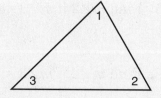

110; obtuse

Use the figure at the right to solve each of the following.

5. Find $m\angle 2$ if $m\angle 3 = 49°$ and $m\angle 1 = 63°$. **68°**

6. Find $m\angle 2$ if $m\angle 3 = 45°$ and $m\angle 1 = 50°$. **85°**

7. Find $m\angle 3$ if $m\angle 2 = 66°$ and $m\angle 1 = 64°$. **50°**

8. Find $m\angle 3$ if $m\angle 2 = 38°$ and $m\angle 1 = 70°$. **72°**

9. Find $m\angle 3$ if $m\angle 2 = 42°$ and $m\angle 1 = 58°$. **80°**

11-5 Study Guide
Congruent Triangles

Student Edition
Pages 573–577

The triangles on the right are **congruent**. The parts of congruent triangles that "match" are called **corresponding parts**.

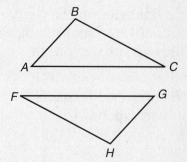

∠A corresponds to ∠G. $\overline{AB}$ corresponds to $\overline{GH}$.
∠B corresponds to ∠H. $\overline{BC}$ corresponds to $\overline{HF}$.
∠C corresponds to ∠F. $\overline{AC}$ corresponds to $\overline{GF}$.

Complete the congruence statement for each pair of congruent triangles. Then name the corresponding parts.

1. △TRS ≅ △ _____

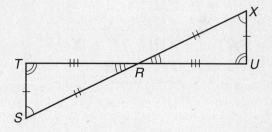

2. △ABD ≅ △ _____

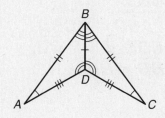

3. △FHG ≅ △ _____

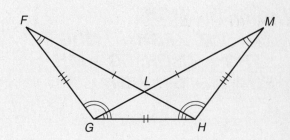

Pre-Algebra

11-5 Study Guide
Congruent Triangles

Student Edition
Pages 573–577

The triangles on the right are **congruent**. The parts of congruent triangles that "match" are called **corresponding parts**.

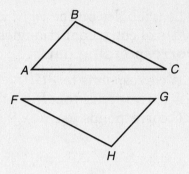

∠A corresponds to ∠G.
∠B corresponds to ∠H.
∠C corresponds to ∠F.

$\overline{AB}$ corresponds to $\overline{GH}$.
$\overline{BC}$ corresponds to $\overline{HF}$.
$\overline{AC}$ corresponds to $\overline{GF}$.

Complete the congruence statement for each pair of congruent triangles. Then name the corresponding parts.

1. △TRS ≅ △ **URX**
   ∠T ≅ ∠U, ∠S ≅ ∠X,
   ∠SRT ≅ ∠XRU; $\overline{TS}$ ≅ $\overline{XU}$,
   $\overline{SR}$ ≅ $\overline{XR}$, $\overline{TR}$ ≅ $\overline{UR}$

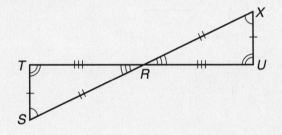

2. △ABD ≅ △ **CBD**
   ∠A ≅ ∠C, ∠ABD ≅ ∠CBD,
   ∠ADB ≅ ∠CDB; $\overline{AB}$ ≅ $\overline{CB}$,
   $\overline{AD}$ ≅ $\overline{CD}$, $\overline{BD}$ ≅ $\overline{BD}$

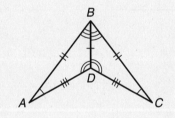

3. △FHG ≅ △ **MGH**
   ∠F ≅ ∠M, ∠FGH ≅ ∠MHG,
   ∠FHG ≅ ∠MGH; $\overline{FG}$ ≅ $\overline{MH}$,
   $\overline{FH}$ ≅ $\overline{MG}$, $\overline{GH}$ ≅ $\overline{GH}$

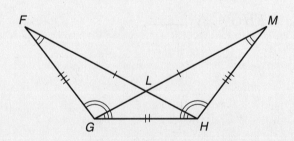

     Pre-Algebra

11-6 Study Guide
Similar Triangles and Indirect Measurement

Student Edition
Pages 578–583

Triangles that have the same shape but not necessarily the same size are **similar**. In similar triangles, the measures of corresponding angles are equal, and the measures of corresponding sides are proportional.

When some measures of the sides of similar triangles are unknown, proportions can be used to find the missing measures.

Example: If $\triangle ABC \sim \triangle DEF$, find the value of x.

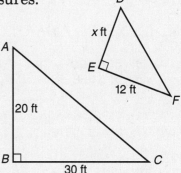

$$\begin{array}{l} \text{width of } \triangle ABC \rightarrow \\ \text{width of } \triangle DEF \rightarrow \end{array} \frac{30}{12} = \frac{20}{x} \begin{array}{l} \leftarrow \text{height of } \triangle ABC \\ \leftarrow \text{height of } \triangle DEF \end{array}$$

$$30 \cdot x = 12 \cdot 20$$
$$30x = 240$$
$$x = 8$$

The height of $\triangle DEF$ is 8 feet.

Write a proportion to find each missing measure x. Then find the value of x.

1.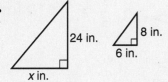

2.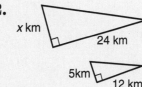

3.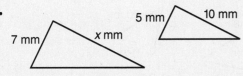

4.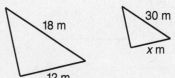

5. A basketball pole is 10 feet high and casts a shadow of 12 feet. A girl standing nearby is 5 feet tall. How long is the shadow that she casts?

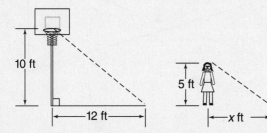

6. Use similar triangles to find the distance across the pond.

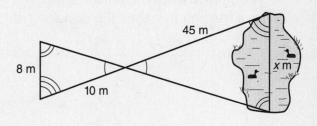

11-6 Study Guide
Similar Triangles and Indirect Measurement

Triangles that have the same shape but not necessarily the same size are **similar**. In similar triangles, the measures of corresponding angles are equal, and the measures of corresponding sides are proportional.

When some measures of the sides of similar triangles are unknown, proportions can be used to find the missing measures.

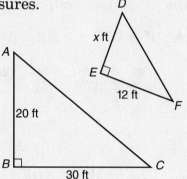

Example: If $\triangle ABC \sim \triangle DEF$, find the value of x.

$$\begin{array}{l}\text{width of } \triangle ABC \rightarrow \\ \text{width of } \triangle DEF \rightarrow\end{array} \dfrac{30}{12} = \dfrac{20}{x} \begin{array}{l}\leftarrow \text{ height of } \triangle ABC \\ \leftarrow \text{ height of } \triangle DEF\end{array}$$

$$30 \cdot x = 12 \cdot 20$$
$$30x = 240$$
$$x = 8$$

The height of $\triangle DEF$ is 8 feet.

Write a proportion to find each missing measure x. Then find the value of x.

1.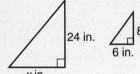

$\dfrac{24}{8} = \dfrac{x}{6}$; **18 in.**

2.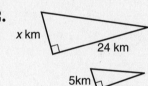

$\dfrac{x}{5} = \dfrac{24}{12}$; **10 km**

3.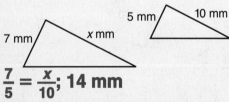

$\dfrac{7}{5} = \dfrac{x}{10}$; **14 mm**

4.

$\dfrac{30}{18} = \dfrac{x}{12}$; **20 m**

5. A basketball pole is 10 feet high and casts a shadow of 12 feet. A girl standing nearby is 5 feet tall. How long is the shadow that she casts?

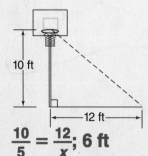

$\dfrac{10}{5} = \dfrac{12}{x}$; **6 ft**

6. Use similar triangles to find the distance across the pond.

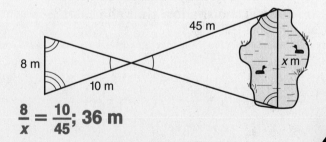

$\dfrac{8}{x} = \dfrac{10}{45}$; **36 m**

11-7 Study Guide
Quadrilaterals

Student Edition
Pages 584–588

You can classify quadrilaterals by their pairs of parallel sides.

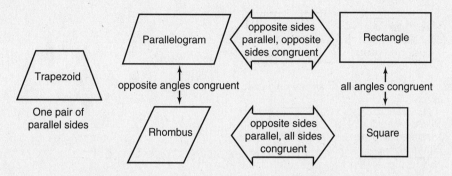

For any quadrilateral, the sum of the measures of the angles is 360°.

Find the value of x.

1.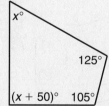

2.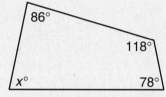

3.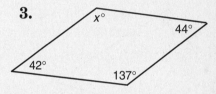

Find the value of x. Then find the missing angle measures.

4.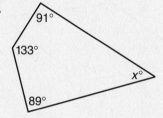

5.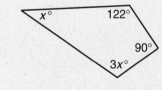

6.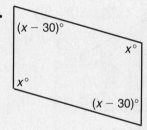

Classify each quadrilateral using the name that best describes it.

7.

8.

9.

Pre-Algebra

11-7 Study Guide

Quadrilaterals

Student Edition
Pages 584–588

You can classify quadrilaterals by their pairs of parallel sides.

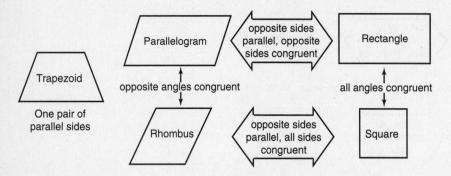

For any quadrilateral, the sum of the measures of the angles is 360°.

Find the value of x.

1. 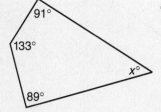   **47°**

2. 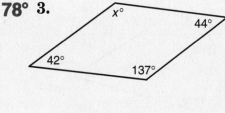   **78°**

3.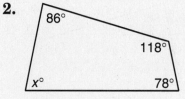

137°

Find the value of x. Then find the missing angle measures.

4. 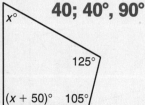   **40; 40°, 90°**

5.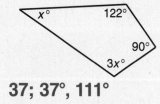

37; 37°, 111°

6. 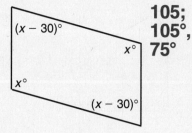   **105; 105°, 75°**

Classify each quadrilateral using the name that best describes it.

7.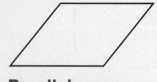

Parallelogram

8.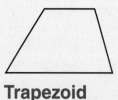

Trapezoid

9.

Rectangle

     Pre-Algebra

11-8 Study Guide
Polygons

Polygons are simple, closed figures formed by three or more line segments, called **sides**. If a polygon has n sides, then the sum of the measures of the interior angles is $(n - 2)180$.

Example: Find the sum of the measures of the angles of a heptagon.

A heptagon has 7 sides. Therefore, $n = 7$.
$(n - 2)180 = (7 - 2)180$ **Replace n with 7**
$\qquad\qquad = 5(180) \text{ or } 900$

The sum of the measures of the angles of a heptagon is 900°.

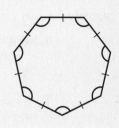

Regular polygons are figures in which all sides are congruent and all angles are congruent. Since the heptagon above is regular, the measure of one **interior** angle is $900 \div 7$, or about 129°.

Interior and **exterior** angles of a polygon are supplementary. In a regular heptagon, the measure of the interior angle is about 129°. Therefore, the measure of the exterior angle is $180 - 129$, or about 51°.

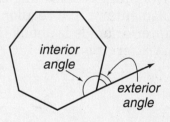

interior angle

exterior angle

Find the sum of the measures of the interior angles of each polygon.

1. hexagon

2. pentagon

3. quadrilateral

4. octagon

5. 16-gon

6. 27-gon

Find the measure of each exterior angle and each interior angle of each regular polygon.

7. regular octagon

8. regular decagon

9. regular 12-gon

10. regular heptagon

11. regular 15-gon

12. regular 24-gon

Find the perimeter of each regular polygon.

13. regular heptagon with sides 12 ft long

14. regular quadrilateral with sides 3.7 m long

15. regular octagon with sides $\frac{1}{2}$ yd long

16. regular pentagon with sides $2\frac{4}{5}$ in. long

Pre-Algebra

11-8 Study Guide
Polygons

Polygons are simple, closed figures formed by three or more line segments, called **sides**. If a polygon has n sides, then the sum of the measures of the interior angles is $(n - 2)180$.

Example: Find the sum of the measures of the angles of a heptagon.

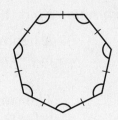

A heptagon has 7 sides. Therefore, $n = 7$.
$(n - 2)180 = (7 - 2)180$ **Replace n with 7**
$= 5(180)$ or 900

The sum of the measures of the angles of a heptagon is 900°.

Regular polygons are figures in which all sides are congruent and all angles are congruent. Since the heptagon above is regular, the measure of one **interior** angle is $900 \div 7$, or about 129°.

Interior and **exterior** angles of a polygon are supplementary. In a regular heptagon, the measure of the interior angle is about 129°. Therefore, the measure of the exterior angle is $180 - 129$, or about 51°.

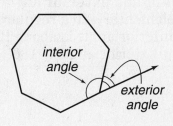

interior angle

exterior angle

Find the sum of the measures of the interior angles of each polygon.

1. hexagon **720°**

2. pentagon **540°**

3. quadrilateral **360°**

4. octagon **1080°**

5. 16-gon **2520°**

6. 27-gon **4500°**

Find the measure of each exterior angle and each interior angle of each regular polygon.

7. regular octagon **135°, 45°**
8. regular decagon **144°, 36°**
9. regular 12-gon **150°, 30°**

10. regular heptagon **129°, 51°**
11. regular 15-gon **156°, 24°**
12. regular 24-gon **165°, 15°**

Find the perimeter of each regular polygon.

13. regular heptagon with sides 12 ft long **84 ft**

14. regular quadrilateral with sides 3.7 m long **14.8 m**

15. regular octagon with sides $\frac{1}{2}$ yd long **4 yd**

16. regular pentagon with sides $2\frac{4}{5}$ in. long **14 in.**

11-9 Study Guide
Transformations

Transformations are movements of geometric figures.

When a geometric figure is moved horizontally, vertically, or both, it is called a **translation**. The figure at the right is moved 6 units to the left.

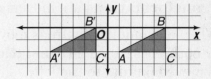
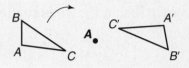

In a **rotation**, a figure is turned about a point.

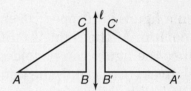

When a figure is "flipped" over a line, it is called a **reflection**. At the right, $\triangle ABC$ is *reflected* about line ℓ. Since the figure can be folded over line ℓ so that the two halves correspond, the figure is **symmetric**. Line ℓ is called a *line of symmetry*. A line of symmetry separates a figure into two congruent parts.

The figure at the right has three lines of symmetry.

Tell whether each transformation is a translation, a rotation, or a reflection. Explain your answer.

1.
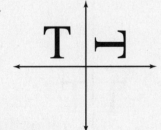

2.
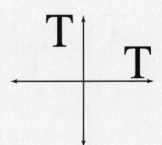

3.
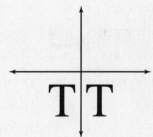

Draw all lines of symmetry.

4.

5.

6.

11-9 Study Guide
Transformations

Student Edition
Pages 595–599

Transformations are movements of geometric figures.

When a geometric figure is moved horizontally, vertically, or both, it is called a **translation**. The figure at the right is moved 6 units to the left.

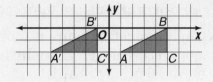

In a **rotation**, a figure is turned about a point.

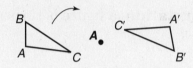

When a figure is "flipped" over a line, it is called a **reflection**. At the right, △ABC is *reflected* about line ℓ. Since the figure can be folded over line ℓ so that the two halves correspond, the figure is **symmetric**. Line ℓ is called a *line of symmetry*. A line of symmetry separates a figure into two congruent parts.

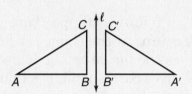

The figure at the right has three lines of symmetry.

Tell whether each transformation is a translation, a rotation, or a reflection. Explain your answer. **Sample answers given.**

1.

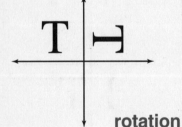

rotation

2.

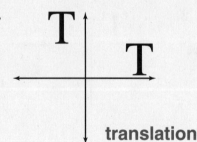

translation

3.

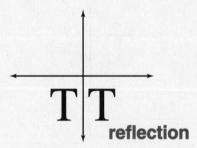

reflection

Draw all lines of symmetry.

4.

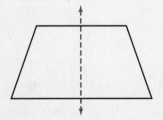

5.

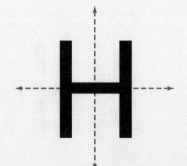

6.

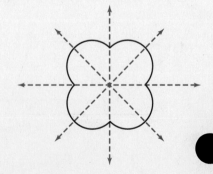

Pre-Algebra

12-1 Study Guide

Area: Parallelograms, Triangles, and Trapezoids

To find the area of a parallelogram, multiply the base by the height.

Example: Find the area of the parallelogram.

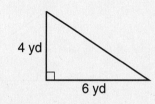

$A = b \times h$
$= 5 \times 3$
$= 15 \text{ ft}^2$

The area of a triangle is half the product of the base and the height.

Example: Find the area of the triangle.

$A = \frac{1}{2} \times b \times h$
$= \frac{1}{2} \times 6 \times 4$
$= 12 \text{ yd}^2$

To find the area of a trapezoid, multiply the sum of the bases by one-half the height.

Example: Find the area of the trapezoid.

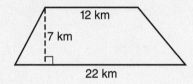

$A = \frac{1}{2} \times h \times (a + b)$
$= \frac{1}{2} \times 7 \times (12 + 22)$
$= \frac{1}{2} \times 238$
$= 119 \text{ km}^2$

Find the area of each figure.

1.

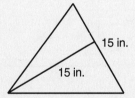
15 in.
15 in.

2.

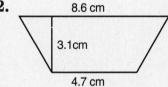
8.6 cm
3.1cm
4.7 cm

3.

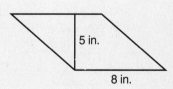
5 in.
8 in.

4.

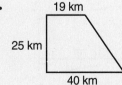
19 km
25 km
40 km

5.

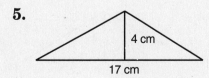
4 cm
17 cm

6.

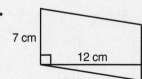
7 cm
12 cm

12-1 Study Guide

Area: Parallelograms, Triangles, and Trapezoids

To find the area of a parallelogram, multiply the base by the height.

Example: Find the area of the parallelogram.

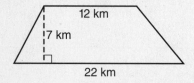

$A = b \times h$
$= 5 \times 3$
$= 15 \text{ ft}^2$

The area of a triangle is half the product of the base and the height.

Example: Find the area of the triangle.

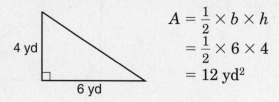

$A = \frac{1}{2} \times b \times h$
$= \frac{1}{2} \times 6 \times 4$
$= 12 \text{ yd}^2$

To find the area of a trapezoid, multiply the sum of the bases by one-half the height.

Example: Find the area of the trapezoid.

$A = \frac{1}{2} \times h \times (a + b)$
$= \frac{1}{2} \times 7 \times (12 + 22)$
$= \frac{1}{2} \times 238$
$= 119 \text{ km}^2$

Find the area of each figure.

1.

15 in.
15 in.

112.5 in²

2.

8.6 cm
3.1cm
4.7 cm

20.615 cm²

3.

5 in.
8 in.

40 in²

4.

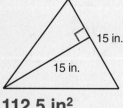

19 km
25 km
40 km

737.5 km²

5.

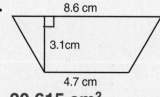

4 cm
17 cm

34 cm²

6.

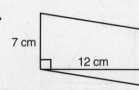

7 cm
12 cm

84 cm²

Pre-Algebra

12-2 Study Guide
Area: Circles

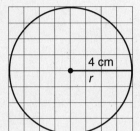

The area of a circle with radius r can be found by using the formula below.

$A = \pi r^2$

Find the area of the circle at the left.

$A = \pi(4)^2$

$\quad = \pi \cdot 16$

$\quad \approx 50.27 \text{ cm}^2$

Find the area of each circle. Round to the nearest tenth.

1.

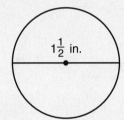

$1\frac{1}{2}$ in.

2.

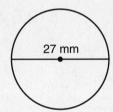

27 mm

3.

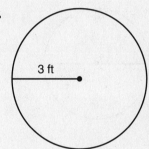

3 ft

4.

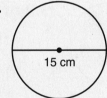

15 cm

5.

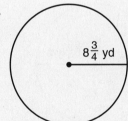

$8\frac{3}{4}$ yd

6.

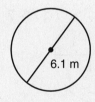

6.1 m

7. diameter, 22 yd

8. radius, 8.4 in.

9. radius $2\frac{1}{4}$ in.

10. diameter, 6.5 ft.

11. diameter, 4 cm

12. radius, 4.6 mm

NAME _____ DATE _____

12-2 Study Guide
Area: Circles

NAME _____ DATE _____

12-2 Study Guide
Area: Circles

NAME _____ DATE _____

12-2 Study Guide
Area: Circles

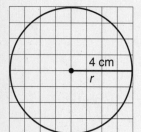

The area of a circle with radius r can be found by using the formula below.

$$A = \pi r^2$$

Find the area of the circle at the left.

$$A = \pi(4)^2$$
$$= \pi \cdot 16$$
$$\approx 50.27 \text{ cm}^2$$

Find the area of each circle. Round to the nearest tenth.

1. 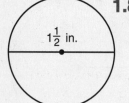 $1\frac{1}{2}$ in. **1.8 in²**

2. 27 mm **572.6 mm²**

3. 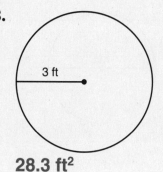 3 ft **28.3 ft²**

4. 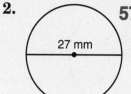 15 cm **176.7 cm²**

5. 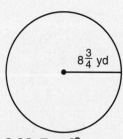 $8\frac{3}{4}$ yd **240.5 yd²**

6. 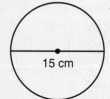 6.1 m **29.2 m²**

7. diameter, 22 yd
380.1 yd²

8. radius, 8.4 in.
221.7 in²

9. radius $2\frac{1}{4}$ in.
15.9 in²

10. diameter, 6.5 ft.
33.2 ft²

11. diameter, 4 cm
12.6 cm²

12. radius, 4.6 mm
66.5 mm²

12-3 Study Guide

Integration: Probability
Geometric Probability

Geometric probability involves using area to find the probability of an event.

Example: The figure at the right represents a dartboard. Assume that a dart will land on the board and that the dart is equally likely to land any place on the board. Find the probability of landing in the shaded region.

$$P(\text{shaded}) = \frac{\text{shaded area}}{\text{area of target}}$$

First find the area of the target and the area of the shaded region. Then write a fraction to represent the probability of the dart landing in the shaded region.

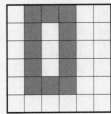
7 ft
3 ft
7 ft
3 ft

The dartboard is a 7-foot by 7-foot square.	Then shaded region is 3 feet by 3 feet.
$A = s^2$	$A = s^2$
$\quad = 7^2$	$\quad = 3^2$
$\quad = 49$ **The dartboard is 49 square feet.**	$\quad = 9$ **The shaded region is 9 square feet.**

So, $P(\text{dart landing in shaded region}) = \frac{9}{49} \approx 0.184$

The probability of landing in the shaded region is $\frac{9}{49}$ or about 18%.

Each figure represents a dartboard. Find the probability of landing in the shaded region.

1.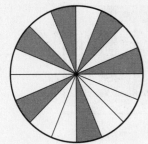

2.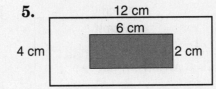

3.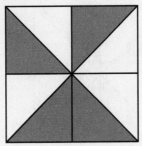

4.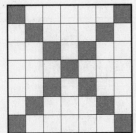

5.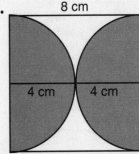
12 cm
6 cm
4 cm
2 cm

6.
8 cm
4 cm
4 cm

12-3 Study Guide

Student Edition
Pages 623–627

Integration: Probability
Geometric Probability

Geometric probability involves using area to find the probability of an event.

Example: The figure at the right represents a dartboard. Assume that a dart will land on the board and that the dart is equally likely to land any place on the board. Find the probability of landing in the shaded region.

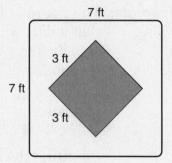

$$P(\text{shaded}) = \frac{\text{shaded area}}{\text{area of target}}$$

First find the area of the target and the area of the shaded region. Then write a fraction to represent the probability of the dart landing in the shaded region.

The dartboard is a 7-foot by 7-foot square.	Then shaded region is 3 feet by 3 feet.
$A = s^2$	$A = s^2$
$= 7^2$	$= 3^2$
$= 49$ **The dartboard is 49 square feet.**	$= 9$ **The shaded region is 9 square feet.**

So, $P(\text{dart landing in shaded region}) = \frac{9}{49} \approx 0.184$

The probability of landing in the shaded region is $\frac{9}{49}$ or about 18%.

Each figure represents a dartboard. Find the probability of landing in the shaded region.

1. 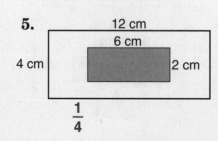 $\frac{3}{8}$

2. 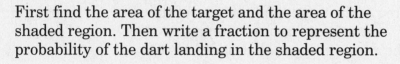 $\frac{1}{2}$

3. 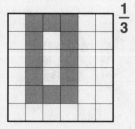 $\frac{1}{3}$

4. 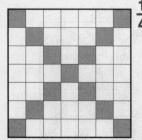 $\frac{13}{49}$

5. 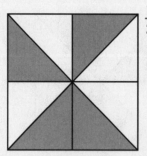 $\frac{1}{4}$

6. 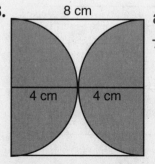 **about** $\frac{79}{100}$

12-4 Study Guide
Problem-Solving Strategy:
Make a Model or Drawing

A rectangular playground is 65 feet long and 35 feet wide. A sidewalk is placed around the playground. If the sidewalk extends 4 feet around the playground, what is the area of the sidewalk?

Explore You know the dimensions of the playground and the width of the sidewalk. You need to find the area of the sidewalk.

Plan Make a drawing to illustrate the problem. You can find the area of the sidewalk by subtracting the area of the smaller section from the area of the larger section.

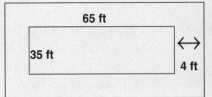

Solve Area of the larger section:
$A = \ell \cdot w$
$= (65 + 4 + 4) \cdot (35 + 4 + 4)$
$= 73 \cdot 43$
$= 3139 \text{ ft}^2$

Area of the smaller section:
$A = \ell \cdot w$
$= 65 \cdot 35$
$= 2275 \text{ ft}^2$

The area of the sidewalk is $3139 - 2275$, or 864 square feet.

Examine An answer of 864 square feet is reasonable, compared to the area of the playground, 2275 square feet.

Solve by making a model or drawing.

1. A 15-foot-by-12-foot room is to be carpeted. There s a 3-foot-by-5-foot area in front of the fireplace where one-foot-square tiles are to be installed. How many square feet of carpet is needed?

2. The Warren's backyard is 50-foot-by-50-foot square. They have attached a 8-foot chain to a back corner fence post to tie up their dog. How much of an exercise area does the dog have?

3. The Keiko Construction Company is building a house. They need to dig a rectangular basement. It will have a length of 32 feet, a width of 24 feet, and a depth of 8 feet. How much dirt must be removed?

4. A wall of the basement is 32 feet by 8 feet. The wall is to be constructed with masonry blocks that have lengths of 16 inches and widths of 8 inches. About how many masonry blocks are needed to build the wall?

12-4 Study Guide
Problem-Solving Strategy:
Make a Model or Drawing

A rectangular playground is 65 feet long and 35 feet wide. A sidewalk is placed around the playground. If the sidewalk extends 4 feet around the playground, what is the area of the sidewalk?

Explore   You know the dimensions of the playground and the width of the sidewalk. You need to find the area of the sidewalk.

Plan   Make a drawing to illustrate the problem. You can find the area of the sidewalk by subtracting the area of the smaller section from the area of the larger section.

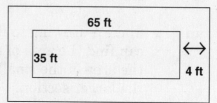

Solve   Area of the larger section:
$$A = \ell \cdot w$$
$$= (65 + 4 + 4) \cdot (35 + 4 + 4)$$
$$= 73 \cdot 43$$
$$= 3139 \text{ ft}^2$$

Area of the smaller section:
$$A = \ell \cdot w$$
$$= 65 \cdot 35$$
$$= 2275 \text{ ft}^2$$

The area of the sidewalk is $3139 - 2275$, or 864 square feet.

Examine   An answer of 864 square feet is reasonable, compared to the area of the playground, 2275 square feet.

Solve by making a model or drawing.

1. A 15-foot-by-12-foot room is to be carpeted. There s a 3-foot-by-5-foot area in front of the fireplace where one-foot-square tiles are to be installed. How many square feet of carpet is needed? **165 ft²**

2. The Warren's backyard is 50-foot-by-50-foot square. They have attached a 8-foot chain to a back corner fence post to tie up their dog. How much of an exercise area does the dog have? **about 50 ft²**

3. The Keiko Construction Company is building a house. They need to dig a rectangular basement. It will have a length of 32 feet, a width of 24 feet, and a depth of 8 feet. How much dirt must be removed? **6144 ft²**

4. A wall of the basement is 32 feet by 8 feet. The wall is to be constructed with masonry blocks that have lengths of 16 inches and widths of 8 inches. About how many masonry blocks are needed to build the wall? **about 288 masonry blocks**

     Pre-Algebra

12-5 Study Guide
Surface Area: Prisms and Cylinders

Student Edition
Pages 632–637

To find the surface area of a solid, find the area of each surface.
Then add the areas.

Rectangular Prism

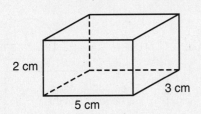

Cylinder

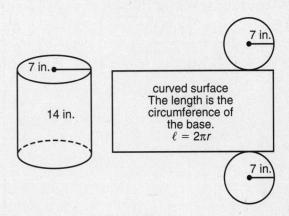

Area:

Top and bottom: ($A = \ell \times w$)	$2 \cdot (5 \cdot 3) = 30$ cm^2
Front and back: ($A = \ell \times w$)	$2 \cdot (2 \cdot 5) = 20$ cm^2
Two sides: ($A = \ell \times w$)	$+ 2 \cdot (2 \cdot 3) = 12$ cm^2
Total surface area	$= 62$ cm^2

Area:

Top and bottom: ($A = \pi r^2$)	$2 \cdot \pi \cdot (7)^2 \approx 307.7$ in^2
Curved surface: ($A = 2\pi r \cdot h$)	$+ 2 \cdot \pi \cdot 7 \cdot 14 \approx 615.8$ in^2
Total surface area	≈ 923.5 in^2

Find the surface area of each solid. Round to the nearest tenth.

1.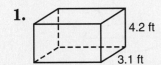

2.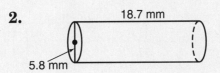

3.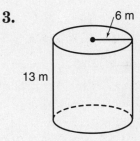

4.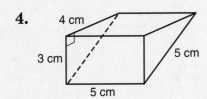

5.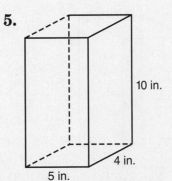

6.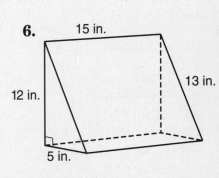

Pre-Algebra

12-5 Study Guide
Surface Area: Prisms and Cylinders

Student Edition
Pages 632–637

To find the surface area of a solid, find the area of each surface.
Then add the areas.

Rectangular Prism

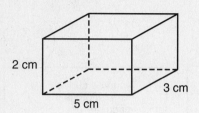

2 cm
3 cm
5 cm

Cylinder

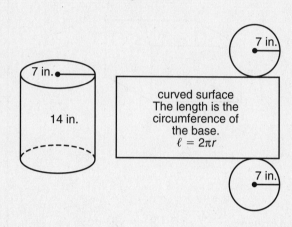

7 in.

7 in.
14 in.

curved surface
The length is the
circumference of
the base.
$\ell = 2\pi r$

7 in.

Area:

Top and bottom: $2 \cdot (5 \cdot 3) = 30$ cm^2
$(A = \ell \times w)$

Front and back: $2 \cdot (2 \cdot 5) = 20$ cm^2
$(A = \ell \times w)$

Two sides: $+ 2 \cdot (2 \cdot 3) = 12$ cm^2
$(A = \ell \times w)$

Total surface area $= 62$ cm^2

Area:

Top and bottom: $2 \cdot \pi \cdot (7)^2 \approx 307.7$ in^2
$(A = \pi r^2)$

Curved surface: $+ 2 \cdot \pi \cdot 7 \cdot 14 \approx 615.8$ in^2
$(A = 2\pi r \cdot h)$

Total surface area ≈ 923.5 in^2

Find the surface area of each solid. Round to the nearest tenth.

1.

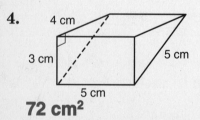

4.2 ft
3.1 ft
7.4 ft
134.1 ft^2

2.

18.7 mm
5.8 mm

393.6 mm^2

3.

6 m
13 m

716.3 m^2

4.

4 cm
3 cm
5 cm
5 cm
72 cm^2

5.

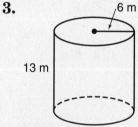

10 in.
4 in.
5 in.
220 in^2

6.

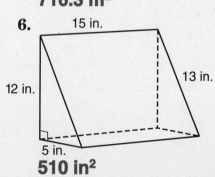

15 in.
12 in.
13 in.
5 in.
510 in^2

Pre-Algebra

12-6 Study Guide

Surface Area: Pyramids and Cones

To find the surface area of a pyramid, add the areas of each of the faces and the area of the base.

To find the surface of a cone, add the area of its circular base and the area of its lateral surface. The area of the lateral surface is $\pi r \ell$.

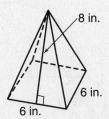

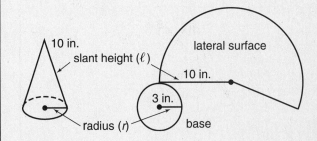

Area:

Square Base	**Four Triangular faces**
$A = s^2$	$A = 4\left(\dfrac{1}{2} \cdot b \cdot h\right)$
$= 6^2$	$= 4\left(\dfrac{1}{2} \cdot 6 \cdot 8\right)$
$= 36 \text{ in}^2$	$= 96 \text{ in}^2$

Surface area is 36 + 96 or 132 in².

Area:

Circular Base	**Lateral Surface**
$A = \pi r^2$	$A = \pi r \ell$
$\approx (3.14)(3)^2$	$\approx (3.14)(3)(10)$
$\approx 28.26 \text{ in}^2$	$\approx 94.2 \text{ in}^2$

Surface area is about 28.26 + 94.2 or 122.46 in².

Find the surface area of each pyramid or cone. Round to the nearest tenth.

1.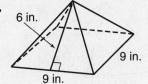

2.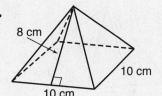

3.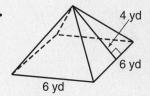

4.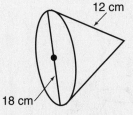

5.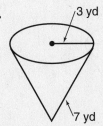

6.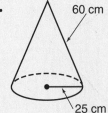

12-6 Study Guide
Surface Area: Pyramids and Cones

To find the surface area of a pyramid, add the areas of each of the faces and the area of the base.

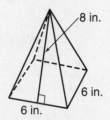

To find the surface of a cone, add the area of its circular base and the area of its lateral surface. The area of the lateral surface is $\pi r \ell$.

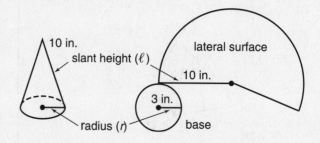

Area:

Square Base

$A = s^2$

$\quad = 6^2$

$\quad = 36 \text{ in}^2$

Four Triangular faces

$A = 4\left(\frac{1}{2} \cdot b \cdot h\right)$

$\quad = 4\left(\frac{1}{2} \cdot 6 \cdot 8\right)$

$\quad = 96 \text{ in}^2$

Surface area is $36 + 96$ or 132 in^2.

Area:

Circular Base

$A = \pi r^2$

$\quad \approx (3.14)(3)^2$

$\quad \approx 28.26 \text{ in}^2$

Lateral Surface

$A = \pi r \ell$

$\quad \approx (3.14)(3)(10)$

$\quad \approx 94.2 \text{ in}^2$

Surface area is about $28.26 + 94.2$ or 122.46 in^2.

Find the surface area of each pyramid or cone. Round to the nearest tenth.

1.

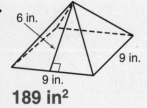

189 in²

2.

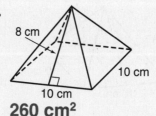

260 cm²

3.

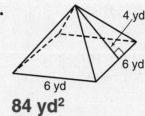

84 yd²

4.

593.8 cm²

5.

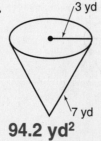

94.2 yd²

6.

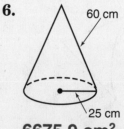

6675.9 cm²

12-7 Study Guide
Volume: Prisms and Cylinders

The **volume (V)** of an object is the amount of space that a solid contains. Volume is measured in cubic units.

To find the volume of any *prism*, multiply the area of the base (B) by the height (h).

Example:
Find the volume of the triangular prism.

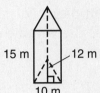

15 m   12 m
10 m

The area of a triangle is $\frac{1}{2} \times b \times h$.

$V = Bh$
$= \left(\frac{1}{2} \cdot 10 \cdot 12\right) \cdot 15$
$= 60 \cdot 15$
$= 900$
The volume is 900 m³.

The base of a circular cylinder is a circle. Therefore, substitute πr^2 for B.

Example:
Find the volume of the cylinder.

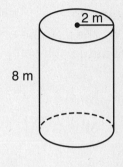

2 m
8 m

$V = Bh$
$= \pi r^2 h$
$= (\pi)(2)^2(8)$
$= \pi \cdot 32$
≈ 100.5
The volume is about 100.5 cm³.

Find the volume of each prism or cylinder. Round to the nearest tenth.

1.

6 in.
6 in.
6 in.

2.

4 m
9 m

3.

4 cm
8 cm
3 cm

4.

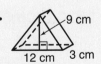

9 cm
12 cm   3 cm

5.

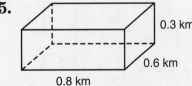

0.3 km
0.6 km
0.8 km

6.

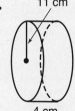

11 cm
4 cm

12-7 Study Guide
Volume: Prisms and Cylinders

The **volume (V)** of an object is the amount of space that a solid contains. Volume is measured in cubic units.

To find the volume of any *prism*, multiply the area of the base (B) by the height (h).

Example:
Find the volume of the triangular prism.

$$V = Bh$$
$$= \left(\frac{1}{2} \cdot 10 \cdot 12\right) \cdot 15$$
$$= 60 \cdot 15$$
$$= 900$$
The volume is 900 m³.

The area of a triangle is $\frac{1}{2} \times b \times h$.

The base of a circular cylinder is a circle. Therefore, substitute πr^2 for B.

Example:
Find the volume of the cylinder.

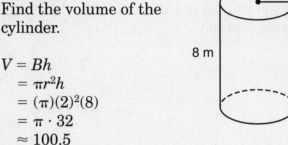

$$V = Bh$$
$$= \pi r^2 h$$
$$= (\pi)(2)^2(8)$$
$$= \pi \cdot 32$$
$$\approx 100.5$$
The volume is about 100.5 cm³.

Find the volume of each prism or cylinder. Round to the nearest tenth.

1. **216 in³**

2. 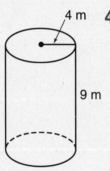 **452.4 m³**

3. **48 cm³**

4. 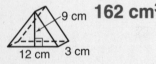 **162 cm³**

5.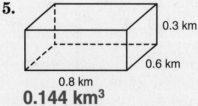

0.144 km³

6. 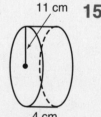 **1520.5 cm³**

12-8 Study Guide

Volume: Pyramids and Cones

Student Edition
Pages 649–653

The volume of a pyramid is one-third the volume of a prism with the same base and height as the pyramid.

 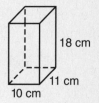

$$V = \frac{1}{3} \times B \times h$$
$$= \frac{1}{3} \times \ell \times w \times h \qquad \mathbf{B = \ell \times w}$$
$$= \frac{1}{3} \times 10 \times 11 \times 18$$
$$= 660 \quad \text{The volume is 660 cm}^3.$$

Pyramid   **Prism**

The volume of a cone is one-third the volume of a cylinder with the same radius and height as the cone.

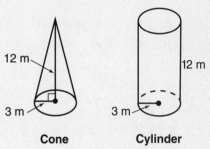

$$V = \frac{1}{3} \pi r^2 h$$
$$\approx \frac{1}{3} \times 3.14 \times 3 \times 3 \times 12$$
$$\approx 113.04 \quad \text{The volume is about 113.04 m}^3.$$

Cone   **Cylinder**

Use the drawings above.

1. The prism has a height of 18 cm and a base that is 11 cm by 10 cm. Find its volume.

2. The cylinder has a height of 12 m and a base with a radius of 3 m. Find its volume. Use $\pi \approx 3.14$.

Find the volume of each pyramid or cone. Round to the nearest tenth.

3.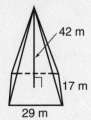
42 m
17 m
29 m

4.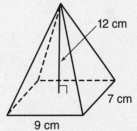
12 cm
7 cm
9 cm

5.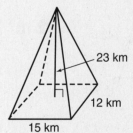
23 km
12 km
15 km

6.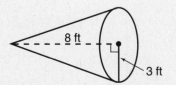
8 ft
3 ft

7.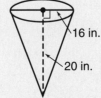
16 in.
20 in.

8.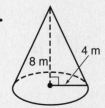
8 m
4 m

Pre-Algebra

12-8 Study Guide

Volume: Pyramids and Cones

Student Edition
Pages 649–653

The volume of a pyramid is one-third the volume of a prism with the same base and height as the pyramid.

Pyramid

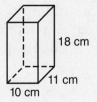
Prism

$$V = \frac{1}{3} \times B \times h$$

$$= \frac{1}{3} \times \ell \times w \times h \qquad \textbf{B} = \boldsymbol{\ell} \times \textbf{w}$$

$$= \frac{1}{3} \times 10 \times 11 \times 18$$

$$= 660 \quad \text{The volume is 660 cm}^3.$$

The volume of a cone is one-third the volume of a cylinder with the same radius and height as the cone.

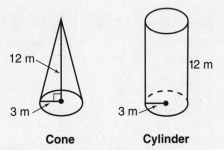
Cone   **Cylinder**

$$V = \frac{1}{3}\pi r^2 h$$

$$\approx \frac{1}{3} \times 3.14 \times 3 \times 3 \times 12$$

$$\approx 113.04 \quad \text{The volume is about 113.04 m}^3.$$

Use the drawings above.

1. The prism has a height of 18 cm and a base that is 11 cm by 10 cm. Find its volume. **1980 cm³**

2. The cylinder has a height of 12 m and a base with a radius of 3 m. Find its volume. Use $\pi \approx 3.14$. **339.12 m³**

Find the volume of each pyramid or cone. Round to the nearest tenth.

3. 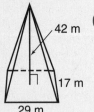 **6902 m³**

4. 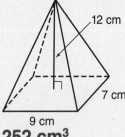 **252 cm³**

5. 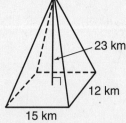 **1380 km³**

6. 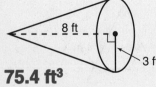 **75.4 ft³**

7. 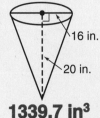 **1339.7 in³**

8. 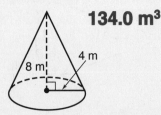 **134.0 m³**

13-1 Study Guide
Finding and Approximating
Squares and Square Roots

Since $6 \times 6 = 36$, a **square root** of 36 is 6.

$$\sqrt{36} = 6$$

Since $-6 \times (-6) = 36$, -6 is also a square root of 36.
A *negative sign* is used to indicate the *negative square root*.

$$-\sqrt{36} = -6$$

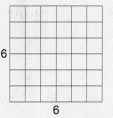

6

6

36 is the square of 6.

If the square root of a number is a whole number, the original
number is called a **perfect square**.
For example, 81 is a perfect square because $9 \times 9 = 81$.
However, 79 and 80 are not perfect squares.

In cases where the square root of a number is not a whole
number, you can estimate the square root by using the two closest
perfect squares. Seventy is between 64 and 81.
So, $\sqrt{70}$ is between $\sqrt{64}$ and $\sqrt{81}$ or between 8 and 9. Since 70 is
closer to 64 than to 81, $\sqrt{70}$ is closer to 8.

Find each square root.

1. $\sqrt{9}$ 2. $\sqrt{25}$ 3. $-\sqrt{4}$ 4. $-\sqrt{64}$

5. $\sqrt{121}$ 6. $-\sqrt{196}$ 7. $\sqrt{225}$ 8. $\sqrt{1.44}$

9. $\sqrt{900}$ 10. $-\sqrt{324}$ 11. $\sqrt{529}$ 12. $\sqrt{100}$

Find the best integer estimate for each square root. Then
check your estimate using a calculator.

13. $-\sqrt{37}$ 14. $\sqrt{90}$ 15. $-\sqrt{50}$

16. $\sqrt{300}$ 17. $-\sqrt{75}$ 18. $\sqrt{69}$

19. $\sqrt{1681}$ 20. $\sqrt{27.96}$ 21. $-\sqrt{11.25}$

13-1 Study Guide

Finding and Approximating
Squares and Square Roots

Since $6 \times 6 = 36$, a **square root** of 36 is 6.

$$\sqrt{36} = 6$$

Since $-6 \times (-6) = 36$, -6 is also a square root of 36.
A *negative sign* is used to indicate the *negative square root*.

$$-\sqrt{36} = -6$$

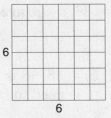

6

36 is the square of 6.

If the square root of a number is a whole number, the original
number is called a **perfect square**.
For example, 81 is a perfect square because $9 \times 9 = 81$.
However, 79 and 80 are not perfect squares.

In cases where the square root of a number is not a whole
number, you can estimate the square root by using the two closest
perfect squares. Seventy is between 64 and 81.
So, $\sqrt{70}$ is between $\sqrt{64}$ and $\sqrt{81}$ or between 8 and 9. Since 70 is
closer to 64 than to 81, $\sqrt{70}$ is closer to 8.

Find each square root.

1. $\sqrt{9}$ **3**

2. $\sqrt{25}$ **5**

3. $-\sqrt{4}$ **-2**

4. $-\sqrt{64}$ **-8**

5. $\sqrt{121}$ **11**

6. $-\sqrt{196}$ **-14**

7. $\sqrt{225}$ **15**

8. $\sqrt{1.44}$ **1.2**

9. $\sqrt{900}$ **30**

10. $-\sqrt{324}$ **-18**

11. $\sqrt{529}$ **23**

12. $\sqrt{100}$ **10**

**Find the best integer estimate for each square root. Then
check your estimate using a calculator.**

13. $-\sqrt{37}$ **-6**

14. $\sqrt{90}$ **9**

15. $-\sqrt{50}$ **-7**

16. $\sqrt{300}$ **17**

17. $-\sqrt{75}$ **-9**

18. $\sqrt{69}$ **8**

19. $\sqrt{1681}$ **41**

20. $\sqrt{27.96}$ **5**

21. $-\sqrt{11.25}$ **-3**

13-2 Study Guide
Problem-Solving Strategy:
Use Venn Diagrams

At Calera City High School, 180 students participate in the band and/or a sport. One hundred thirty-four students are in the band, and 90 play sports. Forty-four students participate in both activities. How many students participate in sports only?

Explore   You know the total amount of students, how many students are in the band, how many play sports, and how many participate in both activities.

Plan   Draw a Venn diagram to organize the data.

Solve   Draw two intersecting circles in a rectangle to represent sports and the band. Write the number of students who participate in both activities. Then subtract to find the number of students who participate only in one activity.

Band = 134 − 44 = 90
Sports = 90 − 44 = 46

There are 46 students that participate in sports only.

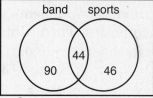

Calera High Students in Band and Sports

Examine   Look at the Venn diagram. Add the number of students in each region.

90 + 44 + 46 = 180   Since the total is 180, the answer is correct.

Solve using a Venn diagram.

1. A television station conducted a survey. They asked 100 viewers which TV series they prefer, Series 1 or Series 2. Sixty-six people preferred Series 1, 50 people liked Series 2, and 16 people preferred both equally. How many people liked Series 1 only?

2. Three hundred fourteen structural engineers were surveyed. One hundred ninety engineers create steel designs, and 216 create wood designs. Ninety-two engineers do both steel and wood designs. How many structural engineers create steel designs but not wood designs?

3. The Venn diagram below represents students' sports preferences.

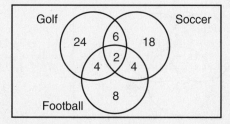

How many students prefer only football?

4. The Venn diagram below represents students' subject preferences.

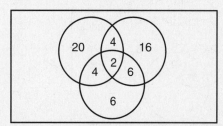

How many students like all three subjects?

13-2 Study Guide

Problem-Solving Strategy:
Use Venn Diagrams

At Calera City High School, 180 students participate in the band and/or a sport. One hundred thirty-four students are in the band, and 90 play sports. Forty-four students participate in both activities. How many students participate in sports only?

Explore   You know the total amount of students, how many students are in the band, how many play sports, and how many participate in both activities.

Plan   Draw a Venn diagram to organize the data.

Solve   Draw two intersecting circles in a rectangle to represent sports and the band. Write the number of students who participate in both activities. Then subtract to find the number of students who participate only in one activity.

Band = 134 − 44 = 90
Sports = 90 − 44 = 46

There are 46 students that participate in sports only.

**Calera High Students
in Band and Sports**

band   sports

44

90   46

Examine   Look at the Venn diagram. Add the number of students in each region.

90 + 44 + 46 = 180   Since the total is 180, the answer is correct.

Solve using a Venn diagram.

1. A television station conducted a survey. They asked 100 viewers which TV series they prefer, Series 1 or Series 2. Sixty-six people preferred Series 1, 50 people liked Series 2, and 16 people preferred both equally. How many people liked Series 1 only?
50 people

2. Three hundred fourteen structural engineers were surveyed. One hundred ninety engineers create steel designs, and 216 create wood designs. Ninety-two engineers do both steel and wood designs. How many structural engineers create steel designs but not wood designs? **98 engineers**

3. The Venn diagram below represents students' sports preferences.

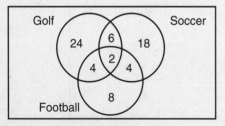

How many students prefer only football? **8 students**

4. The Venn diagram below represents students' subject preferences.

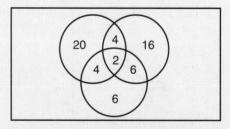

How many students like all three subjects? **2 students**

13-3 Study Guide
The Real Number System

Student Edition
Pages 672–675

Rational numbers are numbers that can be expressed as a quotient of two integers, where the divisor is not zero.

Irrational numbers are numbers that can be named by nonterminating, non-repeating decimals.

The set of **real numbers** includes both the rational numbers and the irrational numbers.

Real Numbers

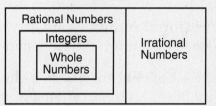

Some equations have solutions that are irrational numbers. To solve an equation that involves squares, take the square root of each side.

Example: Solve $x^2 = 65$

$$x^2 = 65$$
$$x = \sqrt{65} \text{ or } x = -\sqrt{65}$$ Take the square root of each side.
$$x \approx 8.1 \text{ or } x \approx -8.1$$

Name the sets of numbers to which each number belongs: the whole numbers, the integers, the rational numbers, the irrational numbers, and/or the reals.

1. $6.01001\ldots$

2. -2

3. $-\dfrac{3}{5}$

4. $0.\overline{83}$

5. $\sqrt{19}$

6. 0.625

7. $-\sqrt{81}$

8. $4.2342352\ldots$

9. $-\sqrt{7}$

Solve each equation. Round decimal answers to the nearest tenth.

10. $c^2 = 49$

11. $x^2 = 4$

12. $w^2 = 14$

13. $n^2 = 289$

14. $m^2 = 132$

15. $h^2 = 250$

16. $k^2 = 3.24$

17. $r^2 = 1600$

18. $d^2 = 90$

Pre-Algebra

Student Edition
Pages 672–675

13-3 Study Guide

The Real Number System

Rational numbers are numbers that can be expressed as a quotient of two integers, where the divisor is not zero.

Irrational numbers are numbers that can be named by nonterminating, non-repeating decimals.

The set of **real numbers** includes both the rational numbers and the irrational numbers.

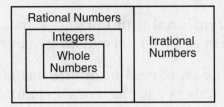

Some equations have solutions that are irrational numbers. To solve an equation that involves squares, take the square root of each side.

Example: Solve $x^2 = 65$
$x^2 = 65$
$x = \sqrt{65}$ or $x = -\sqrt{65}$ **Take the square root of each side.**
$x \approx 8.1$ or $x \approx -8.1$

Name the sets of numbers to which each number belongs: the whole numbers, the integers, the rational numbers, the irrational numbers, and/or the reals.

1. $6.01001\ldots$ **irrational, real**

2. -2 **integer, rational, real**

3. $-\dfrac{3}{5}$ **rational, real**

4. $0.8\overline{3}$ **rational, real**

5. $\sqrt{19}$ **irrational, real**

6. 0.625 **rational, real**

7. $-\sqrt{81}$ **integer, rational, real**

8. $4.2342352\ldots$ **irrational, real**

9. $-\sqrt{7}$ **irrational, real**

Solve each equation. Round decimal answers to the nearest tenth.

10. $c^2 = 49$ **c = 7 or c = -7**

11. $x^2 = 4$ **x = 2 or x = -2**

12. $w^2 = 14$ **w ≈ 3.7 or w ≈ -3.7**

13. $n^2 = 289$ **n = 17 or n = -17**

14. $m^2 = 132$ **m ≈ 11.5 or m ≈ -11.5**

15. $h^2 = 250$ **n ≈ 15.8 or n ≈ -15.8**

16. $k^2 = 3.24$ **k = 1.8 or k = -1.8**

17. $r^2 = 1600$ **r = 40 or r = -40**

18. $d^2 = 90$ **d ≈ 9.5 or d ≈ -9.5**

13-4 Study Guide
The Pythagorean Theorem

Student Edition
Pages 676–681

In a right triangle, the square of the hypotenuse, c, is equal to the sum of the squares of the lengths of the other two sides, a and b.

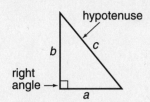

$$c^2 = a^2 + b^2$$
$$5^2 = 3^2 + 4^2$$
$$5^2 = 9 + 16$$
$$25 = 25$$

Example: How long must a ladder be to reach a window 13 feet above ground? For the sake of stability, the ladder must be placed 5 feet away from the base of the wall.

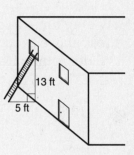

$$c^2 = (13)^2 + (5)^2$$
$$c^2 = 169 + 25$$
$$c^2 = 194$$
$$c^2 = \sqrt{194} \approx 13.9 \text{ ft}$$

Solve. Round decimal answers to the nearest tenth.

1. In a softball game, how far must the catcher throw to second base?

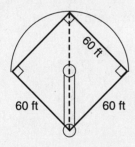

2. How long must the brace be on a closet rod holder if the vertical side is 17 cm and the horizontal side must be attached 30 cm from the wall?

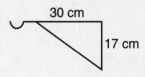

3. If Briny is 32 miles due east of Oxford and Myers is 21 miles due south of Oxford, how far is the shortest distance from Myers to Briny?

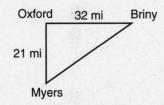

4. In a baseball game, how far must the shortstop (halfway between second base and third base) throw to make an out at first base?

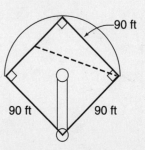

13-4 Study Guide
The Pythagorean Theorem

Student Edition
Pages 676–681

In a right triangle, the square of the hypotenuse, c, is equal to the sum of the squares of the lengths of the other two sides, a and b.

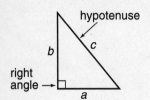

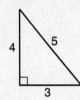

$$c^2 = a^2 + b^2$$
$$5^2 = 3^2 + 4^2$$
$$5^2 = 9 + 16$$
$$25 = 25$$

Example: How long must a ladder be to reach a window 13 feet above ground? For the sake of stability, the ladder must be placed 5 feet away from the base of the wall.

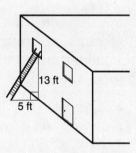

$$c^2 = (13)^2 + (5)^2$$
$$c^2 = 169 + 25$$
$$c^2 = 194$$
$$c^2 = \sqrt{194} \approx 13.9 \text{ ft}$$

Solve. Round decimal answers to the nearest tenth.

1. In a softball game, how far must the catcher throw to second base?

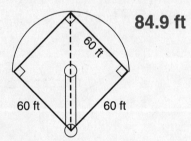

84.9 ft

2. How long must the brace be on a closet rod holder if the vertical side is 17 cm and the horizontal side must be attached 30 cm from the wall?

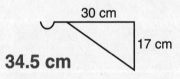

34.5 cm

3. If Briny is 32 miles due east of Oxford and Myers is 21 miles due south of Oxford, how far is the shortest distance from Myers to Briny?

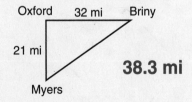

38.3 mi

4. In a baseball game, how far must the shortstop (halfway between second base and third base) throw to make an out at first base? **100.6 ft**

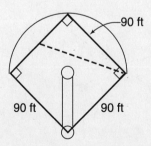

13-5 Study Guide
Special Right Triangles

Student Edition
Pages 683–686

In any 30°–60° right triangle, the length of the shortest side is one-half the length of the hypotenuse.
The side opposite the 60° angle is $\sqrt{3}$ times the length of the other leg.

Example:

Find the lengths of sides a and b in the triangle below.

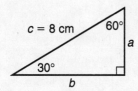

Side a is one-half of side c, 8 cm.
Therefore, side $a = \frac{1}{2} \cdot 8$, or 4 cm.

Side b is $\sqrt{3}$ times side a. Thus, side $b = \sqrt{3} \cdot 4$, or about 6.9 cm.

In any 45°–45° right triangle, the length of the hypotenuse is $\sqrt{2}$ times the length of a leg.

Example:

Find the lengths of sides a and b in the triangle below.

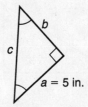

Side b is the same length as side a, 5 in.
Therefore, side $c = \sqrt{2} \cdot 5$, or about 7.1 in.

Find the lengths of the missing sides in each triangle. Round decimal answers to the nearest tenth.

1.

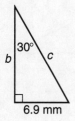

2.

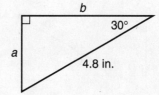

3.

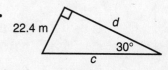

4.

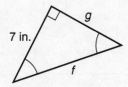

5.

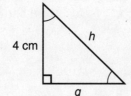

6.

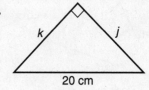

Pre-Algebra

13-5 Study Guide
Special Right Triangles

In any 30°–60° right triangle, the length of the shortest side is one-half the length of the hypotenuse.
The side opposite the 60° angle is $\sqrt{3}$ times the length of the other leg.

In any 45°–45° right triangle, the length of the hypotenuse is $\sqrt{2}$ times the length of a leg.

Example:

Find the lengths of sides a and b in the triangle below.

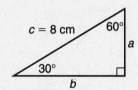

Side a is one-half of side c, 8 cm.
Therefore, side $a = \frac{1}{2} \cdot 8$, or 4 cm.
Side b is $\sqrt{3}$ times side a. Thus, side $b = \sqrt{3} \cdot 4$, or about 6.9 cm.

Example:

Find the lengths of sides a and b in the triangle below.

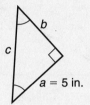

Side b is the same length as side a, 5 in.
Therefore, side $c = \sqrt{2} \cdot 5$, or about 7.1 in.

Find the lengths of the missing sides in each triangle. Round decimal answers to the nearest tenth.

1.
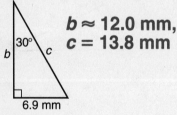
$b \approx 12.0$ mm, $c = 13.8$ mm

2.
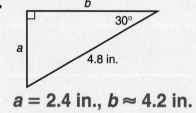
$a = 2.4$ in., $b \approx 4.2$ in.

3.
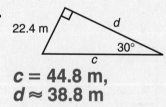
$c = 44.8$ m, $d \approx 38.8$ m

4.
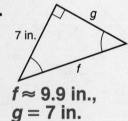
$f \approx 9.9$ in., $g = 7$ in.

5.
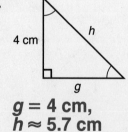
$g = 4$ cm, $h \approx 5.7$ cm

6.
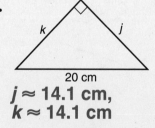
$j \approx 14.1$ cm, $k \approx 14.1$ cm

Pre-Algebra

13-6 Study Guide

The Sine, Cosine, and Tangent Ratios

Student Edition
Pages 688–692

In the triangle at the right, the measures of the sides are used to find the following **trigonometric ratios**.

$$\text{sine of } \angle R = \frac{\text{measure of the leg opposite } \angle R}{\text{measure of the hypotenuse}}$$

$$= \frac{4}{5} \text{ or } 0.8$$

$$\text{cosine of } \angle R = \frac{\text{measure of the leg adjacent to } \angle R}{\text{measure of the hypotenuse}}$$

$$= \frac{3}{5} \text{ or } 0.6$$

$$\text{tangent of } \angle R = \frac{\text{measure of the leg opposite } \angle R}{\text{measure of the leg adjacent to } \angle R}$$

$$= \frac{4}{3} \text{ or about } 1.333$$

If a trigonometric ratio is known, then the degree measure of an angle can be determined by using a calculator. For example, in the triangle above, sin $R = 0.8$. Therefore, the measure of $\angle R$ is 0.8 [sin⁻¹] or about 53.1°.

For each triangle, find sin A, cos A, and tan A to the nearest thousandth.

1.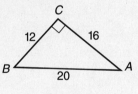

2.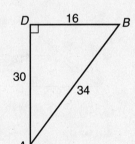

3.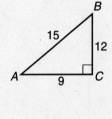

4.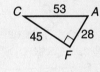

For each triangle, find the measure of the marked acute angle to the nearest degree.

5.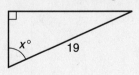

6.

7.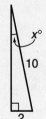

8.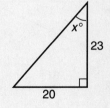

13-6 Study Guide
The Sine, Cosine, and Tangent Ratios

In the triangle at the right, the measures of the sides are used to find the following **trigonometric ratios**.

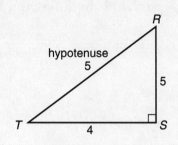

$$\text{sine of } \angle R = \frac{\text{measure of the leg opposite } \angle R}{\text{measure of the hypotenuse}}$$

$$= \frac{4}{5} \text{ or } 0.8$$

$$\text{cosine of } \angle R = \frac{\text{measure of the leg adjacent to } \angle R}{\text{measure of the hypotenuse}}$$

$$= \frac{3}{5} \text{ or } 0.6$$

$$\text{tangent of } \angle R = \frac{\text{measure of the leg opposite } \angle R}{\text{measure of the leg adjacent to } \angle R}$$

$$= \frac{4}{3} \text{ or about } 1.333$$

If a trigonometric ratio is known, then the degree measure of an angle can be determined by using a calculator. For example, in the triangle above, sin R = 0.8. Therefore, the measure of $\angle R$ is 0.8 [sin⁻¹] or about 53.1°.

For each triangle, find sin A, cos A, and tan A to the nearest thousandth.

1.
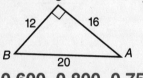
0.600, 0.800, 0.750

2.
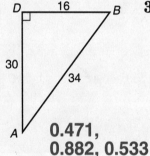
0.471, 0.882, 0.533

3.
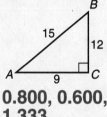
0.800, 0.600, 1.333

4.
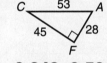
0.849, 0.528, 1.607

For each triangle, find the measure of the marked acute angle to the nearest degree.

5.
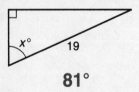
81°

6.
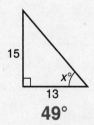
49°

7.
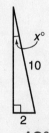
12°

8.
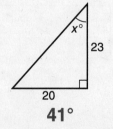
41°

13-7 Study Guide
Using Trigonometric Ratios

Student Edition
Pages 694–697

The ski run at Mad River Mountain rises at an angle of 25°. The length of the run is 500 meters. How high is the run?

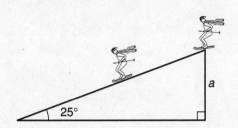

$$\sin 25° = \frac{a}{500}$$

$$0.4226 \approx \frac{a}{500}$$

$$0.4226 \times 500 \approx \frac{a}{500} \times 500$$

$$211.3 \approx a$$

The run is approximately 211.3 meters high.

Write an equation that you could use to solve for x. Then solve. Round decimal answers to the nearest tenth.

1.

2.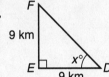

3.

Use trigonometric ratios to solve each problem.

4.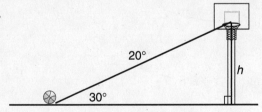

How high is the basketball hoop?

5.

How long is the tent pole?

6.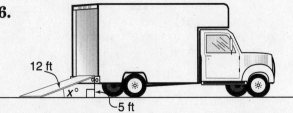

What is the angle of the ramp?

7.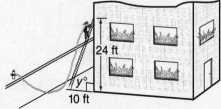

What is the angle of the ladder?

13-7 Study Guide
Using Trigonometric Ratios

The ski run at Mad River Mountain rises at an angle of 25°. The length of the run is 500 meters. How high is the run?

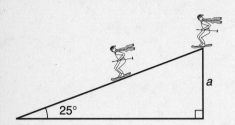

$$\sin 25° = \frac{a}{500}$$

$$0.4226 \approx \frac{a}{500}$$

$$0.4226 \times 500 \approx \frac{a}{500} \times 500$$

$$211.3 \approx a$$

The run is approximately 211.3 meters high.

Write an equation that you could use to solve for x. Then solve. Round decimal answers to the nearest tenth.

1. 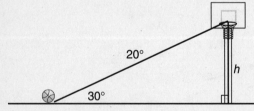 **Sin 36° = $\frac{x}{12}$; 7.1cm**

2. **Tan x° = $\frac{9}{9}$; 45°**

3.  **Cos x° = $\frac{3}{8}$; 68.0°**

Use trigonometric ratios to solve each problem.

4. How high is the basketball hoop? **10 ft**

5. 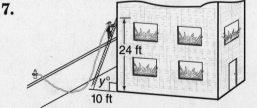 How long is the tent pole? **7 ft**

6. 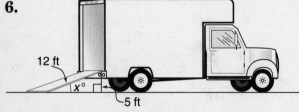 What is the angle of the ramp? **25°**

7. What is the angle of the ladder? **67°**

14-1 Study Guide
Polynomials

Student Edition
Pages 706–709

A **polynomial** is an algebraic expression that contains one or more monomials. A **binomial** is a polynomial with two terms. A **trinomial** is a polynomial with three terms.

A term of a polynomial *cannot* be a quotient with the variable in the denominator or the square root of a variable.

Monimials			
-36	x^3	$0.5y$	$\frac{-z}{10}$

Binomials			
$3x + \sqrt{2}$	$-4a + b^2$	$\frac{c}{3}$	$-\frac{d}{4}$

Trinomials	
$x^2 - 3x + 4$	$4a^2b^3 + 2ab^2 - b$

To find the degree of a monomial, add the exponents on the variables. The monomial $5x^5y^3$ has a degree of $5 + 3$ or 8.

The degree of a polynomial the same as that of the term with the highest degree.

Example: Find the degree of $y^3 + 2y^3z + 4x$.

y^3 has degree 3.
$2y^3z$ has degree $3 + 1$ or 4.   **Greatest degree**
$4x$ has degree 1.

The degree of $y^3 + 2y^3z + 4x$ is 4.

State whether each expression is a polynomial. If it is, classify it as a monomial, bionomial, or trinomial.

1. $r^2 - 2$

2. $\frac{-10}{c}$

3. $\frac{w}{2} - 24$

4. $b^2 + 1$

5. $-14m^2n$

6. $4x^2 - 2xy - 4y^2$

7. $\frac{1}{x} - \frac{1}{y} - \frac{1}{z}$

8. $a^2 - b^3 - c^4$

9. $\sqrt{b - 4ac}$

Find the degree of each polynomial.

10. $5d^4 + 13a^2b^4c$

11. $7g^2h - 2h$

12. $2x^4 - 6xy^3 + 3x^3z^2$

13. -36

14. $12a + 3$

15. $-34r^2s^4t^6$

115

14-1 Study Guide
Polynomials

Student Edition
Pages 706–709

A **polynomial** is an algebraic expression that contains one or more monomials. A **binomial** is a polynomial with two terms. A **trinomial** is a polynomial with three terms.

A term of a polynomial *cannot* be a quotient with the variable in the denominator or the square root of a variable.

Monimials			
-36	x^3	$0.5y$	$\frac{-z}{10}$

Binomials		
$3x + \sqrt{2}$	$-4a + b^2$	$\frac{c}{3} - \frac{d}{4}$

Trinomials	
$x^2 - 3x + 4$	$4a^2b^3 + 2ab^2 - b$

To find the degree of a monomial, add the exponents on the variables. The monomial $5x^5y^3$ has a degree of $5 + 3$ or 8.

The degree of a polynomial the same as that of the term with the highest degree.

Example: Find the degree of $y^3 + 2y^3z + 4x$.

y^3 has degree 3.
$2y^3z$ has degree $3 + 1$ or 4.   **Greatest degree**
$4x$ has degree 1.

The degree of $y^3 + 2y^3z + 4x$ is 4.

State whether each expression is a polynomial. If it is, classify it as a monomial, bionomial, or trinomial.

1. $r^2 - 2$ **yes, bionomial**

2. $\frac{-10}{c}$ **no**

3. $\frac{w}{2} - 24$ **yes, binomial**

4. $b^2 + 1$ **yes, bionomial**

5. $-14m^2n$ **yes, monomial**

6. $4x^2 - 2xy - 4y^2$ **yes, trinomial**

7. $\frac{1}{x} - \frac{1}{y} - \frac{1}{z}$ **no**

8. $a^2 - b^3 - c^4$ **yes, trinomial**

9. $\sqrt{b - 4ac}$ **no**

Find the degree of each polynomial.

10. $5d^4 + 13a^2b^4c$ **7**

11. $7g^2h - 2h$ **3**

12. $2x^4 - 6xy^3 + 3x^3z^2$ **5**

13. -36 **0**

14. $12a + 3$ **1**

15. $-34r^2s^4t^6$ **12**

Pre-Algebra

14-2 Study Guide
Adding Polynomials

To add two or more polynomials, look for **like terms**. Like terms are those that have exactly the same variables to the same powers.

Method 1:
Add Vertically

$$\begin{array}{l} 5x + 1 \\ \underline{+\ 4x + 3} \\ 9x + 4 \end{array}$$ **Align the terms.**
        Add.

In Method 1, notice that the terms are aligned and added.

Method 2:
Add Horizontally

$(3x + 2y + 1) + (5x + 2)$
$\qquad = (3x + 5x) + (2y) + (1 + 2)$
$\qquad = 8x + 2y + 3$

In Method 2, notice that there is nothing to add to the term $2y$. That is, the second polynomial does not include a term having the variable y.

Find each sum.

1. $\begin{array}{l} 2x + 3 \\ \underline{+\ 3x + 9} \end{array}$

2. $\begin{array}{l} 8y\ -\ 7 \\ \underline{+\quad x + 13} \end{array}$

3. $\begin{array}{l} 12y + 7x \\ \underline{+\ 7y - 2x} \end{array}$

4. $\begin{array}{l} 3x^2 -\ x + 7 \\ \underline{+\ 2x^2 + 3x + 3} \end{array}$

5. $\begin{array}{l} 6x\quad + 12 \\ \underline{+\quad 8y -\ 2} \end{array}$

6. $\begin{array}{l} 8x\qquad + 9 \\ \underline{+\quad x + 4y + 11} \end{array}$

7. $(4y + 2x) + (6y - x)$

8. $(6x + 2y) + (4x - 8y)$

9. $(11m - 4n) + 3n$

10. $(x + y + 8) + (5x + 2y + 3)$

11. $(3x^2 - 12x + 7) + (3 + 2x - 6x^2)$

12. $(5y^2 + 3y + 2) + (2y^2 + 9)$

13. $(4y^2 - y + 6) + (3y - 4)$

14-2 Study Guide
Adding Polynomials

Student Edition
Pages 711–714

To add two or more polynomials, look for **like terms**. Like terms are those that have exactly the same variables to the same powers.

Method 1:
Add Vertically

$$5x + 1 \quad \text{Align the terms.}$$
$$\underline{+\ 4x + 3} \quad \text{Add.}$$
$$9x + 4$$

In Method 1, notice that the terms are aligned and added.

Method 2:
Add Horizontally

$$(3x + 2y + 1) + (5x + 2)$$
$$= (3x + 5x) + (2y) + (1 + 2)$$
$$= 8x + 2y + 3$$

In Method 2, notice that there is nothing to add to the term $2y$. That is, the second polynomial does not include a term having the variable y.

Find each sum.

1. $2x + 3$
    $\underline{+\ 3x + 9}$
    $\mathbf{5x + 12}$

2. $8y \quad -\ 7$
    $\underline{+\quad x + 13}$
    $\mathbf{8y + x + 6}$

3. $12y + 7x$
    $\underline{+\ 7y - 2x}$
    $\mathbf{19y + 5x}$

4. $3x^2 - \ x + 7$
    $\underline{+\ 2x^2 + 3x + 3}$
    $\mathbf{5x^2 + 2x + 10}$

5. $6x \quad +\ 12$
    $\underline{+\quad 8y - \ 2}$
    $\mathbf{6x + 8y + 10}$

6. $8x \qquad +\ 9$
    $\underline{+\quad x + 4y + 11}$
    $\mathbf{9x + 4y + 20}$

7. $(4y + 2x) + (6y - x)$
    $\mathbf{10y + x}$

8. $(6x + 2y) + (4x - 8y)$
    $\mathbf{10x - 6y}$

9. $(11m - 4n) + 3n$
    $\mathbf{11m - n}$

10. $(x + y + 8) + (5x + 2y + 3)$
    $\mathbf{6x + 3y + 11}$

11. $(3x^2 - 12x + 7) + (3 + 2x - 6x^2)$
    $\mathbf{-3x^2 - 10x + 10}$

12. $(5y^2 + 3y + 2) + (2y^2 + 9)$
    $\mathbf{7y^2 + 3y + 11}$

13. $(4y^2 - y + 6) + (3y - 4)$
    $\mathbf{4y^2 + 2y + 2}$

14-3 Study Guide
Subtracting Polynomials

A rational number can be subtracted by adding its **additive inverse** or opposite. You can find the additive inverse of a number by multiplying the number by -1. For example, the additive inverse of 3 is $(-1)3$, or -3. You can also subtract binomials and trinomials by adding their additive inverse.

To find the additive inverse or binomials and trinomials, replace each term with its additive inverse.

binomial	additive inverse
$x + 2y$	$x - 2y$
$2x^2 + 4x$	$-2x^2 - 4x$

trinomial	additive inverse
$2x^2 - 3x + 5$	$-2x^2 + 3x - 5$
$-8x + 5y - 7z$	$-8x - 5y + 7z$

Examples

a.
$$\begin{array}{r} 4x^2 + 5xy \\ -\ 6x^2 + 8xy \\ \hline \end{array}$$
additive inverse
$-(6x^2 + 8xy)$
$$\begin{array}{r} 4x^2 + 5xy \\ (+)\ -6x^2 - 8xy \\ \hline 2x^2 - 3xy \end{array}$$

b.
$$\begin{array}{r} 12a^2 - 3a + 3 \\ -\ 6a^2 - 12a - 4 \\ \hline \end{array}$$
additive inverse
$-(6a^2 - 12a - 4)$
$$\begin{array}{r} 12a^2 - 3a + 3 \\ (+)\ -6a^2 + 12a + 4 \\ \hline 6a^2 + 9a + 7 \end{array}$$

Find each difference.

1. $(2x + 6) - (x + 4)$

2. $(6x - 1) - (2x + 5)$

3. $(14y + 2) - (6y - 1)$

4.
$$\begin{array}{r} 9x + y + 8 \\ (-)5x + 3y - 3 \\ \hline \end{array}$$

5.
$$\begin{array}{r} 6x\quad + 7 \\ (-)-x - 4y - 12 \\ \hline \end{array}$$

6.
$$\begin{array}{r} x^2 + 2x + 4 \\ (-)x^2 - 6x + 3 \\ \hline \end{array}$$

7. $(5y^2 + 3y + 2) - (2y^2 - 9)$

8. $(4y^2 - y + 6) - (-3y - 5)$

9. $(9x + 12) - (5y + 3)$

14-3 Study Guide
Subtracting Polynomials

A rational number can be subtracted by adding its **additive inverse** or opposite. You can find the additive inverse of a number by multiplying the number by -1. For example, the additive inverse of 3 is (-1)3, or -3. You can also subtract binomials and trinomials by adding their additive inverse.

To find the additive inverse or binomials and trinomials, replace each term with its additive inverse.

binomial	additive inverse
$x + 2y$	$x - 2y$
$2x^2 + 4x$	$-2x^2 - 4x$

trinomial	additive inverse
$2x^2 - 3x + 5$	$-2x^2 + 3x - 5$
$-8x + 5y - 7z$	$-8x - 5y + 7z$

Examples

a.

$$\begin{aligned} 4x^2 + 5xy \\ -\ 6x^2 + 8xy \end{aligned}$$

additive inverse
$^-(6x^2 + 8xy)$

$$\begin{array}{r} 4x^2 + 5xy \\ (+)\ -6x^2 - 8xy \\ \hline 2x^2 - 3xy \end{array}$$

b.

$$\begin{aligned} 12a^2 -\ 3a + 3 \\ -\ 6a^2 - 12a - 4 \end{aligned}$$

additive inverse
$^-(6a^2 - 12a - 4)$

$$\begin{array}{r} 12a^2 -\ 3a + 3 \\ (+)\ -6a^2 + 12a + 4 \\ \hline 6a^2 +\ 9a + 7 \end{array}$$

Find each difference.

1. $(2x + 6) - (x + 4)$
$x + 2$

2. $(6x - 1) - (2x + 5)$
$4x - 6$

3. $(14y + 2) - (6y - 1)$
$8y + 3$

4.
$$\begin{array}{r} 9x +\ y + 8 \\ (-)5x + 3y - 3 \\ \hline \end{array}$$
$4x - 2y + 11$

5.
$$\begin{array}{r} 6x\ \ \ \ \ + 7 \\ (-)-x - 4y - 12 \\ \hline \end{array}$$
$7x + 4y + 19$

6.
$$\begin{array}{r} x^2 + 2x + 4 \\ (-)x^2 - 6x + 3 \\ \hline \end{array}$$
$8x + 1$

7. $(5y^2 + 3y + 2) - (2y^2 - 9)$
$3y^2 + 3y + 11$

8. $(4y^2 - y + 6) - (-3y - 5)$
$4y^2 + 2y + 11$

9. $(9x + 12) - (5y + 3)$
$9x - 5y + 9$

Pre-Algebra

14-4 Study Guide
Powers of Monomials

Student Edition
Pages 719–723

To find a **power of a power**, multiply the exponents.

$$(4^2)^3 = 4^{2 \cdot 3} \qquad (x^3)^4 = x^{3 \cdot 4}$$
$$= 4^6 \qquad\qquad\quad = x^{12}$$

To find a **power of a product**, multiply the individual powers.

$$(ab)^4 = a^4 b^4 \qquad (xy)^{-3} = x^{-3} y^{-3}$$

Use the previous rules to find a **power of a monomial**.

$$(2a^4 b^5)^2 = (2)^2 (a^4)^2 (b^5)^2 \qquad (d^2 e^6 f^3)^{-3} = (d^2)^{-3} (e^6)^{-3} (f^3)^{-3}$$
$$= 2^2 a^{4 \cdot 2} b^{5 \cdot 2} \qquad\qquad\qquad = d^{-6} e^{-18} f^9$$
$$= 4a^8 b^{10}$$

Simplify.

1. $(ab)^7$

2. $(2^4)^2$

3. $(6m)^3$

4. $(-4m^2 n)^2$

5. $(k^6)^3$

6. $[(-2)^4]^2$

7. $(-3y^5)^2$

8. $(-h^4)^5$

9. $(d^6 e^3)^8$

10. $(4a^2 b)^4$

11. $(-pq^2)^9$

12. $6x(4x)^3$

13. $(-2x^4 y^3)^6$

14. $-4t(t^4)^5$

15. $[(4)^2]^3$

16. $(-w^8)^{-4}$

17. $(-m^9)^{-2}$

18. $7(u^6 v)^{-4}$

Evaluate each expression if x = -1 and y = 4.

19. $3x^2 y$

20. $-2xy^3$

21. $(x^3 y)^3$

22. $2x(2y^2)^{-2}$

23. $(x^2 y)^4$

24. $-(xy)^{-2}$

14-4 Study Guide
Powers of Monomials

To find a **power of a power**, multiply the exponents.

$$(4^2)^3 = 4^{2 \cdot 3}$$
$$= 4^6$$

$$(x^3)^4 = x^{3 \cdot 4}$$
$$= x^{12}$$

To find a **power of a product**, multiply the individual powers.

$$(ab)^4 = a^4 b^4$$

$$(xy)^{-3} = x^{-3} y^{-3}$$

Use the previous rules to find a **power of a monomial**.

$$(2a^4 b^5)^2 = (2)^2 (a^4)^2 (b^5)^2$$
$$= 2^2 a^{4 \cdot 2} b^{5 \cdot 2}$$
$$= 4a^8 b^{10}$$

$$(d^2 e^6 f^3)^{-3} = (d^2)^{-3} (e^6)^{-3} (f^3)^{-3}$$
$$= d^{-6} e^{-18} f^9$$

Simplify.

1. $(ab)^7$ $a^7 b^7$

2. $(2^4)^2$ 2^8

3. $(6m)^3$ $216m^3$

4. $(-4m^2 n)^2$ $16m^4 n^2$

5. $(k^6)^3$ k^{18}

6. $[(-2)^4]^2$ 256

7. $(-3y^5)^2$ $9y^{10}$

8. $(-h^4)^5$ $-h^{20}$

9. $(d^6 e^3)^8$ $d^{48} e^{24}$

10. $(4a^2 b)^4$ $256a^8 b^4$

11. $(-pq^2)^9$ $-p^9 q^{18}$

12. $6x(4x)^3$ $384x^4$

13. $(-2x^4 y^3)^6$ $64x^{24} y^{18}$

14. $-4t(t^4)^5$ $-4t^{21}$

15. $[(4)^2]^3$ 4096

16. $(-w^8)^{-4}$ w^{-32}

17. $(-m^9)^{-2}$ m^{-18}

18. $7(u^6 v)^{-4}$ $7u^{-24} v^{-4}$

Evaluate each expression if x = -1 and y = 4.

19. $3x^2 y$ 12

20. $-2xy^3$ 128

21. $(x^3 y)^3$ -64

22. $2x(2y^2)^{-2}$ $\dfrac{-1}{512}$

23. $(x^2 y)^4$ 256

24. $-(xy)^{-2}$ $-\dfrac{1}{16}$

Pre-Algebra

14-5 Study Guide

Multiplying a Polynomial by a Monomial

To multiply a polynomial by a monomial, use the distributive property. First, multiply each term of the polynomial by the monomial. Then combine any like terms.

Example: Find the product of $4x^2y\,(3x - 2xy^3 + 4y^2 + 2x)$.

$$4x^2y\,(3x - 2xy^3 + 4y^2 + 2x)$$

$$= 4x^2y(3x) - 4x^2y(2xy^3) = 4x^2y(4y^2) + 4x^2y(2x) \qquad \textbf{Distributive property}$$

$$= 12x^3y - 8x^3y^4 + 16x^2y^3 + 8x^3y \qquad \textbf{Multiplying monomials}$$

$$= 20x^3y - 8x^3y^4 + 16x^2y^3 \qquad \textbf{Combine like terms.}$$

Find each product.

1. $2(3x - 4)$

2. $-3z(z + 9)$

3. $4(x - 3)$

4. $7w(3w + 2)$

5. $-2c(c + 7)$

6. $x(y^2 - z)$

7. $3p(p^3 + p^2)$

8. $xy(xy - 3x)$

9. $5y^3(2xy - 3y^2)$

10. $-xy(xy + x^2 - 3)$

11. $2x(xy + x^2 - 3)$

12. $-xy(2xy - 3y^2)$

13. $2x(2xy - 3y^2 + 4)$

14. $5(-2x^2 + 3x - 3)$

15. $-4x^2(y^2 + 4x + 1)$

16. $-3x(3x^4 + 2x^3 - 7x^2 + 1)$

17. $2x^2(3x^3 - 2x^2 + 9x - 4)$

14-5 Study Guide
Multiplying a Polynomial by a Monomial

To multiply a polynomial by a monomial, use the distributive property. First, multiply each term of the polynomial by the monomial. Then combine any like terms.

Example: Find the product of $4x^2y(3x - 2xy^3 + 4y^2 + 2x)$.

$$4x^2y(3x - 2xy^3 + 4y^2 + 2x)$$

$$= 4x^2y(3x) - 4x^2y(2xy^3) = 4x^2y(4y^2) + 4x^2y(2x) \quad \text{Distributive property}$$

$$= 12x^3y - 8x^3y^4 + 16x^2y^3 + 8x^3y \quad \text{Multiplying monomials}$$

$$= 20x^3y - 8x^3y^4 + 16x^2y^3 \quad \text{Combine like terms.}$$

Find each product.

1. $2(3x - 4)$ $6x - 8$

2. $-3z(z + 9)$ $-3z^2 - 27z$

3. $4(x - 3)$ $4x - 12$

4. $7w(3w + 2)$
$21w^2 + 14w$

5. $-2c(c + 7)$ $-2c^2 - 14c$

6. $x(y^2 - z)$ $xy^2 - xz$

7. $3p(p^3 + p^2)$ $3p^4 + 3p^3$

8. $xy(xy - 3x)$
$x^2y^2 - 3x^2y$

9. $5y^3(2xy - 3y^2)$
$10xy^4 - 15y^5$

10. $-xy(xy + x^2 - 3)$
$-x^2y^2 - x^3y + 3xy$

11. $2x(xy + x^2 - 3)$
$2x^2y + 2x^3 - 6x$

12. $-xy(2xy - 3y^2)$
$-2x^2y^2 + 3xy^3$

13. $2x(2xy - 3y^2 + 4)$
$4x^2y - 6xy^2 + 8x$

14. $5(-2x^2 + 3x - 3)$
$-10x^2 + 15x - 15$

15. $-4x^2(y^2 + 4x + 1)$
$-4x^2y^2 - 16x^3 - 4x^2$

16. $-3x(3x^4 + 2x^3 - 7x^2 + 1)$
$-9x^5 - 6x^4 + 21x^3 - 3x$

17. $2x^2(3x^3 - 2x^2 + 9x - 4)$
$6x^5 - 4x^4 + 18x^3 - 8x^2$

14-6 Study Guide
Multiplying Binomials

Student Edition
Pages 728–731

Use the distributive property to multiply two binomials.

$$(a + b)(c + d) = ac + ad + bc + bd$$

Example: Find the product $(x + 6)(x + 2)$.

$$
\begin{aligned}
(x + 6)(x + 2) &= x(x + 2) + 6(x + 2) & \text{Distributive property} \\
&= x \cdot x + x \cdot 2 + 6 \cdot x + 6 \cdot 2 & \text{Distributive property} \\
&= x^2 + 2x + 6x + 12 & \text{Multiply polynomials} \\
&= x^2 + 8x + 12 & \text{Combine like terms}
\end{aligned}
$$

Find each product.

1. $(x + 1)(x + 2)$ **2.** $(y + 4)(y + 5)$ **3.** $(z + 7)(z + 7)$

4. $(y + 2)(y - 9)$ **5.** $(y + 3)(y - 3)$ **6.** $(x + 1)(x + 1)$

7. $(x + 5)(x - 1)$ **8.** $(y + 8)(y - 3)$ **9.** $(3x + 8)(2x + 1)$

10. $(4x + 3)(x - 6)$ **11.** $(x - 7)(3x + 4)$ **12.** $(6y + 3)(4y - 6)$

13. $(3y - 2)(6y + 3)$ **14.** $(3x + 8)(3x - 8)$ **15.** $(2x + 4)(2x + 4)$

14-6 Study Guide
Multiplying Binomials

Student Edition
Pages 728–731

Use the distributive property to multiply two binomials.

$$(a + b)(c + d) = ac + ad + bc + bd$$

Example: Find the product $(x + 6)(x + 2)$.

$$
\begin{aligned}
(x + 6)(x + 2) &= x(x + 2) + 6(x + 2) && \text{Distributive property} \\
&= x \cdot x + x \cdot 2 + 6 \cdot x + 6 \cdot 2 && \text{Distributive property} \\
&= x^2 + 2x + 6x + 12 && \text{Multiply polynomials} \\
&= x^2 + 8x + 12 && \text{Combine like terms}
\end{aligned}
$$

Find each product.

1. $(x + 1)(x + 2)$
$x^2 + 3x + 2$

2. $(y + 4)(y + 5)$
$y^2 + 9y + 20$

3. $(z + 7)(z + 7)$
$z^2 + 14z + 49$

4. $(y + 2)(y - 9)$
$y^2 - 7y - 18$

5. $(y + 3)(y - 3)$
$y^2 - 9$

6. $(x + 1)(x + 1)$
$x^2 + 2x + 1$

7. $(x + 5)(x - 1)$
$x^2 + 4x - 5$

8. $(y + 8)(y - 3)$
$y^2 + 5y - 24$

9. $(3x + 8)(2x + 1)$
$6x^2 + 19x + 8$

10. $(4x + 3)(x - 6)$
$4x^2 - 21x - 18$

11. $(x - 7)(3x + 4)$
$3x^2 - 17x - 28$

12. $(6y + 3)(4y - 6)$
$24y^2 - 24y - 18$

13. $(3y - 2)(6y + 3)$
$18y^2 - 3y - 6$

14. $(3x + 8)(3x - 8)$
$9x^2 - 64$

15. $(2x + 4)(2x + 4)$
$4x^2 + 16x + 16$